The Oratory School
* 0 0 0 0 7 0 5 1 *

COLERIDGE

MASTERS OF WORLD LITERATURE

General Editor: Louis Kronenberger

Published:

GEORGE ELIOT by Walter Allen
JOHN KEATS by Douglas Bush
JOHN MILTON by Douglas Bush
JONATHAN SWIFT by Nigel Dennis
DANTE by Francis Fergusson
THOMAS HARDY by Irving Howe
HONORE DE BALZAC by E. J. Oliver

In Preparation:

PROUST by William Barrett
FLAUBERT by Jacques Barzun
MATTHEW ARNOLD by Douglas Bush
SAMUEL JOHNSON by James L. Clifford
YEATS by F. W. Dupee
JOYCE by Leon Edel
STENDHAL by Wallace Fowlie
CONRAD by Elizabeth Hardwick
EMERSON by Alfred Kazin
SHAKESPEARE by Frank Kermode
JANE AUSTEN by Louis Kronenberger
POE by Dwight Macdonald
CHEKHOV by Howard Moss
FIELDING by Midge Podhoretz
HENRY JAMES by Richard Poirier
OLIVER GOLDSMITH by Ricardo Quintana
TOLSTOY by by Philip Rahv
MELVILLE by Harold Rosenberg
BEN JONSON by Raymond Rosenthal
WORDSWORTH by Lionel Trilling

COLERIDGE

Walter Jackson Bate

WEIDENFELD AND NICOLSON
5 Winsley Street London W1

ACKNOWLEDGEMENTS

Acknowledgement for permission to quote material from *The Notebooks of S. T. Coleridge,* edited by Kathleen Coburn, Bollingen Series L, Volume 1 (1794–1804), copyright 1957 by Bollingen Foundation, New York, is gratefully made to Routledge & Kegan Paul, Ltd., and to the Bollingen Foundation. For quotations from the *Letters of S. T. Coleridge,* edited by E. L. Griggs, acknowledgement is gratefully made to the Clarendon Press.

First published in Great Britain 1969

SBN 297 17407 X

Printed in Great Britain by
Lowe & Brydone (Printers) Ltd., London

To
Jerome H. Buckley
David Perkins
and
I. A. Richards
Friends and Coleridgeans

Contents

Preface

Coleridge has fascinated the English-speaking world for over a century and a half. To begin with, he had at least three different careers, and if our attention is not caught up by him in one way, it is in another. He is a major poet, though to the writing of poetry he devoted only a fraction of his time and abilities. Then, during the painful years from thirty-five to his late forties, he emerged as one of the supreme critics and interpreters of literature, partly because his interests extended so far beyond literature in the narrower sense of the word. With his fifties, he turned more directly to religious speculation, and became—as we are beginning to realize even more than before—one of the seminal religious thinkers of modern times.

In addition he was versed in the sciences and in the history of philosophy as few men have been who are not specialists in those subjects; he was a political thinker of considerable influence in the century after his death; and as a psychologist he had as clairvoyant an intelligence as any of which we have record.

Finally there is the moving—in some ways deeply disturbing—story of his life, which presents so many baffling problems, especially if we refuse to take up the personal details of his life in reductive isolation and apart from the manysidedness of his mind and achievement.

But exactly this variety of interest presents difficulties for anyone attempting a critical biography of Coleridge. How do we begin to notice all the interests, as well as the personal life, of so richly endowed a talent? And even supposing this could be done, how do we keep them all in proportion as we seek the underlying unity? But it seemed to me that a work as necessarily short as this could take heart, especially if one viewed it as only a prefatory exercise to a longer work. It would be taken for granted that we were here following his life and thought only in its main and general character, suppressing the argument, substantiation, and nuance that a longer book would be expected to supply. And if we thus far lack a comprehensive and full-scale treatment to support and protect a mere essay in critical biography like this, there was the liberty that resulted from the fact that the subject had not yet jelled. One was freer to speculate.

Yet everyone who attempts a short critical biography of a complex figure ends his work with less jauntiness than he began it. As he restudies his subject, he finds that much he had earlier thought could be left out or drastically summarized now demands not only recognition but emphasis, even if he hopes to deal with the matter later in more detail. Moreover at each step interrelations between the man's life and work are discovered or need revision. But the writer then finds that to insert discussion of them means that something else has to be left out or further condensed that he and others already take for granted as necessary.

My list of obligations is embarrassingly long for so short a book. But this is perhaps inevitable in a work that distils so much from others and lacks the extensive annotative apparatus in which specific obligations can be detailed as they arise. I am particularly indebted to Professor Earl Leslie Griggs, whose magisterial edition of the *Letters,* with its wealth of commentary, is the basis for any biography or general study of Coleridge. His personal interest has greatly heartened me; and, with typical generosity, he sent me the proofs of his concluding volumes of the *Letters* and allowed me to draw on them. For permission to consult the still unpublished later notebooks and the manuscript of the *Opus Maximum,* I thank Miss Kathleen Coburn, who is so brilliantly editing the *Notebooks,* and the authorities of the Victoria University Library, Toronto. For allowing me to use in Chapter VII an earlier discussion of Coleridge as a critic (in *Perspectives of Criticism,* ed. Harry Levin), I am indebted to Professor Levin and the authorities of the Harvard University Press. For permission to use a copy of the report of Coleridge's autopsy, I thank Dr. John Spiegel and the library of the Michael Reese Hospital, Chicago, to which Dr. Spiegel presented it, and, for help in interpreting it, Dr. Louis Zetzel and Dr. Lincoln Clark, who I hope will forgive me for condensing into a few sentences their detailed analyses. I should also thank Dr. Clark, one of the foremost American authorities on the psychological effect of drugs, for advising me on the subject at several stages of this book. For many favors, and for allowing me to exceed somewhat the length ordinarily expected for the books in this series, I am grateful to Mr. Louis Kronenberger, the general editor, and to Mr. Arthur Gregor of Macmillan. For permission to quote from Coleridge's *Notebooks,* I wish to thank the Bollingen Foundation and Routledge and Kegan Paul, Ltd., London. For helpful criticism of my pages on Coleridge's later religious thought, I am indebted to J. Robert Barth, S.J., whose own book, *Coleridge and Christian Doctrine,* is soon to be published.

From the time I first began to read Coleridge with some care, the influence of two teachers has remained with me and to some extent—however different they were from each other—coalesced. I hope I may be allowed to speak of them briefly here. One was John Livingston Lowes, the memory of whom has been constantly present as I tried to reconsider the poetry and the earlier years of Coleridge. Like so many others, I also learned from him to prize the union of style and erudition as well as the Longinian ideal of genius. The other teacher was Alfred North Whitehead, whose majestic reinterpretation of the organic philosophy of nature for the modern era lit up for us an immense zone of possibilities, cleared the ground of trivia, and led us toward the level of generality for which Coleridge himself hungered. I should add that neither of these men would have thought it strange that a student concerned primarily with the eighteenth century should also be interested in the greater Romantics, who after all were born in that century and were very much the products of it. They assumed that one of the principal interests of a period was the youth it produced and educated.

Finally I express my debt, extending over many years, to the following friends: Professors Douglas Bush, Harry Levin, Earl Wasserman, Robert Penn Warren, Harold Bloom, René Wellek, M. H. Abrams, Geoffrey Tillotson, and the three colleagues to whom I inscribe this small book—Jerome H. Buckley, David Perkins, and I. A. Richards. Here I should especially mention the notable Harvard seminars in Coleridge conducted by Professor Perkins in 1964 and 1965, in which his detailed reconsideration of Coleridge as a mind helped to shake us free of routine conceptions and brought us back to a renewed and deeper sense of Coleridge's own quest for unity.

W. J. B.

Cambridge, Massachusetts
May, 1967

I

Early Years; Christ's Hospital and Cambridge; Marriage

SAMUEL TAYLOR COLERIDGE WAS BORN on October 21, 1772, in Ottery St. Mary, Devonshire, a market town on the left bank of the little river Otter with a population at that time of about 2,500. He was the youngest of fourteen children. His father, John Coleridge, the vicar of the parish and master of the grammar school, had married twice, having four children by his first wife and ten (one of which died in infancy) by his second wife, Anne Bowden. This lovable, learned, and absentminded clergyman, whom his famous son was to compare with Fielding's Parson Adams, was fifty-three when his last child was born, and his wife was forty-five; and they both, especially the father, treated the boy with an indulgence that often irritated the older children.

Overshadowed in age by all around him, the young Benjamin of the family quickly developed habits that we find persisting throughout his later life. Dependent as he was on almost everyone else and with practically no one dependent on him, the need to ingratiate himself became especially strong, and with it, as corollaries, a readiness of guilt, a chronic fear of disappointing others, and a fascinated admiration for people of firm—or at least apparently self-sufficient—character. Though there were occasional outbursts of frustration, his general defense before this formidable array of older brothers was to retreat into passiveness: a passiveness by no means sullen but of a pliable, good-natured sort, quick in apology, benevolent protest, and occasional self-abasement. At the same time another part of him became resourceful in appealing over the heads of the older brothers to those still older—to those who seemed even more truly adult—by displays of knowledge or sentiment that won approval, even admiration. There, whether in talking with his father or with other adults, he was on ground that he felt could be trusted. He became very precocious, "flattered," as he said, "and wondered at by all the old women. And before I was eight years old I was a *character*." Constantly, in his mature years, his hunger for approval or love and his dread of disapproval were to lead him to oscillate between these two extremes: on the one hand an apologetic self-effacement, in which he could stand aside and find his satisfactions vicariously; on the other hand, an impetuous brilliance of discourse, usually in support of the most approved sentiments. In his most successful work we find some interplay of both, and it is when something very different from either is needed that hesitation and paralysis of will begin to appear.

When he entered his father's grammar school (he was then in his sixth year), he rapidly outstripped the other students of his age. He had already exhausted the stock of books at the small Everything shop kept by his aunt, including *Robinson Crusoe, Belisarius,* and the *Arabian Nights;* and using for audience the gravestones in the churchyard next to the vicarage, he would often act out scenes from what he had been reading. One tale from the *Arabian Nights* particularly struck the boy, who for most of his adult life was to feel compelled to search for a single-minded purity of doctrine—a quest for which he felt so unqualified in his wayward interests and his love of variety. This was "the tale of a man who was compelled to seek for a pure virgin," which "made so deep an impression on me (I read it in the evening while my Mother was mending stockings), that I was haunted by spectres, whenever I was in the dark." He was later to defend (and very effectively) the value of fairy tales and stories of romance and magic as a means of exercising a child's imaginative curiosity and habituating him to conceptions beyond the routine. From them he was to pass easily to other reading. Delighted by the boy's imaginative openness, so much greater than that of the other children, his father used to take the boy on his knee and "hold long conversations with me." Coleridge especially remembered that, as they walked home one winter evening from a farmhouse,

> he told me the names of the stars—and how Jupiter was a thousand times larger than our world—and that the other twinkling stars were Suns that had worlds rolling round them—& when I came home, he shewed me how they rolled round—. I heard him with a profound delight & admiration; but without the least mixture of wonder or incredulity. For from my early reading of Faery Tales, & Genii &c &c—my mind had been habituated *to the Vast*— & I never regarded my *senses* in any way as the criteria of my belief. I regulated all my creeds by my conceptions not by my sight—even at that age.

When he was eight an incident occurred that seems to have lain more heavily on his conscience than anything else that happened in his childhood. Indeed he felt years later that what followed it affected his health permanently, creating a disposition for a sort of neuralgia, or, as he often thought it, rheumatic fever, from which he was to suffer off and on for the rest of his life. His sense of guilt must have been enormous; for, whatever the physical effects, there was almost certainly nothing so serious as rheumatic fever.[1] The incident began trivially enough. He asked his mother that the piece of cheese allotted him one evening be cut entire so he could toast it. "This was no easy matter, it being a *crumbly* cheese." But his mother, with some care, did what he requested. When they were out of the room, his brother Francis snatched the cheese and minced it, resolved "to disappoint the favorite." Returning, Samuel flew at the older brother and struck him. Pretending to be seriously hurt, Francis fell to the floor. Moaning, the frightened boy bent over him, when suddenly his brother rose with a laugh and struck him in the face. Samuel in turn seized a

[1] See p. 104.

knife and was starting toward Francis when his mother returned. Expecting a flogging, he ran from the house, stopping at a small hill a mile away, just above the river Otter. He had in his pocket a little book that contained, at the end, morning and evening prayers. He got it out, repeated them, thinking at the same time with "gloomy satisfaction how miserable my mother would be." Finally, in the damp cold of the October night, he fell asleep. All through the night men from the village searched for him. Early in the morning he awoke, cried out for help, and at length was found. He was always to remember vividly his parents' relief—his father's "tears stealing down his face," his mother "outrageous with joy." He was put to bed but was "subject to the ague for many years after."

• 2 •

A year later (October, 1781), shortly before the boy's ninth birthday, his father suddenly died. His mother, eager to carry out her husband's wish that Samuel prepare for the clergy, had little confidence in John Coleridge's successor, whose slips in grammar were eagerly recounted by her son. Through the help of a former student of the vicar (Francis Bulwer, later famous as a judge), Coleridge was admitted to the great London school, Christ's Hospital, attended at that time by over seven hundred students.

Because the change for the boy might otherwise be too abrupt, and because he appeared to be getting little or nothing at the local grammar school, it was arranged that he leave several weeks early (April, 1782), go to London, and stay for the interim with Mrs. Coleridge's brother, John Bowden, a tobacconist in Threadneedle Street. This entrance into a world so different from the little market town of Ottery was immensely stimulating. For his genial uncle, delighted by the volubility and knowledge of the boy, proudly escorted him to his own favorite haunts. There, at taverns and coffee-houses, the nine-year-old Samuel talked to men of the City as he had talked to his father and to the adults he encountered in Ottery. Even in this larger and shrewder world, he found the same approval, interest, possibly delight, when he exerted himself, when he spread his wings. Within another fifteen years the thought of a wide wingspread would be associated (as in the albatross, in the "Ancient Mariner") not only with openness and innocence, but with vulnerability to the unpredictable hostilities of human nature. But now there was only an intoxication with the experience that he could express the best that he was able to express, drawing on every resource, and be given in return what seemed a cordial welcome.

When summer came, he was sent (July 18) for six weeks to the Christ's Hospital Junior School out at Hertford. After this preparatory period, he was brought back to London and was entered at the Under Grammar School. In later years, he (and even more his friends Charles Lamb and Wordsworth) romanticized the friendless youth torn from his native village to the great city of London ("pent 'mid cloisters dim,/And saw nought lovely but the sky and stars"). But he soon found friends, and, through a happy chance, access to a large number of books. Walking through the crowded Strand, his arms outstretched since he was pretending to be Leander swimming the Hellespont, he touched the coat of a stranger who suspected him to be a pickpocket. The frightened Coleridge, in justifying himself, so won the heart of the stranger that he was given a free ticket to a circulating library in King Street, Cheapside. A visitor to the library could get two books at a time. Daily, Coleridge would rush from school to do so. Starting at the beginning of the library's catalogue, he continued until he had finished everything there. The eagerness to read, no matter what, had already become one of the distinctive qualities of Coleridge by the age of six, and was to remain so, especially until his fifties. "Curiosity," as Johnson said, "is one of the permanent and certain characteristics of a vigorous intellect," and "perhaps always predominates in proportion to the strength of the contemplative faculties." At the same time the boy had an equal eagerness to communicate whatever he had read, at least with those who would not receive it in too unfriendly a way. Drawing on only a fraction of his daily interest and effort, he meanwhile rose to the top of his classes in the great school just as he had earlier done at the little grammar school in Ottery.

By his sixteenth year he was admitted into the small group of students called the Grecians, the best classical scholars at Christ's Hospital, who were working for a university scholarship or fellowship. They were taught directly by the celebrated master of the upper school, the Rev. James Boyer, whose use of the birch rod was considered firm and frequent even for the time. Reading the verse compositions of his students, he showed no mercy to inflated or stock phrases:

> In fancy I can almost hear him now [wrote Coleridge twenty-five years later], exclaiming, "Harp? Harp? Lyre? Pen and ink, boy, you mean! Muse, boy, Muse? Your Nurse's daughter, you mean! Pierian spring? Oh, aye! the cloister-pump, I suppose."

Such expressions (especially apostrophes and quasi-poetic "O thou's") Boyer dismissed as "the grimaces of lunacy." One of his customs, praised by Coleridge, was to permit the student's exercises to accumulate until there were four or five of them. Spreading them out on the desk, he would then ask why this or that expression could not be just as appropriately used in any of the other exercises. If the student could not justify himself and two faults of the same kind were found in one exercise, the exercise was torn up and a new one on the same subject assigned in addition to the other tasks of the day. In time, said Coleridge,

> I learnt from him, that Poetry, even that of the loftiest and, seemingly, that of the wildest odes, had a logic of its own, as severe as that of science; and more difficult, because more subtle, more complex, and dependent on more, and more fugitive causes.

The close encounter with Boyer proved immensely valuable. For the first time Coleridge faced a taskmaster who was both intelligent and stern. Hitherto he had been a little spoiled by the readiness with which older people would listen to him; and the circle was now widening to include people of his own age (among his friends were Charles Lamb, Thomas Fanshawe Middleton, the Le Grice brothers, Charles and Samuel, Robert Allen, and Hartwell Horne). Much of his growing ability to attract so many different kinds of people is explained by his genuine enthusiasm for the subject, whatever it might be. There was comparatively little of self. Above all there was nothing personally aggressive or competitive. He was merely soliciting others to share in his delight, and with his generous sympathies he shunned anything that might put others on the defensive. From his twenties till his late forties he could move into any circle and talk with equal ease to a group of butchers, to scholars and critics, to political gatherings, to Unitarian meetings, or to people assembled in an inn or a hall for a lecture on anything—education, Shakespeare, the history of philosophy. Usually, at least until his middle years, he would captivate his audience not only by a transparency of self before subject (this remained with him to the end) but to some extent by his instinctive empathy with those to whom he talked, alone or in groups. So with his letters. This most pliable of spirits bends himself at once to the thoughts and interests of those to whom he is writing (though often, it must be admitted, with the result of saying merely what he thinks they would like to have him say).

Of these later years at Christ's Hospital, Lamb's account is always, and justifiably, quoted:

> Come back into memory, like as thou wert in the dayspring of thy fancies, with hope like a fiery column before thee—the dark pillar not yet turned—Samuel Taylor Coleridge—Logician, Metaphysician, Bard!—How have I seen the casual passer through the Cloisters stand still, intranced with admiration (while he weighed the disproportion between the *speech* and the *garb* of the young Mirandula), to hear thee unfold, in thy deep and sweet intonations, the mysteries of Iamblichus, or Plotinus (for even in those years thou waxedst not pale at such philosophic draughts), or reciting Homer in his Greek, or Pindar—while the walls of the old Grey Friars re-echoed to the accents of the *inspired charity-boy!*

What Lamb is saying here is expressed by one person after another throughout most of Coleridge's life, the difference being that, during his thirties and forties, there was a general feeling that the "dark pillar" *had* turned, though perhaps not permanently.

• 3 •

In considering the life of Coleridge one of the commonplaces of experience is often forgotten. Even with more robust and independent spirits, the constant pressure to live up to what is expected will produce periods of inner rebellion or lassitude. With a nature habitually dependent on others—above all dependent for praise or affection—the pressure is far more concentrated. While encouraging precocity it can become as much of a burden as a challenge. Since too much of the self is bound up in the ideals to reject them openly, the response is frequently to retreat rather than rebel. Hence the history of precocity often carries with it a later history of periodic lassitude or indifference, and of avocations, distractions, or temptations radically different from the persistent and highly specialized self-demand. Constantly from his late twenties to the end of his life, though so acute a psychologist himself, Coleridge was haunted and puzzled by his lack of "will" or motivation. What was wrong? Sometimes, as he was to tell Robert Southey, he had

> a haunting sense, that I was an herbaceous Plant, as large as a large Tree, with a Trunk of the same Girth, & Branches as large & shadowing—but with *pith within* the Trunk, not heart of Wood/—that I had *power* not *strength*—an involuntary Imposter.

The moments of self-dissatisfaction were to increase from the time he entered Cambridge (at the age of twenty), and by his middle thirties were almost to have exceeded his control.

But now, at Christ's Hospital, the "dark pillar," as Lamb said, had "not yet turned." There was too much hope for the future. Any number of things seemed possible. True, the thought of the vocation for which he was destined, the Church, could at times weigh heavily. But there were alternatives. He became infatuated (he was now about thirteen or fourteen) with the thought of devoting his life to manual labor, a thought that was often to recur to him. He persuaded a friendly shoemaker named Crispin to ask Boyer's permission to take him as an apprentice. The unhappy Crispin withdrew in terror from his interview (" 'Ods my life, man, what d'ye mean?" said Boyer, as he rose and pushed Crispin from the room). Soon afterward Coleridge decided to become a doctor, and read every book he could find on medicine. Through his brother Luke, who was now studying medicine, he secured entrance as a general helper in the public wards of the hospital. He was always quick to empathize at the sight of physical suffering, and the public wards of a London hospital at this time, when the anaesthetics now taken for granted were unknown, could shake a far more self-sufficient nature than his. Medicine was put aside, though he was to continue to read widely in medical literature for the next thirty years.

On leave days at the school, he would strike up an acquaintance with clergymen he met on the street, turn the discussion to philosophy and religion, and question and dispute with them. He had been reading Voltaire's *Philosophical Dictionary,* Erasmus Darwin, and Cato's *Letters.* He decided that he was coming close to atheism, and so informed Boyer, who simply gave him a flogging. Coleridge later felt the flogging was altogether justified.

He was approaching the end of his time at Christ's Hospital when his friend T. F. Middleton, now at Cambridge, sent him a small volume of sonnets by the Rev. William Lisle Bowles *(Sonnets Written Chiefly on Picturesque Spots).* On the brilliantly articulate Coleridge, these simple, reflective poems made a lasting impression. He had learned much about poetry from Boyer; and he was never to forget that either. But here was a poetry completely without some of the qualities he had come to expect as necessary in good writing—logic, tightness of structure, inevitability and intensity of phrase—and yet a poetry that deeply appealed to him. It was in its own way direct and simple —something Boyer himself prized (though Boyer was thinking of a more intellectually rigorous simplicity). At the same time it was *familiar.* It had in it the kind of thing one could associate with family or with friends. What was wrong with occasionally prizing literature when it was simply a "friend"—a friend that could comfort while it informed and uplifted? The great English poets could not be viewed (at least not yet) in exactly that way. Only the best were studied—and the best part written by that best. Around them was an inevitable association of demand. In this respect they offered no essential contrast to his other reading—the reading in Greek literature and philosophy, the Neoplatonists, the metaphysical writers generally, the skeptics, the modern writers on science and epistemology. But here, in these mild sonnets of Bowles, the contrast was obvious, and all the more because Bowles was a human being now alive and not one of the assemblage of the great, unapproachable dead. "The great works of past ages," said Coleridge in the *Biographia,* "seem to a young man things of another race, in respect to which his faculties remain passive and submiss, even as to the stars and mountains." But the works of a man not much older than himself, and in similar circumstances, can "possess a *reality* for him, and inspire an actual friendship as of a man for a man." Coleridge wanted immediately to share with all he knew this discovery (it really was one of the great discoveries of his life—a discovery that poetry *could* be loved as a "friend"). Lacking money to buy the books, he made more than forty handwritten copies himself, during the next year and a half, and presented them to friends.

During all this time he seems to have returned to Ottery for only one short visit at the age of twelve. It was probably just after this that Boyer had seen him crying and said: "Boy! the school is your father! Boy! the school is your mother! . . . and all the rest of your relations! Let's have no more crying." When, three years later, Coleridge was at last to have some experience of a home life, a large internal fund of devotion was tapped. A school friend, Tom Evans, to whom he had been kind, introduced him to his widowed mother and three sisters (Mary, Anne, and Elizabeth). The atmosphere created by the mother was one of common sense, humor, and affection. Coleridge's discussion of abstruse metaphysical problems did not much interest either her or the children. He quickly found that he had no need to prove himself. The feeling of relief was enormous. Within a few months he had fallen in love with the eldest sister, Mary. On Saturdays he and his friend Robert Allen, carrying "the pillage of the flower-gardens within six miles of town, with Sonnet or Love Rhyme wrapped round the nosegay," would show up to the milliner's shop where Mary and Anne worked, and they would then escort the girls home. Mary treated his attentions with lighthearted kindliness, and his own feelings—at least until he had left London—were perhaps generally sentimental rather than intense. Certainly his last three or four years at Christ's Hospital were his happiest there, and largely because of the Evans family.

• 4 •

In February of his last year at school (1791), he was admitted to Jesus College, Cambridge, and went up for residence the following October 16, five days before he became twenty. The scholarship funds he received (a Christ's Hospital Exhibition of £80 a year and a Rustat Scholarship of about £25) presupposed a career in the Church of England.

For much of his first year he tried to cling to a schedule in which he would study mathematics for three hours a day and classics for another four or five. Evenings were often spent working in the rooms of his old school friend, T. F. Middleton, at Pembroke, who was reading for a fellowship. Unfortunately, Middleton, who was a steadying influence, left after a few months. Coleridge competed for several prizes, and won a medal for a Greek ode on the slave trade. The dampness of the college rooms brought on a neuralgic or rheumatic attack, and a letter to his brother George (November 28) contains his first reference to opium, which we should remember was prescribed very commonly at the time. The Christmas vacation was spent in London with the Evans family.

From the spring of his first year through that of his second, the resolutions with which he had started university life began to erode. He read as widely as ever, perhaps more so, but as curiosity led him. Intervals without regular work grew longer. His acquaintance was broadening, and friends from Christ's Hospital also began to appear at Cambridge. Charles Le Grice, now at Trinity, said that Coleridge "was ready at any time to unbend in conversation," and his room became "a constant rendezvous of conversation-loving friends." He speaks of the small suppers they had together,

> when Aeschylus, and Plato, and Thucydides were pushed aside, with a pile of lexicons, to discuss the pamphlets of the day. Ever and anon, a pamphlet issued from the pen of Burke. There was no need of having the book before us. Coleridge had read it in the morning, and in the evening he would repeat whole pages verbatim.

Like many other undergraduates, Coleridge became an admiring supporter of William Frend, a Fellow of Jesus College whose strong Unitarian beliefs and political liberalism so annoyed the authorities that he was finally tried (May, 1793) for sedition and defamation of the Church and then dismissed. Coleridge, with other students, appeared at the trial and was conspicuous in his applause for Frend. During these months—certainly within another year—he looked into the work of David Hartley, himself a Jesus College man, and found for the first time a philosophical system to which he could give a complete commitment. Hartley's *Observations on Man* (1749) had virtually founded (or at least systematized) what was by now the dominant British school of psychology, which interpreted all intellectual and emotional processes through the "association" of ideas, impressions and feelings. Hartley himself was far more thoroughgoing than his followers, who had since modified his work. But it was precisely this systematic inclusiveness that so appealed to Coleridge. It seemed to explain everything, from the most elementary physiological facts to the highest states of consciousness, benevolence, and religious apprehension. Man, as Hartley conceives him, is a sort of computer capable of progressive development. When an object is encountered, vibrations carry the impression through the white medullary substance of the nerves to the brain, after which fainter vibrations ("vibratiuncles") remain ready in the brain to coalesce with others. Memory begins, and man develops step by step as more complex and refined reactions take place. From primitive responses and self-interested feelings, moral values of disinterested purity progressively evolve.

In short, unlike his fellow associationists in France, Hartley—however thoroughgoing in his psychology and physiology—seemed able, in the traditional British spirit of compromise, to unite this frank materialism, even mechanism, with moral and even religious ideals. If one did not inquire too closely into the logic (and had not experience always proved to the British that the abstractions of logic are not to be completely trusted?), here was a philosophy that could unite the "head and the heart." Coleridge was altogether captivated. Greek philosophy—and he was widely read in it—offered no alternative: it was too open, tentative, capable of any number of interpretations; and Coleridge, though himself so open and speculative, hungered for the experience of a comprehensive system. In any case he had approached classical philosophy in another spirit: with curiosity and imaginative delight, but with the knowledge that it was something generally venerated. Hartley, however, was more his own discovery. Above all, Hartley was a modern man. He was aware of what modern science had done and could do—indeed warmly championed it; and he was also concerned with the problems of modern society. Christianity, modern science, and the present-day situation of man were brought together and interpreted through each other.

• 5 •

Coleridge's older brothers had meanwhile become disturbed not only by his enthusiasm for the controversial William Frend but by his requests for money. His debts were beginning to mount. During his first month at Cambridge he had incurred one that was still hanging over him. When he had first arrived, an upholsterer had asked him how he wished his rooms furnished. Assuming the man was employed by the college, Coleridge had replied, "Just as you please, sir." The brothers still did not know of this. Unsuccessful in his competition for an additional scholarship, he tried to ingratiate himself with them in advance. We now have the first of his projected works that are "about to go to the press." He was engaged, he said, on a translation of Greek and Latin lyrics, which he was planning to publish within six months. The skeptical brothers advanced him some money during the summer vacation of 1793. During his leisurely return to Cambridge by way of London, most of the money seemed to dissolve. While in London, hoping to recoup his fortunes, he bought a ticket in the Irish Lottery, and, waiting for the result, passed the time at Cambridge in nervous conviviality. With Le Grice he formed a literary society (one of the members of which was Christopher Wordsworth, the youngest brother of William) at the first meeting of which (November 13) Coleridge, having neglected to prepare the paper that was expected, recited poems instead and promised a paper for the following week. Actually he was about to leave for London for the drawing of the lottery. Hurrying there, he drew a blank and fell into despair. He was convinced he could never return. He felt the more miserable since his love for Mary Evans had now become almost a passion, and with his affairs in so hopeless a state, he dared not avow his feelings "even in a whisper." To what sort of work, however humble, could he turn?

Coming upon a recruiting officer in Chancery Lane, he impetuously enlisted in the 15th Light Dragoons, and was sworn in at Reading as a trooper (December 4). In order to keep his identity hidden lest his family know what he had done, but reluctant to sacrifice his initials (he was always fond of referring to himself as S. T. C.), he gave his name as Silas Tomkyn Comberbacke. He was of course hopeless as a dragoon. He could not ride, groom a horse, or even keep his accouterments in order. His fellow-dragoons liked and helped him. In return he occasionally wrote their love letters for them or prescribed medicines for them when they were ill. But the officers soon gave him up and assigned him work cleaning the stables and serving as hospital orderly.

Within a month or so after joining the dragoons, he revealed his presence there to some friends still at Christ's Hospital, obviously hoping they would relay the information to someone who could help him. Soon he was in correspondence with his favorite brother, George. His capacity for self-abasement when he felt guilty and helpless had always been great. He now writes George (February 23): "My more than brother. . . . I have been a fool even to madness. What shall I dare to promise? . . . One wish only can

I read distinctly in my heart, that it were possible for me to be forgotten as though I had never been! . . . O that without guilt I might ask of my Maker annihilation." To his still older brother, James, now the head of the family, he wrote a formal letter of confession and repentance. The brothers, after some involved negotiations with the authorities, secured his release (April 7), and arranged to pay his college debts. Back in Cambridge, four days later, filled with new resolution, Coleridge wrote George that he is up at five every morning, plans to compete for all prizes, and is cherishing as ideals "correctness" and "severe economy." He issued proposals for publishing by subscription *Imitations from the Modern Latin Poets* together with a "Critical and Biographical Essay on the Restoration of Literature." The work never appeared. He may have written one or two poems. The essay remained in limbo. The rest of his career at Cambridge, in fact, was to prove a complete anticlimax. His feeling of guilt because of it, after his brothers had rescued him as they had, was to contribute to a growing pattern of life.

• 6 •

Two months after his return to Cambridge (he was still twenty-one and in his third year at the university), he set off with a friend, Joseph Hucks, for a walking tour through Wales (June 9). They stopped at Oxford to visit Coleridge's school friend Robert Allen, who introduced them to Robert Southey, a student at Balliol. Southey had never met a man so brilliant. Coleridge, in turn, was attracted by the apparent firmness of Southey's character (though Southey was two years younger) and by his liberal political opinions. Southey, who had been reading Plato's *Republic,* had been thinking generally of the attractions of emigrating to the New World and trying to live in a somewhat similar way. Coleridge at once began to develop the idea with an eloquence that seemed to transform it from a mere possibility to an immediate practicable goal. For the rest of June the walking tour was deferred while Coleridge, Southey, Allen and two other friends constructed a plan for an ideal republican community to which (probably Coleridge is responsible for the word) they gave the name "pantisocracy"—equal government by all.

If not at the start, at least within a few months, the project, as described by Coleridge's new friend Tom Poole, was as follows. They would get together a group of twelve educated men, all of liberal political sentiments, and migrate to America. An attractive spot could be found in Pennsylvania on the banks of the Susquehanna (the melodious name of which delighted Coleridge). With each man laboring two or three hours a day in the fields or at other manual work, the wants of the group would be supplied. Their wives would tend to the households and look after the smaller children. A library of good books would be collected. Complete freedom of religious and political opinion was to be encouraged, and there would be philosophical discussion in free hours. Selfishness would be gradually extinguished. They could provide an example of what could be done in order to free man to become his best self. They would indeed be as a city set on a hill. A mere £125 from each member would suffice to start up the settlement. When we smile at the thought—and it has its comic side—we forget that many similar projects were actually carried out in America during the first half of the nineteenth century. They may not have lasted, but they left an effect and are rightly remembered with some tenderness and even admiration for the idealism shown.

Throughout the Welsh walking tour that summer, Coleridge thought constantly of the new plan, speaking about it to everyone he met. He had never been so caught up with an idea. Here was the promise of a completely new life that could satisfy some of his highest moral ideals and at the same time offer freedom from so much that oppressed the spirit. Here there would be no debts, no demanding tradesmen, no political tyrannies, no vested interests and prejudices, no heavy thought of a lifelong career in the Church of England. Nor was it mere "vacant liberty" that was attracting him. A definite course of *action* and specific duties was involved to which he could surrender himself with commitment and relief.

Returning to Bristol from Wales in early August, in order

to meet Southey, he found further developments had taken place. At their center was the Fricker family—a widow with five daughters (Sarah, Mary, Edith, Martha, Eliza) and a son, George. The older sisters supported themselves with their needles. Southey, long in love with Edith, had now become engaged to her in preparation for the adventure ahead. Mary's husband, Robert Lovell, a young Quaker poet, had also become an enthusiastic recruit. Indeed the whole Fricker family seemed prepared to go, and within a few months was regarding itself as not only the nucleus but probably the future breeding center for the enterprise. The Frickers welcomed Coleridge with warmth. As always when people were kind to him, he responded with gratitude. Southey and he then went to the farm of their fellow-pantisocrat George Burnett, in Somerset, to discuss the next step. While there they also briefly visited Thomas Poole, later to become a close friend and helper of Coleridge. They could not make a convert of him, though he sympathized with their general ideals. Back in Bristol again, Coleridge and Southey together with Robert Lovell decided to turn their talents as poets to a use both practical and idealistic. They suddenly agreed to write a play, *The Fall of Robespierre,* Coleridge writing the first act, Southey the second, and Lovell the third, to be finished by the next evening. Southey completed his dutifully. Coleridge showed up with only a part. Lovell's was finished in time, but Southey felt compelled to redo it. Eventually the work was put together. No Bristol bookseller would take it.[2]

• 7 •

At some point during these weeks in August Coleridge took, or was helped to take, a decisive step. He became engaged to the oldest, still unattached daughter of the Fricker family, Sarah. At least Southey was soon to tell Coleridge that it was considered as a firm engagement. (Southey may have courted Sarah before his interest in Edith—so Mrs. Coleridge implied years later—and if so,

[2] Coleridge managed to get it published that autumn in Cambridge. With the hope that it would sell better, since he was known there, it was decided to issue it only under his name.

it could help to explain his eagerness to get her settled in a way that would relieve his own conscience). There may have been merely a general understanding that, when the group embarked, Coleridge would be committed to Sarah, the formalities of engagement seeming to him inappropriate for pantisocrat idealists. More probably Coleridge himself, if only during an impetuous moment, made a proposal of sorts, though soon afterward the reins passed to the hands of Southey. During Coleridge's summer walk through Wales, he had briefly seen Mary Evans. The sight of her had shaken him. In his irregular life, what seemed to him now lacking was the sympathetic companionship and care of a woman. Who else was available except Sarah? Moreover, for the project ahead everyone was expected to be married so that the little colony could increase. The Frickers were of the true faith. Southey had shown the way and had ample opportunity to encourage his suggestible friend. Yes, Coleridge would join in and become one of them.

After spending some convivial evenings with Lamb and others at the Salutation and Cat in London, he arrived in Cambridge in mid-September, preached pantisocracy to everyone he knew, started in spare moments to learn carpentry, published *The Fall of Robespierre,* wrote some poems, and sent long letters to Southey about the general ideals involved in the new project ("My head, my heart, are all alive"). His correspondent, however, was becoming more concerned with Coleridge's reluctance to write to Sarah. Obviously the Fricker family gave Southey little peace, and he in turn continued to hound Coleridge and demand that he show the personal solicitude expected of an engaged man. Coleridge hastily tried to reassure Southey and also himself. But he was becoming uneasy. An affectionate letter from Mary Evans saying she had heard of the plan to emigrate, thought it "absurd and extravagant," and begging him to reconsider it, aroused all his feeling for her. Could there be more than sisterly affection in her concern? Was there after all a possible alternative to Sarah? But that would mean an alternative also to pantisocracy —Sarah and it were now bound up together. What was he to do?

Within a short time the decision seemed taken out of his hands. He discovered that Mary Evans was herself engaged to be married. He disclosed this to Southey: "To lose her! I can rise above that selfish pang! . . . O Southey! bear with my weakness . . . But to marry a woman whom I do *not* love . . ." True enough, he adds, "Mark you, Southey! *I will do my duty.*" But it is plain that he would be relieved if Southey would use his influence to help to free him.

He was supposedly by this time on his way to join Southey and the Frickers. (He had left Cambridge permanently, around the middle of December, without taking a degree.) But instead he lingered in London, contributed to the *Morning Chronicle* a series of sonnets on eminent figures of the day, began his longer poem, "Religious Musings," and took refuge in evenings at the Salutation and Cat, where he and Lamb would talk of religion, metaphysics, and poetry. With the help of a friend he began negotiations for a position as tutor in a Scottish noble family. Meanwhile, as the weeks passed, the Frickers were becoming more restive. Coleridge, who should have been with them by now, was writing to neither Southey nor Sarah.

Finally, in the latter part of January, the resolute Southey appeared in London, traced the stray sheep to an inn, the Angel (so fascinated were the guests by Coleridge's talk that the landlord was prepared to offer him free lodging if he remained), and escorted him back to Bristol. Sarah, appealing to his sense of duty, now informed him that because of her commitment to him she had since "rejected the Addresses of two Men, one of them of large Fortune," and in doing this on his behalf she had annoyed her relatives. These circumstances, said the guilt-stricken Coleridge, "she had with her usual Delicacy concealed from me till my arrival at Bristol."

Other complications had arisen that also tempered the joy of his return to the fold. Southey, Lovell, and another recruit, Charles Wynn, were concluding that the American venture was too drastic as a start. Far better to make a trial first at a co-operative farm in Wales. This distressed Coleridge. It would not be the same thing at all. In the meantime, whichever place they went, money was needed. He agreed to join Southey and Burnett in the same lodgings, and to begin writing (in a room where Southey, industriously at work, kept an eye on him). Coleridge was to write and lecture on politics and religion and Southey on history. Coleridge gave several lectures, including a series of six on "Revealed Religion," and then continued to work at a slower pace. With some irritation Southey said later that his earnings, during the half year that followed, were as four to one of those of Coleridge—that indeed he actually had to support Coleridge at this time. He was already beginning to have second thoughts about the idea of communal property. Sternly he noted the desultory, roundabout way in which Coleridge would get to work, sauntering about the room, often repeating ideas or phrases that fascinated him. Soon other alternatives would be opening for Southey that were to prove very attractive.

• 8 •

As for Coleridge himself, he could never live for long in an atmosphere not completely friendly. When confronted with feelings of hostility or annoyance, his first impulse was to approach them directly, half admit their reasonableness, and seek to palliate them with resolves of reform and with open and generous admiration of the other person. If this proved hopeless, he would turn away and try to forget the unpleasantness through an enthusiastic and sympathetic interest in other things. In the presence of firm characters, his procedure was the former for as long as was possible. Such people fascinated him in their freedom from the dubieties and self-questionings with which his own life was habitually spent. Southey had already wounded him in several ways. But he writes of him now to a friend: "You will esteem and love him. His Genius and acquirements are uncommonly great yet they bear no proportion to his Moral Excellence—He is truly a Man of *perpendicular Virtue.*"

So with Sarah. Faced now with no alternative, he sought to

welcome the situation. If not she herself, at least circumstance was being stern in its demand for duty. Very well—he had crossed the Rubicon. And did he not in a way really love her? She had shared the ideals that had meant so much to him. She had made the sacrifice of which she had been too delicate to inform him beforehand. He told himself he was privileged, and should be—indeed was—grateful for it.

On October 4 of that year they were married. Meanwhile, a month before, he had found a cottage for them near the village of Clevedon, a few miles from Bristol.

II

Nether Stowey

He was now twenty-two. His moorings had been cut, and in almost every possible way. Ottery, the older brothers, the years at Christ's Hospital, Cambridge, the intended career in the Church of England, Mary Evans, were all behind him. Here he was instead in a cottage with a newly married wife, without funds, and—for the first time—permanent obligations that could not be met by theory or sentiment only.

But then the claim of specific actions and duties—if only it could be in a cause he believed—was what he had been needing. True, the scheme of pantisocracy had been facing unforeseen difficulties, and Southey was wavering. A little patience was needed. This could be a period of preparation. He could learn much that might help them later. He compiled a long list of all the household objects still needed at the cottage—candlesticks, glasses, spoons, a teakettle, a dustpan. Into the house were also welcomed, in the spirit of pantisocracy, Sarah's sister Martha, and George Burnett. Then distressing news arrived. Southey, in order to secure a legacy left him if he entered the law, had dropped the whole project of pantisocracy. The anguished Coleridge—he had not been able during the previous weeks to believe Southey would really do this—replied in a letter that fills a dozen printed pages, in which he poured out the whole history of their hopes.

What was he to do now, in this crowded little cottage, with the bills coming in, with Southey's delusively firm back removed, and the hope of pantisocracy—on which Coleridge had gambled everything—punctured? He was completely naked. To tell himself that he had always been thrown on his own resources, at least since his father's death, gave no consolation. Very different resources were now needed. To what immediate practical use could he turn that wealth of reading of the past fourteen years—a full two-thirds of his life thus far—and the philosophical discourse, the range of reference and constant habit of speculation, that had caught the interests of his elders at Ottery, and won him friends and approval at Christ's Hospital and Cambridge?

• 2 •

The result was the beginning, during the next three years, of his career as a writer. It was a career never planned, indeed hardly thought of, at Christ's Hospital and Cambridge. Hence the literary historian and critic, accustomed to a more cleanly focused ambition in the youth of writers, naturally finds something bizarre in the scattered, confused efforts of Coleridge at this time (and for that matter the next few years). We should continue to remind ourselves that, until the advent of pantisocracy, the expected career had been the Church or something close to it, and that the expertise acquired had been scholarly, critical, speculative. He was not seeking to be a poet or even a "literary" writer in the more specialized sense of the word. True, he could write rapidly, at least at times, though he preferred conversation. Naturally he had written several poems. Educated people often did write poems as a by-product of other interests. In short, the writing throughout the next few years should not be viewed as that of a committed young poet, unable or reluctant to concentrate on poetry we might otherwise be anthologizing or discussing. It is the writing of a scholar and clergyman *manqué,* idealistic, anxious, pliable, suddenly forced to swim in unaccustomed waters.

Robert Lovell had introduced him to a young publisher at Bristol, Joseph Cottle, who, entranced by Coleridge, had offered him thirty guineas, payable in advance, for a volume of poems and soon followed it up with another offer for an unlimited amount of verse to be paid for at a guinea and a half for every hundred lines. Coleridge now started to assemble what he had for Cottle and to write some new poems (a volume was published the following March). A collection of political writing was also published this winter, *Conciones ad Populum* or *Addresses to the People* (1795), which incorporated some of the lectures he had given the previous spring. In December he began to make plans for a periodical, *The Watchman* (to be published every eight days instead of weekly in order to avoid the newspaper tax). Liberal, anti-Pitt, advocating general suffrage, it would give a "History of the domestic and foreign Occurrences of the preceding days," print selections of speeches in Parliament, and provide discussions of governmental policy. There would also be book reviews and some poetry. In order to secure subscriptions, he set off in January on a tour through the Midlands (Birmingham, Sheffield, Manchester, Liverpool) where people with liberal political and religious views were especially concentrated. During the tour, which is vividly described in the *Biographia Literaria,* he preached in Unitarian chapels (in Birmingham to a congregation of 1,400), thus securing lodging and also arousing considerable interest in the new magazine. When he returned to Bristol (February 13) after receiving news of his wife's illness, he brought with him the names of about a thousand probable subscribers.

He was now prepared to start, though in surroundings that left something to be desired. Mrs. Coleridge, during her illness, had moved to her mother's house at Redcliffe Hill in Bristol, and was not eager to return to the cottage. Coleridge was too full of plans to object, and there was an advantage anyway in being near the Bristol library. In a poem written at this time, "Reflections on Having Left a Place of Retirement," he bids the cottage a nostalgic farewell. With a natural desire to make a virtue of it, he tells himself that he is leaving the place

> to join head, heart, and hand,
> Active and firm, to fight the bloodless fight
> Of science, freedom, and the truth in Christ.

For the first number of *The Watchman* (March 1) he wrote attacks on Pitt's budgetary loan and on the slave trade, as well as discussions of Burke, the essays of Count Rumford, the writings of Godwin (about whom he was revising his earlier admiring opinion), and the religion and manners of the ancient German tribes. In his second issue an unfortunately flippant essay "On National Fasts" (with its motto from Isaiah, "Wherefore my bowels shall sound like an harp") lost him, he said, half his subscribers. He probably exaggerated. In general *The Watchman* was dull reading. The Midland manufacturers who had subscribed to it, expecting something like the eloquent sermons Coleridge had preached in the Unitarian chapels, were disappointed. Moreover, while pleasing his liberal readers by attacking the repressive measures of Pitt, he was alienating them by attacking the hero of many of them, William Godwin. As for news of current events, one could read that well in advance of this eight-day paper.

Coleridge was trying to do too many things, and not simply in *The Watchman*. Cottle had been demanding copy for the *Poems,* for which a preface had been promised. Sarah was ill for a while and this preyed on Coleridge's mind. The constant presence of Mrs. Fricker was a trial. Indeed he was now expected to help support her and her son George. His brother-in-law, Robert Lovell, who had assured him help with *The Watchman,* proved worse than useless. Coleridge himself, distracted in so many ways and with the future so uncertain, became unwell. He began, in order to help him at this distressing time, to take some laudanum, at one period every night for two weeks. It was soon plain that *The Watchman* would fold, and at a considerable loss. (The final and tenth number appeared on May 13.) That Josiah Wade should later have made up the loss was a lucky thing, though it did not help Coleridge's self-respect.

• 3 •

Coleridge had meanwhile, using the Bristol library, been reading everything he could in spare hours, and with his usual speed of assimilation. Was there any possibility of going back to the kind of thing he did best, bearing in mind that money was an immediate problem? He had been studying German. Why not translate the complete works of Schiller? On the proceeds he could then go to Germany, study chemistry and anatomy, and, more slowly, the German philosophers and theologians. Thus equipped he could return and open a school. He was always an educator at heart. The problem was how to get a publisher interested enough to advance him the funds. The second alternative was to become a Dissenting minister. He did not believe in preaching for hire, but under the circumstances it might be permissible now. An offer to work for the *Morning Chronicle* in London was only halfheartedly pursued. Far more interesting was the chance to serve as a tutor to the sons of a wealthy widow named Evans (no relation of Mary Evans). Investigating this opportunity, he completely captivated Mrs. Evans. She had never met anyone like him. The Coleridges were to move in with the Evans family. He was to receive £150 a year. At this point the legal guardians of the children, wanting them to attend a regular school, interfered. The plan was dropped, as much to the regret of Mrs. Evans as of Coleridge. "Farewell, pure and benevolent spirit," she wrote him, "Brother in the family of soul." She insisted on giving him £95 and presented Sarah with baby clothes worth £40.

While Coleridge was still debating what next to do, a youth named Charles Lloyd, who had been fascinated by Coleridge during the *Watchman* tour and wanted to escape the family banking business and become a philosopher and poet, nagged his father for permission to become Coleridge's student. Coleridge, invited to interview the father, quickly won over the whole family. Why should not the youth (though he was only two years younger than Coleridge) be taken into the Coleridge family and given daily personal instruction in all the sciences and arts? The Lloyd family agreed, offering £80 a year. Taking his new charge with him, Coleridge hastened home on receiving news that he had just become a father (the baby, a boy, was christened Hartley Coleridge in honor of the philosopher his father admired). The unexpected epileptic fits of Lloyd created some anxiety in the house. As the weeks passed, Coleridge began to suffer again from the neuralgia that so often seemed to plague him. It was again checked by laudanum and in rather heavy doses.

• 4 •

Despite his gift for Micawberlike optimism, Coleridge's whole situation began to weigh on him. In exchanging one set of obligations—those associated with the family at Ottery, Christ's Hospital, and Cambridge—for another that had seemed more welcome, he could never have expected the grotesque result with which he now found himself: the constant worry about money, the Fricker family attached to his coattails, *The Watchman* and its failure, the advent of Charles Lloyd. The reading to which he turned for relief—philosophy, science, travel, poetry—only accentuated by contrast his sense of loss. The truth is that the collapse of pantisocracy had left an enormous void. He had been so used to looking forward to it; it had pushed aside and replaced most of his earlier expectations; and now it too was gone.

Increasingly his thoughts turned to the village of Nether Stowey where Thomas Poole lived. If pantisocracy was dead—and if it was dead it was because Southey had abandoned it (significantly it had never occurred to Coleridge that he himself might lead such a group)—some version of it might still be possible, perhaps a better one. At Nether Stowey he could grow most of the food for his family. The manual labor would clear the head and keep the heart close to essentials. If the Stowey was a far cry from the Susquehanna, there would at least be no Mrs. Fricker. She would be left behind in Bristol. And there would be a moral leader, a firmer back even than Southey's on which to lean: that remarkable man Tom Poole, practical but kind, efficient but liberal. Everyone, from gentry down to the humblest folk, turned to this sturdy, simple-hearted bachelor with confidence in his solid judgment and his disinterested altruism. He could direct effectively the business of his tannery, his farm, his other enterprises; he could work as well with his hands as any of his help; and he approached the sciences and arts with an interest all the more genuine because it was self-earned. The man was blessed, as few people Coleridge had met, with "integrity, i.e. *entireness* of character." One could see this at once in the "originality and raciness of his intellect," the "practical value of his remarks . . . truths plucked as they are growing . . . the fair earning, of an observing eye." And how Coleridge envied the man's steadiness, his calm, confident ability "to do one thing at a time"! Tom Poole was all that Coleridge would himself wish to be: respectable and firm (like his brother George, or like that former "sheet anchor" of virtue, Southey), and yet, unlike Southey, tolerant and open-minded. Coleridge's praise of Poole was by no means unjustified. Everything we know about Poole—and a great deal is known—confirms it. But Coleridge's anxious need for the approval of the respectable, the self-sufficient and "integrated," was especially acute now. Poole had long since shown his confidence in Coleridge. Back in May, just as *The Watchman* collapsed, he had tactfully informed Coleridge that he and six other admirers wished him to accept a small annuity of £35 for seven years that might help him over this difficult period. To be near such a bulwark would strengthen Coleridge's resolve to justify himself. Do we not catch by infection the virtues of those we admire, at least if we see them frequently?

Yes, Nether Stowey was the answer, at least for the time being. Could Poole, he asked, get the Coleridges a cottage near his own place? Delighted by the thought but finding nothing good available, Poole delayed. Then other complications occurred to him. Coleridge had a naïvely romantic view of village life. Because of his political views, the neighbors might be hostile. He would lack the friends with whom he was accustomed to talk at Bristol. Poole suggested that he reconsider. Coleridge's desperation at this time is shown in his long and frantic reply. What could be the cause of such a rebuff? Obviously Poole would be embarrassed to have such a person as himself for a neighbor!

> Mrs. Coleridge has observed the workings of my face, while I have been writing, and is intreating to know what is the matter; I dread to shew her your Letter.

Naturally Poole at once dropped all objections, and secured for the Coleridges the famous cottage (now changed and enlarged).

The house into which the Coleridges moved on December 31, was as poor as Tom Poole had said—cold, draughty, with a chimney that failed to draw the smoke. Mice were everywhere about the house, though Coleridge thought it cruel to set traps. But the rent was only £7 a year. The long narrow garden behind it joined that of Poole, who soon put a gate in the dividing wall. Coleridge for a while plunged into the manual work of which he had been thinking nostalgically since, at thirteen, he had tried to get the shoemaker near Christ's Hospital to take him as an apprentice. He grew vegetables, fed the pigs and poultry, wrote reviews for magazines, and prepared his poems for a second edition.

His health improved dramatically, perhaps more from peace of mind than from physical exercise. Charles Lloyd continued with the Coleridges for a while, returning home in the spring after a series of epileptic seizures. A request arrived from Richard Brinsley Sheridan for a play that might, if satisfactory, be produced at Drury Lane. Coleridge, without hesitation, began a tragedy *(Osorio)*. Whatever he thought now, or was to think, about the quality of his own poetry (he was certainly the most modest of the major English poets—modest at least about his poetry, if only because his real effort lay elsewhere), the activity of working on it diverted his thoughts from pantisocracy or even its present shadow version. The vegetable garden was gradually neglected. The tragedy *Osorio* went forward briskly. There were no inhibitions, no crippling standards of what a tragedy should be. He was simply turning out what he thought Sheridan and Drury Lane might want. On Sundays he would preach at the Unitarian chapels in nearby Bridgewater or Taunton.

• 5 •

It is during this first year at Nether Stowey (1797), when he is twenty-four, that the Coleridge who has passed into legend again returns, after the eight-year hiatus since the accounts of "the inspired charity-boy" of Christ's Hospital. Our rapid summary of external events has inevitably neglected the inner life of Coleridge, except by suggestion. Until later writings, later expressions, allow us to take them up as something of a unit, the fluidities of his inner life resist the rapid categorization to which we are forced. The poetry, until we come to the later months of his first year at Nether Stowey, is much of a piece. The political writing and the reviews are not among the works for which he is remembered. In our sketch of Coleridge's life from the time he left Cambridge to the autumn of 1797, our need to proceed briskly is heightened when we remember that his three principal careers as a writer still lie before us—the major poems, the literary criticism, and the religious writing.

But we must recognize that, beneath the flurry of external events, Coleridge's philosophical interests had rapidly begun to widen. Here we have to do with a far more essential Coleridge than we find in the journalistic writing on political and social subjects—now or later—or even in much of the poetry. This is the Coleridge whose religious and philosophical pilgrimage must serve as one of the principal themes, perhaps the central theme, in any true account of his life. In the enthusiastic commitment and speed with which he appeared to move from system to system throughout his twenties, indeed his thirties, there are continuities we often overlook. For like Robert Southey, who is so often quoted,[1] most of us live at a more sedate tempo, and feel that serious thinking should involve not only one system of thought at a time but at a pace that should preferably not exceed one decade at a time.

The overriding philosophical interest of Coleridge, from the time he became a disciple of David Hartley at Cambridge until the end, was in unity of interpretation, unity of feeling, unity of relationship of every sort, but with no sacrifice of the claims of diversity. At the same time this lifelong hunger for unity, which so often tempts most of us to put our fingers in our ears to shut out objections or reservations, and seek the security of an imposed and restrictive neatness, is counterbalanced in Coleridge (at every stage of his life) by his openness to the obdurate detail, the unexpected nuance, the resistant qualification, and by his eagerness in every case to rescue it into a richer synthesis. As he moves within this pattern of hope and interest, his procedure is dialectic. He goes from one side of the path to the other (as Hazlitt noticed of him when he was walking): from the empirical and scientific to the spiritual and idealistic; then back again, with further insights, in the hope of finding a more capacious frame of reference.

What had caught his imagination when he had read David Hartley back in Cambridge was not what we remember now of Hartley (his importance in the history of mechanist psychology) but the comprehensiveness of the man's thought as he faced the modern setting. Hartley seemed to make place not only for religious faith and moral ideals but for the discoveries and methods of the scientist and pragmatic psychologist. Then, during the spring of 1796, while working on the ill-fated *Watchman*, Coleridge studied the works of George Berkeley, whose idealism reopened a world on which Hartley (as Coleridge was now beginning to feel) had prematurely closed the door. About this time

[1] His remark about Coleridge in 1808: "Hartley was ousted by Berkeley, Berkeley by Spinoza, and Spinoza by Plato; when last I saw him [1804] Jacob Behmen [Boehme] had some chance of coming in. The truth is that he plays with systems, and any nonsense will serve him for a text from which he can deduce something new and surprising."

he records in a notebook, while listing other future works, a series of "Hymns" or odes, one of which would contain "a sublime enumeration of all the charms or Tremendities of Nature—then a bold avowal of Berkeley's System!!!!" From December 1796, when he is about to move to Nether Stowey, through the months ahead, he continues to tell his friends that he is a "Berkleian." Naturally we think of the rectilinear Southey's remark. Hartley is as much of a prototype for conventional mechanism as we could find, while Berkeley is perhaps the supreme exemplar of subjective idealism in the history of philosophy. What greater leap could there be? But psychologically, at least, the enthusiasm for Berkeley was a development and not a radical change. In a way, the two could be considered counterparts to each other, as concave is to convex. The old joke about the monist comes to mind: one variety of monist puts mind inside matter, and the other puts matter inside mind. Hartley did the former, and Berkeley, a far greater intellect, appeared to do the latter. The change, at least for Coleridge at this time, was one of emphasis, reflected in the fact that he named his first son Hartley and his second Berkeley. Soon Berkeley would not be enough. Within another two years Coleridge was to discover Spinoza. (He may have known something about Spinoza before, but by 1799 he was reading him with the excitement of the young German romantics.) In a notebook entry (November, 1799), he states that if he were ever to write a poem that could build on the thought of this philosopher, who himself so hungered for unity,

> thus it should begin/ I would make a pilgrimage to the burning sands of Arabia, or &c &c &c to find the Man who could explain to me there can be oneness, there being infinite Perceptions—yet there must be *one*ness, not an intense Union but an Absolute Unity.

He had been only indirectly expressing such thoughts in the poetry he had been writing. Was it because of the *formality* of a poem? There, because one assumed a kind of public role, one always seemed to be on trial for approval. Except for some lines in his "Religious Musings," he had been surrounding—was more often than not to continue to surround—poetic expressions of the thought of the "one life" with a filter of self-protection. (Of course—as he could tell himself—he was not trying to be a poet, least of all at this time. If he wrote verse, was it not simply to celebrate incidental occasions or in order to have something to sell?) So in the "Eolian Harp," which he wrote when he and Sarah had moved to their cottage in Clevedon. The very title expressed the receptivity, the openness he thought typical of himself. (His conversation, he once said, compared with that of Samuel Johnson, was like an "Eolian Harp" in contrast to a drum.) He was later to insert a direct expression of his almost pantheistic sense of entirety:

> O! the one Life within us and abroad,
> Which meets all motion and becomes its soul.

But now—as if fearing that a thought so close to pantheism would annoy the respectable and orthodox—he puts it only as a question:

> And *what if* all of animated nature
> Be but organic Harps diversely fram'd,
> That tremble into thought, as o'er them sweeps
> Plastic and vast, one intellectual breeze,
> At once the Soul of each, and God of all?

Even as a question this went too far. With the "ventriloquism" he was later to attack as a critic, he suddenly introduces, in the role of orthodox censor, his wife Sarah, whose opinions he really far from respected: "But thy *more serious* eye" expresses a "mild reproof," and bids "me walk humbly with my God":

> Well hast thou said and holily disprais'd
> These shapings of the unregenerate mind.

What we are confronting here, as Coleridge almost grotesquely hobbles his thought in this innocent poem, is in its mild way a direct anticipation of the self-division with which he was to live for at least the next twenty years—a self-division in which some of his central philosophical interests are feared to be outside the pale of a respectability that he felt compelled to solicit, not because he himself respected it in turn, but because he so deeply craved the security of its approval, associated as it was with memories of the Ottery vicarage, the general thought of home, simple benevolence and piety.

• 6 •

Meanwhile the circumference of his reading continued to expand. It can be seriously argued that no Englishman of his time read more widely and at the same time more tenaciously in so many different fields of learning than had Coleridge by the time he was thirty. This would be in 1802, three years after his return from Germany, and five after the spring of 1797 at which we are now pausing.

He was only too aware himself of the incongruity between his intellectual interests and his external life at Nether Stowey (or for that matter what he had done generally with his life for the past eight years). Just before moving to Nether Stowey, Coleridge had described himself quite objectively to a man whom he had been getting to know through correspondence. This was the ardent revolutionary, John Thelwall (Citizen Thelwall, as he was called), who had been interested in some of Coleridge's political writing and had asked him to send some personal account of himself. In his answer Coleridge described his face as one that, unless momentarily animated by the spur of immediate eloquence, "expresses great Sloth, and great, indeed almost ideotic, good nature":

> a mere carcase of a face: fat, flabby, and expressive chiefly of inexpression. . . . As to my shape, 'tis a good shape enough, if measured —but my gait is awkward, & the walk, & the *Whole man* indicates *indolence capable of energies.*—I am, & ever have been, a great reader —& have read almost everything—a library-cormorant—I am *deep* in all out of the way books, whether of the monkish times, or of the puritanical aera—I have read & digested most of the Historical Writers —; but I do not *like* History. Metaphysics, & Poetry, & 'Facts of mind'— (i.e. Accounts of all the strange phantasms that ever possessed your philosophy-dreamers from Tauth [Thoth], the Egyptian to Taylor, the English Pagan,) are my darling Studies.—In short, I seldom read except to amuse myself—& I am almost always reading.

—Of useful knowledge, I am a so-so chemist, & I love chemistry—all else is *blank,*—but I *will* be (please God) an Horticulturist & a Farmer. I compose very little—& I absolutely hate composition. Such is my dislike, that even a sense of Duty is sometimes too weak to overpower it.

Finally, he had begun keeping the notebooks, now so famous—his "flycatchers," as he later called them—into which he jotted down every interest (phrases that struck him, psychological or scientific facts, notes of his reading in travel books, recipes for food and drink, future plans, self-condemnations and self-assurances).[2] Of special interest, for the years 1796-97, are two lists of works that he would like to write (they total about forty): "The Origin of Evil, An Epic Poem"; a discussion of William Paley, author of the famous *View of the Evidences of Christianity* (1794); an essay on the Book of Tobit, and another on the German Neoplatonist, Jakob Boehme; a liturgical drama "On the different Sects of Religion and Infidelity," with a "philosophical analysis of their Effects on mind and manners"; "Carthon, an Opera," and two satires in the manner of John Donne; editions, with critical commentary, of the eighteenth-century poets, Akenside, Collins, and Gray; six hymns "to the Sun, the Moon, and the elements"—"in one of them to introduce a dissection of Atheism," and in the last of them his "bold avowal of Berkeley's System." Also included is the two-volume "Imitations of the Modern Latin Poets," which back at Cambridge he had told his brother George was about to be sent to the press, together with a biographical and critical essay on the "Restoration of Literature" in the Renaissance.

At the close of the second and longer list is jotted a reflection that was to recur to him in the years ahead: "Our quaint metaphysical opinions in an hour of anguish [are] like playthings by the bedside of a child deadly sick."

[2] The *Notebooks* are now being authoritatively edited by Professor Kathleen Coburn (Bollingen: Pantheon Books). The first two volumes have thus far appeared (1957, 1961).

III

Wordsworth's Arrival; Coleridge as a Poet

NEAR THE END OF MARCH, Wordsworth, whom he had met briefly back in the autumn of 1795, stopped by on his return from Bristol to Racedown, in Dorset, where he was living with his sister Dorothy. In June, Coleridge repaid the visit, stayed almost a month, and the famous friendship began.

When Coleridge arrived, said Dorothy, he did not "keep to the high road, but leapt over a gate and bounded down the pathless field, by which he cut off an angle." He had indeed leapt into their hearts. The conversation of this "wonderful man," wrote Dorothy, "teems with soul, mind, and spirit." In particular she was struck with the cheerful benevolence through which his brilliance shone. (Years later she was still to wonder at the quickness with which it could reappear even in the darkest trials.) At first she thought him "very plain," with his

> wide mouth, thick lips, and not very good teeth, longish loose-growing half-curling rough black hair. But if you hear him speak for five minutes you think no more of them. His eye is large and full, not dark but grey; such an eye as would receive from a heavy soul the dullest expression; but it speaks every emotion of his animated mind; it has more of the "poet's eye in a fine frenzy rolling" than I ever witnessed. He has fine dark eyebrows, and an overhanging forehead.

Her reserved and cautious brother also began to thaw before this radiant goodwill, this ready and generous sympathy, combined with an astonishing power "of throwing out in profusion grand central truths from which might be evolved the most comprehensive systems."

Throughout most of his life the unconfident Coleridge—inhibited when he tried to write directly and formally in his own voice (inhibited, that is, when he was trying to write anything he felt was really important)—became most completely alive and the resources of his mind most open when he could talk or write vicariously: when he could speak on behalf of another, as a champion or defensive critic, or appropriate and embellish arguments from another in order to show what they could lead to, if helped along the way, or could give to another a deeper sense of the aims and supports for which he had been groping. With the other person in the foreground, any blame that could arise was deflected. Coleridge's own pent-up abilities then flowed freely. All that he himself felt incapable of expressing, poetically or systematically (for who knew to what it might lead?), could now be turned to use by another. And it was a special joy when his speculations or suggestions could find secure harbor—approval, interest, above all direct use—within the mind of a person of more "rectitude" than himself. Here, if anywhere, was proof that he was on the right track. It was like going home, but with the confidence now that he would really be welcomed at home. What reassurance he had felt when he had met the firm Southey! Since then things had slipped; Southey was not what he should be. But Tom Poole had understood (this wonderful man was even now helping him again financially, and in his usual self-effacing, indirect way). And now Coleridge was coming to know this dour Northcountryman, Wordsworth, the very embodiment of rectitude and himself a poet (a poet in the heroic British puritan vein of Milton), who prized the simplest virtues but who needed a more comprehensive aim, a more general philosophy, if he was to succeed in what he hoped to do. And was it not what Coleridge himself would have hoped to do if he himself had been a real poet?

In deepening Wordsworth's beliefs, Coleridge induced the slowly assimilative nature of the older man to turn from what Keats called "small pieces" to larger ambitions, and to begin a major philosophical poem. Wordsworth's own sense of his mission as a poet was given new meaning in a way he was just beginning to feel as Coleridge's long visit to Racedown came to its end. Years later, after all the difficulties that arose between them, he was to continue to think of Coleridge, uniquely among all he had known, as one "Placed on this earth to love and *understand.*" Meanwhile Coleridge wrote to his friends about Wordsworth. "I speak with heart-felt sincerity & (I think) with unblinded judgement," he writes Joseph Cottle, "when I tell you, that I feel myself *a little man by his side.*" And he tells Southey: "Wordsworth is a very great man—the only man, to whom *at all times* & in *all modes of excellence* I feel myself inferior."

• 2 •

With the Wordsworths in tow, both of them completely captivated by their new friend, Coleridge returned to Nether Stowey in early July. They were ostensibly coming for just a visit but Coleridge was hoping they would remain as neighbors. A mansion, Alfoxden, with beautiful grounds and a mere three miles away, was to let. The owner seemed unapproachable. But could not Tom Poole help them? The obliging Poole immediately made inquiries. Such was Poole's influence that difficulties evaporated. The place was indeed available, and at only £23 a year.

While Poole was looking into Alfoxden for the Wordsworths, Charles Lamb, receiving a week's vacation from India House, suddenly arrived for a visit at the crowded cottage. It was a joyous time for everyone except Mrs. Coleridge. She trudged about, doing the work, and looked askance at Dorothy, who sat talking freely with the men and in her Bohemian manner seemed herself, to the glum Sarah, a kind of man. Long walks were planned, but then "dear Sara," said Coleridge, "accidentally emptied a skillet of boiling milk on my foot." Forced to remain at home while the

Wordsworths and Lamb took a walk over the neighboring hills, he wrote one of the finest of his conversation poems, "This Lime-Tree Bower My Prison," in which he imaginatively follows their walk and shares *in absentia* their delight in the surroundings, especially that of the city-bred Charles Lamb, whom he addresses throughout, much to Lamb's annoyance, as "my gentle-hearted Charles."

After Alfoxden was secured for the Wordsworths, the friends visited each other constantly, extending their walks together throughout the whole area. A fly in the ointment was the unexpected visit of the revolutionary and atheist, John Thelwall, with whom Coleridge had been corresponding. He was well known to the villagers by reputation. There were complaints from as far away as Bristol. The government was naturally worried about French spies. Invasion was expected; the mutinies in the fleet had taken place in Portsmouth and Sheerness. A detective was appointed to watch the activities of this strange group that roamed about the countryside, portfolio in hand, obviously interested in the inlets of the shore. One of Coleridge's plans was for a future poem to be called "The Brook," tracing a stream from its origin to the sea, symbolically developing from it a reflective poem on life. It was a thought that often recurred to him but, except for a brief use in "Kubla Khan," it was left to Wordsworth, who later used it in the "River Duddon" sonnets. The government spy was suspicious as Coleridge jotted down descriptive notes during his walks with the Wordsworths. A reference to Spinoza, said Coleridge, was overheard by the man and interpreted as "Spy Nosy"—a reference to himself (the spy had a prominent nose). Coleridge may have embellished the story for comic effect. But the disturbance of the villagers was real enough, especially after Thelwall appeared. Mrs. St. Albyn, the owner of Alfoxden, censured the tenant who had sublet the place to the Wordsworths in the first place—the arrangement was not to be renewed—and Poole was blamed by everyone, including members of his family, for bringing this traitorous nest into the quiet, respectable countryside of Somerset. Thelwall, delighted by his new friends and the scenery, announced that he would like to settle there. Poole decided things had gone far enough. He would do anything for Coleridge himself and was beginning to admire Wordsworth, but Thelwall was different. There was also the fact that, while the others might be birds of passage, this was Poole's home; he had to live among these people for the rest of his life. Coleridge naturally understood the situation, and, delighted that he could cite a firm opinion from another for what he himself already thought, so informed Thelwall. The Wordsworths themselves were not much disturbed. They knew that they were there only for a while. It was the hope of Coleridge's company that had brought them there in the first place. Sooner or later they would be returning to the northern part of England to which they were so deeply drawn.

As the summer passed into autumn, Wordsworth and Coleridge saw each other almost daily. Naturally they began to talk in general terms about a volume of poems on which they might collaborate. Meanwhile Coleridge finished off his tragedy (*Osorio*) and sent it to Drury Lane, with no real confidence it would be accepted (it was not). He was also planning other projects, especially poems, partly because of the contagion of Wordsworth's own interests.

• 3 •

Coleridge's career as a poet has no parallel among the major European poets since the Renaissance (we are not here speaking of the quality of the poetry). There is in fact nothing quite like it in the other arts.

To begin with, no other poet of comparable stature has devoted so little time and effort to his poetry. Second, and more important, none has considered it so incidental to his other interests, hopes, or anxieties. Failure to recognize these two facts alone, at the start, has led to misinterpretations of his career that are still accepted and passed on without examination. Most common among them is the stock premise that one of the major modern poets, after being delayed by domestic and personal troubles, hit his true stride in the "Ancient Mariner," "Christabel," and "Kubla Khan," and then, because of opium and general weakness of will, was forced to fritter away the next thirty-five years in chasing philosophical and theological will-of-the-wisps, to which he would not have resorted unless his true talent had deserted him. A third and subtler interest to the psychologist and historian of genius is that the three poems that especially give him the place he has among the great English poets (all written, when put together, within a fraction of a year) are not at all in the mode or style in which he habitually wrote verse, either before or afterwards. The final incongruity is that neither his general mode of poetry nor the short-lived brilliantly exceptional one that we find in the famous three is closely connected with what one of the greatest critics in the history of literature himself most prized in poetry and, with so much sympathetic insight, understood. We are not speaking here of a mere disparity in quality between performance and ideal. This could be taken for granted. The real disparity, to use a distinction of which Coleridge himself was so fond, is in *kind* rather than *degree.*

Repeatedly, as the years passed, Coleridge kept protesting that he was not really a poet—that in particular he felt he had "no title to the name of poet according to my own definition of poetry." Among his many other remarks is a note he jotted down in his copy of Heinrich's *Commentary on the Apocalypse:* "I have too clearly before me the idea of a poet's genius to deem myself other than a very humble poet; but in the very possession of the idea, I know myself so far a poet as to feel assured that I can understand and interpret a poem in the spirit of poetry, and with the poet's spirit." Then, with the delightful humor of exaggeration and the sudden release of metaphor and image we so often find in his prose, he adds: "Like the ostrich, I cannot fly, yet have I wings that give me the *feeling* of flight"; and he goes on to picture himself running along the plain, looking up, a "bird of the earth," and expressing his appreciation and sympathy to the birds that can really fly, from the eagle to the humble skylark. And always there is the tone of apology with which he speaks of his poems or escorts them into print, as in the subtitle to "Religious Musings" ("A Desultory Poem"), or as in the original title for his "Reflections on having left a Place of Retirement"—"Reflections on entering into Active Life: A Poem which Affects not to be Poetry"—or as in his note to the fine conversation poem, "Fears in Solitude," applicable to so much of the other verse he wrote: "The above is perhaps not Poetry—but rather a sort of middle thing between Poetry and Oratory—*sermoni propriora.* Some parts are, I am conscious, too tame even for animated prose."

More than any English poet of his time except Keats—perhaps more than any other poet of the last two centuries—Coleridge from the beginning looked back with almost overwhelming admiration to what the eighteenth century had called the "greater genres"—the epic and, above all, the tragic drama: poetry that could unite scope and depth, philosophical range and immediacy of detail, psychological insight and emotional suggestiveness of phrase and image. It was the coalescence of all of these that he most prized and in fact understood with a clairvoyance that came from a genuine kinship of mind and temperament. It was this that was to serve later as the fulcrum with which he was to approach both his criticism of Shakespeare and his general theory of the function and uses of art and poetry. The potentially inhibiting effect of so pressing an ideal on so brilliantly self-conscious a nature might be taken for granted. But it is not. Constantly, in biographies and psychological interpretations of genius, almost every other factor is plucked into prominence and given precedence over those factors that have to do with a man's craft and what he was most concerned with. We are all, as Johnson said, more comfortable when we can level a man "down" to ourselves rather than level ourselves "up," and we prefer to look among more rudimentary experiences for a lower common denominator that could conceivably apply to us all (as if every "deerstealer," as Coleridge once said, had it in him to become a Shakespeare). That literary biography has always been more guilty of this reductionism than has the biography of statesmen or scientists is a salutary reminder to the critic of the slippery, elusive nature of the arts, and the ease with which we can use them for any purpose.

George Coleridge, reflecting long afterwards on the earlier poetry of his younger brother, made a perceptive remark. The verse showed little of the "exuberance of fancy" that had been one of the principal characteristics of his brother since early boyhood. In his school days, George continued, Coleridge showed an unrivalled talent "in the facility with which he construed the most difficult Classics, and in his various and deep English reading." And George goes on to speculate whether Samuel's understanding and admiration of great writing did not intimidate him—whether "his practice in writing did not keep pace with his knowledge" because he found it inevitably "embarrassing every moment to be confronted in his progress" with so high a standard.

• 4 •

In Coleridge's early poems we find two conventional eighteenth-century styles, one of which has completely faded by the time he is twenty-five, while the other persists to the end, remaining as the vehicle for most of the poetry he ever wrote. The first is the declamatory odal style that descends from Dryden.[1] This is the official poetic style of the century for what we may call occasional *celebrative* verse. That it had been disdained by Pope made it the more attractive. Here was no association with neoclassic delicacy, artifice, or didacticism. Hence its persistence in the minor poetry of the century, and the ready use of it, in their first poetic exercises, by most of the young Romantics. The virtue of the style lay in the ease with which vigor could be expressed or suggested. The weakness lay in the ease with which the style could harden into the gestures of rhetoric.

But far more alluring to Coleridge from the beginning was the reflective mode of the later eighteenth century—familiar, casual,

[1] Examples would be the "Destruction of the Bastile" (1789), the first version of the "Monody on the Death of Chatterton" (1790), the ode "Music" (1791), and the "Ode to the Departing Year" (1796).

uninvolved, often elegiac in tone.[2] This proved so congenial and made such good use of his inhibitions as well as some of his hopes that it could, in fact, be described as Coleridge's general and habitual poetic style, the flowering of which we see in the best of the conversation poems, especially "Frost at Midnight" (February, 1798). By this, we must again remind ourselves, is not meant the form of expression in which he achieved his greatest success (the "Mariner" or "Kubla Khan"), still less the kind of poetry he most admired and by the age of forty felt it to be one of the purposes of his life to interpret, but rather that in which the overwhelming bulk of his poetry is written: that is, a meditative mode, deliberately relaxed in manner, in which the poet, though speaking in the first person, stands aside and views things somewhat *ab extra* (to use one of Coleridge's favorite distinctions), "feeling *for*" rather than "with" the object. As the years passed, he was to become increasingly impatient of the poet who stands *ab extra,* and was to prize by contrast—though feeling himself unable to exemplify it—the direct sympathetic involvement, the dramatic portrayal of subject organically and *ab intra* (from the "germ within"). Here, as in so many of his critical values, he was personally spurred by his reaction to the poetry he himself had written and by his sense of the chasm between it and the forms of poetry he valued most.

Of all the major English Romantic poets, from the oldest of them, Blake, to the youngest, Keats, Coleridge is by far the most conservative—almost defensively so—in the idiom he accepts and with which he in general remains. No interpretation of him can even begin to get beneath the surface without the frank recognition of this fact. It is a fact of the greatest psychological interest in a man who is in so many ways an innovator—far more interest-

[2] As in most of the sonnets and poems in short stanzas, but principally in the blank verse "effusions," of which "Religious Musings: a Desultory Poem . . ." (1794-96) is the first important example, followed by "The Destiny of Nations" (1796), "To a Friend [Lamb]" (1796), and the conversation poems generally. "Religious Musings" and "The Destiny of Nations," probably because they are more pretentious in aim, also incorporate some of the props and stiff brocade of the declamatory style, which are then shed, almost permanently, in the conversation poems.

ing than the minor personal details to which we often reductively attach our conception of the "psychological." If it has not been much noticed, it is partly because of the unhappy historical compartmentalization of our approach to literature. The student of the Romantics tends to leap over the period from 1660 to 1790. The phrase "eighteenth-century poetry" conjures up for him memories of the couplets of Dryden and Pope and perhaps a few names that suggest something a little different. The student of the eighteenth century, in turn, repays the compliment with what Johnson, rebuking Mrs. Thrale, called "the superiority of inattention," and thinks, when confronted with the name of Coleridge, of little more than the "Ancient Mariner," "Christabel," "Kubla Khan," and some of the critical writing.

By the middle of the eighteenth century English poetry had already begun the great transition in idiom and style that was to create a rough norm that lasted at least until World War I. The Romantics—the entire nineteenth-century achievement in poetry—are very much the offspring of the eighteenth century, an offspring already adolescent by 1800. True, most of the major Romantics—Wordsworth, Shelley, Keats, even Byron at times—transcended the convention, though working through it rather than against it. (Blake, when he was not working through it, did not deliberately work against it, as the twentieth century was to do, but simply forgot it.) Coleridge alone retained the relaxed Augustan mode in its pristine state for most of the poetry he wrote—and not merely that with which he began. Its appeal and the protection it offered were irresistible (at least it was irresistible to the more passive side of his nature—always the principal side of him when challenge and ideal became too active). For it did not claim much. It was obviously not aspiring to the "greater genres" of an earlier period—the epic and the tragic drama. It had not yet evolved the ideal of what Keats called "intensity" as a quality that could be attained within this familiar, popularly "open" idiom. (This was something that was to happen very suddenly within the next thirty years, from 1790 to 1820.) At the same time it had virtues. It was accessible to almost everyone. It could fulfill the functions of a "friend." And there were opportunities for improvement. It could be made even more personal and direct ("a man speaking to men," in Wordsworth's phrase). There were also opportunities for "philosophy," for the expression of genuine thought. Granted that the poet tended to stand *ab extra,* as compared with the Shakespearean poet-dramatist. This was a problem. But there were possibilities of moving closer. And in any case, Coleridge could tell himself that he was not yet seriously getting to work on poetry. No one could expect him to be unaware of what was really needed. He was not completely joking when he told Joseph Cottle (April, 1797):

> I should not think of devoting less than 20 years to an Epic Poem. Ten to collect materials and warm my mind with universal science. I would be a tolerable Mathematician, I would thoroughly know Mechanics, Hydrostatics, Optics, and Astronomy, Botany, Metallurgy, Fossilism, Chemistry, Geology, Anatomy, Medicine—then the *mind of man*—then the *minds of men*—in all Travels, Voyages and Histories. So I would spend ten years—the next five to the composition of the poem—and the five last to the correction of it.

• 5 •

Easily the finest things he wrote in the Augustan vein are the so-called conversation poems—a group of at least six poems in blank verse: "The Eolian Harp" (August, 1795), "Reflections on Having Left a Place of Retirement" (winter, 1795), "This Lime-Tree Bower My Prison" (June, 1797), "Frost at Midnight" (February, 1798), "Fears in Solitude" (April, 1798), and "The Nightingale" (April, 1798). The term is sometimes stretched to include a few other, shorter poems of the time. It does not embrace but is sharply applicable to two later poems, "Dejection: an Ode" (April, 1802) and "To William Wordsworth" (January, 1807).

We violate chronology in jumping ahead through the next year to speak of the conversation poems as a whole. But they may be most conveniently discussed as the culmination of his earlier and habitual mode. Their novelty, within their limits, should be recognized. The most rapid survey of the poetry of the second half of the eighteenth century (including even Coleridge's admired William Cowper—an admiration that tells a good deal about Coleridge the poet) will show that, in Coleridge, the verse becomes more flexible, the idiom still more colloquial (the lute, in the "Eolian Harp," placed "length-wise" in the casement; "Well, they are gone"; the "goings-on of life"; "It was a spot which you might aptly call"; "And we *were* bless'd," "One Benefit-Club for mutual flattery"; "I hurried with him to our orchard-plot"). Moreover the interplay and development of association is on a higher plane. What is being considered is more interesting; it assumes more mind.

In writing these poems, Coleridge was not consciously creating or hoping to establish a genre. When he used the term ("The Nightingale: A Conversation Poem, April, 1798"), it was with a half-humorous apology as if to say it was a "middle thing" between poetry and conversation. Yet by not claiming too much, by setting his sights deliberately (even ostentatiously) low and therefore feeling free to regard these frankly minor poems as only casual "effusions," he was able, in the release this brought him, to lift almost effortlessly the late Augustan reflective mode into something that could fulfill many of the poetic needs and interests of the next century and a half. And by this is meant not merely the "purer" form of the blank-verse conversation poem, from Wordsworth (particularly "Tintern Abbey") to Robert Frost—this is only the most obvious line of descent—but the colloquial-ruminative mode generally, which persists in a variety of forms even after the twentieth-century shift in idiom. Significantly Eliot, after attacking it in his early years, found it indispensable for much of his culminating work, the *Four Quartets*.

We cannot hope to pursue this subject historically through the next century and a half, though there is a large uncharted area here for the critic of modern poetry who wishes to examine the brute fact that *reflective* verse has become inevitable to the poet since the middle eighteenth century, however much he may secretly or openly yearn for poetic drama, the epic, or for lyrical intensity (though the last has continued longer as an attainable ideal). Our concern is with only a fraction of the work of a great writer—his poetry—and at the moment with only a part of that fraction. The point to be stressed is that in this group of poems, released from the burden of self-demand (here as in so many other ways he proves to be a barometer for later poets), he became fluent and inventive, and in the process transmitted to Wordsworth and to the nineteenth-century generally an effective voice for the more colloquial and ruminative uses of poetry.

• 6 •

But the very congeniality of the conversation poem to Coleridge's own dialectical habit of mind had its liabilities, far more for him than others who were to use it. He was refreshingly free—or so it seemed at first—to move from one side of the path to the other. But for this very reason, lacking the excuses as well as the challenges that an imposed form can provide, the writer is naturally more vulnerable. Permitted to "walk naked" (as Yeats put it), a Wordsworth—confident of himself and even more of his convictions—had little to fear. Poets less confident than Wordsworth could also exploit the obvious advantages of this form that seemed not to be a "form." But to Coleridge, so apprehensive of criticism, so quick to take steps to forestall or deflect it, the lack of a protective, superimposed form—protective because it could itself serve as a lightning rod for blame, as an excuse for saying (or having to say) what he did—compelled him to construct his own protections or, more accurately, allowed some of his habitual, personal defenses to enter bodily into the poem. He saw this quickly enough. By the summer of 1798, a year after the months on which we are lingering, he was becoming convinced he could do nothing with this particular kind of poetry that the "Giant Wordsworth," as he called him, could not do better.

Hence the conversation poems, however admirable in their own right, have less value as the direct expression of his actual or formal thought than they at first appear to have. They are transparent expressions of the writer, to be sure, but not so much of what he really thought (though this is to some extent present), nor of the whole of what he would really have wished to be, as of a particular way in which he would wish—in fact needed—to be considered by others. There was nothing really hypocritical here. He needed, for example, to show to others, and to reassure himself, that he was a benevolent man. And he *was* benevolent. The constant protest that this was so, from the boyhood years at Ottery, was not because he was trying to hide any deep aggressions. It was because he had quickly learned—or felt—that in his thinking, reading, and imaginings, he was outside the pale of an older, more respectable company of human beings. What was "wrong" with him, what made him suspect to himself and as he imagined to others, was not any desire to harm. It was the deeply ingrained fear that his inner life was not really what *they* wanted—the *Arabian Nights,* which he had read in his aunt's Everything shop, *Robinson Crusoe,* the tales of the supernatural, and later, at Christ's Hospital and Cambridge, the Neoplatonists, Voltaire, Hartley, Unitarianism, pantisocracy: the eccentric generally, the out-of-the-way, the constant craving for new horizons, new knowledge—whether fanciful, or philosophic, or pragmatically scientific.

His deepest need was to prove that in this waif-like irregularity there was nothing harmful or vicious: as little harmful or vicious as the friendly albatross when, also from outside the pale—from unknown and mysterious regions—it appears on the ship of human voyagers: able, with its wide spread of wing, to travel so far; awkward when not in flight; unaccustomed to the habits of men, but eager for their company; and altogether well-meaning. Wordsworth's casual suggestion about the use of the albatross in a poem of exploration caught his imagination as no symbol had ever done in any poetry he had yet written. The need was to prove that any excursions Coleridge himself might be making—these "shapings" of an apparently "unregenerate mind"—were on behalf of others. And was he not, in his own way, always seeking to return home—return to the hearth, the domestic and simple virtues, the humanly direct and unpretentious? So at Christ's Hospital he might (the "inspired charity-boy") quote Homer, Plotinus, and Iamblichus. But his heart was stirred when he was taken into the Evans family, or when he had encountered Bowles's sonnets—that poetry that could serve as a "friend"—and had made forty handwritten copies of them. Was not his life since then—the ideals of society when at Cambridge, pantisocracy, even the simple life at Nether Stowey—indication enough where his heart really lay?

With the completely open form of the conversation poem, therefore, a recurring pattern is noticeable in which, however free he ostensibly is, he falls into his habitual role as usher—as benevolent and understanding usher: a role he was to fulfill brilliantly in the literary criticism, was to fall into (at times rather jerkily) during his exhilarating encounter with German thought, and then continued to adopt, partly out of old habit and partly because of uncertainty, even in the later years when, in the religious writing, he must first introduce another on the stage (Archbishop Leighton in the *Aids to Reflection*), and then, in his own voice, only champion or nuance. It was not he who could receive the "blessing." Hence the premise of some of the conversation poems (suggestively noted by R. A. Durr): the release, the happiness or confidence, the opportunity for insight, are either given or presumed to be possible only to another. What is involved here—at least we can say this when we think of his life as a whole—is an act of "blessing," and in the older meaning of that term: a surrender, a giving, which assumes sacrifice (the word "blessing" is connected with "blood"—with "bleeding"). Through surrender, Coleridge himself—the incorrigible waif—can acquire his own vicarious release of heart, his own security and confidence in what he thinks and hopes. So in the "Eolian Harp," where, as we noticed, it is the young wife Sarah who is brought in, with "more serious eye," to check the roving fancies of the "unregenerate mind" that is his own. And in "This Lime-Tree Bower My Prison," the poem written when he was forced to stay at home because of his lame foot, when Charles Lamb and the Wordsworths took their walk from the Stowey cottage through the Quantock Hills, the release of imagination comes in picturing the city-bred Lamb's feeling of novelty and joy in these new surroundings.

So, again, in "Frost at Midnight," easily the finest of the "conversation" poems. The poet's musings, as he sits before the fire in his cottage, become focused on his cradled son, Hartley. The film on the firegrate—"the stranger" as it was called—had in folk tradition been a symbol that an absent friend would be coming. This hunger for friendship and understanding, as the poet watches the fluttering flame (the stranger), leads him back in memory to his childhood, his days at school. The hope, year after year, to find both the stranger and the friend—"the *stranger's* face" that turns out to be the familiar "more beloved"—is now given to the sleeping infant: "I was rear'd / In the great city, pent 'mid cloisters dim / . . . But *thou,* my babe, shalt wander like a breeze," and learn the shapes and sounds

> Of that eternal language, which thy God
> Utters, who from eternity doth teach
> Himself in all, and all things in himself.

• 7 •

On the afternoon of November 13, 1797, Wordsworth, his sister Dorothy, and Coleridge set off on a short walking tour along the southern coast of the Bristol Channel. During this walk, and for a few months afterwards, some of the psychological problems Coleridge faced as a poet were suspended, deflected, or turned to brilliant, unanticipated use.

Coleridge and Wordsworth had planned beforehand to defray the expenses of this walking tour by writing jointly a poem that might be sold to a magazine. Interests from each side of the joint enterprise coalesced. The poem was to be written as a ballad, the simple, traditional form to which Wordsworth was so attracted. But it would involve, to please Coleridge, the theme of exploration. He had in mind, for that matter, a dream told him by his neighbor, John Cruikshank, of "a skeleton ship, with figures on it." He had also been thinking again of the outcasts-

of society: those figures of guilt, of unthinking or unintentional sin, like the Wandering Jew, that are found throughout literature. Naturally he was drawn to them. But the apologetic treatments of them to which he was inclined were out of the question, at least at the moment. The "Wanderings of Cain," the archetype of the outcast, made a better subject. Culpability could there be taken for granted. No moral question would be involved. He had broached this to Wordsworth as a subject for joint effort. Wordsworth was not enthusiastic. Nor was Coleridge himself when he stopped to reflect on it. What would one do with the subject? The man was really guilty of murder. No drama of extenuation was possible, at least from Coleridge, though Byron was later to write one. The whole thing broke up in a laugh. Wordsworth, however, had been reading in Shelvocke's *Voyages* that a man who killed an albatross—that awkward bird of good omen that could appear on ship from the Antarctic—could bring on himself the vengeance of the tutelary spirits of the region.

Together, as they walked along the seacoast, they worked out the plan of the ballad, which if finished was to be published (and this was both a reassurance and incentive to Coleridge) with some other poems of Wordsworth. Coleridge's interest and imagination took so fertile a hold on the idea that, as Wordsworth later said, he himself felt it presumptuous to continue with his own contributions and withdrew "from an undertaking upon which I could only have been a clog." When they returned home from the walking tour, Coleridge, even more caught up with the subject and with a sense that Wordsworth's and Dorothy's eyes were on him, continued to work on it for some weeks, with a single-mindedness almost unique in his career as a writer until the desperate days, twenty years later, when he forced himself to put together the *Biographia Literaria*.

• 8 •

Yes, he had fallen into something here that was altogether different and yet in its own way strangely familiar: different from his own previous ways of writing, different from the way he generally thought he ought to write, different from Wordsworth himself. It was a pleasure to find that he could write a poetry that would in no way seem to rival Wordsworth. The field could be left completely free for Wordsworth, with Coleridge present only as philosophical assistant and general encourager—and for a kind of poetry that was really more relevant to the modern age: a poetry in which we should have the colloquial in language, the familiar and homely in image and sentiment, the deliberative and reflective (as contrasted with Coleridge's own impulsiveness), and, above all (it was here that he felt himself so lacking) the combination of moral rectitude with personal self-confidence.

Encouraging Wordsworth, helping him to find a ground for further self-clarification, Coleridge himself laid the basis for the famous division of labor in which he himself would play the lesser role. The results were the "Ancient Mariner," "Christabel," and "Kubla Khan," of which the subjects, interests, style, indeed the entire conception, are almost the reverse of Wordsworth's, or for that matter of Coleridge's own poetry thus far. And if Coleridge's eagerness to play the minor—at least more specialized—partner seemed to create limitations, it also proved to be a genuine release. Limitation of any sort has that advantage to a nature clogged by too rich a diversity of sympathies and hesitant before the demands of conflicting choice. This particular form of limitation proved especially fruitful, if only in the short run. No moral or religious censor intruded before every line. Technical claims (of plot, atmosphere, general theme, meter) were paramount. His habitual need to demonstrate the writer's personal goodwill was, if not anesthetized, made obviously irrelevant, at least until he was midway at work on "Christabel."

If some of the inhibitions with which he had been living now stood aside, it was partly because of the psychological transfer that had taken place in his need for a moral basis. The benevolent gesture, instead of entering bodily into the poem, could now take another form: assistance to an admired friend through a cooperation that involved some self-effacement, a more specialized and restricted effort, on Coleridge's part. In addition there was also the appeal of novelty, as he found himself making rapid progress with the "Ancient Mariner," and then, caught up by the momentum, began "Christabel." But there was a release also because this new, specialized mode was deliberately remote and symbolic. Here Coleridge exemplifies the sense of release that the symbolic was to give poets a century later. In the process a surprisingly large internal fund was tapped. He suddenly attained a power of expression—a condensation and suggestiveness of phrase, image, and music—that gave him the position he now has among the major English poets.

At the same time something very curious happened that suggests how pent-up his creative life had been thus far, how little it had been released by his other poetry. For at least a fraction of his unrivaled reading (and when we speak of his reading we should remember that he was still only in his middle and later twenties) was tapped and brilliantly exploited. The subject is treated in detail by the greatest of literary detective studies, indeed one of the monuments of literary scholarship—*The Road to Xanadu* (1927) by John Livingston Lowes.[3] In this one respect if in no other, these three poems of Coleridge are almost unique. Nothing quite like this sudden release of so large a range of reading has yet been found in any other poem of comparable length.[4]

[3] Lowes was concerned with the "Ancient Mariner" and "Kubla Khan." The same method has been applied to "Christabel" by Arthur H. Nethercot, in *The Road to Tryermaine* (1939).

[4] During the fifteen years before and the twenty years after the *Road to Xanadu,* Lowes tried to apply the same approach to other poets (his own reading, rarely equalled in the twentieth century, embraced every major literature beginning with Greek and Hebrew). But as this greatest of literary sleuths often admitted, he could find nothing really comparable. The combined effort of forty years of scholarship since the *Road to Xanadu* has had to confess the same thing. Eliot's "Waste Land" is occasionally mentioned as an interesting parallel. But it is not really comparable since the use of literary echoes and allusions is there a self-conscious device.

IV

"The Ancient Mariner," "Christabel," and "Kubla Khan"

THE FIRST OF THE THREE POEMS, "The Rime of the Ancient Mariner," is indeed greatly conceived. For whatever its more specific themes, the general premise, pervading every aspect and interest of the poem, is the mystery of human life and conscience. To stress this at the start is obviously not to deny that much else is involved. The wider the circumference of our experience in anything, the more points at which we begin to encounter what Wordsworth called the "burden of the mystery."

As a result the poem has eluded reductionism into pat formula more triumphantly than any other comparable poem in English—more than any other poem of similar length and quality, that is, which has been completed and not left as a fragment, which has been composed with obvious care, and which, just as obviously, is deeply moral in theme. Hence both the wealth of possible interpretations and, conversely, the skeptical refusal to admit the possibility of any at all.[1] Specialized interpretation is at once chal-

[1] Throughout the nineteenth century, indeed almost until World War II, discussions of the "Ancient Mariner" tended more often than not to deny meanings beyond the surface of the poetry. The turning point in the interpretation of the "Ancient Mariner" came with Robert Penn Warren's brilliant and extended analysis (1946), to which most of the later studies of the poem are indebted either directly or indirectly.

lenged and frustrated. Both the challenge and the frustration are increased by a further peculiarity of the poem. For while as a whole it is so open in what it includes and even more suggests, much of what the classical critic would call its "machinery" seems deceptively closed and specific, virtually crying out for allegorical interpretation. This was doubtless the real reason for any uneasiness that Coleridge had about the poem, and his reluctance to talk much about it (with the significant exception of his remark to Mrs. Barbauld, in which he implied that the machinery of the avenging spirits was too morally obtrusive, thus oversimplifying the conception of the poem).[2] Meanwhile in his critical writing—so much of which answers or indirectly censures his own poetry—he was to have a personal incentive to make his crucial distinction between "allegory"—the straight one-for-one translation of thought into "picture language"—and "symbol."

But once incorporated, the machinery, much of it suggested by Wordsworth, could hardly be removed without disrupting the whole structure of the last third of the "Ancient Mariner." Moreover this was a finished poem, and one of obvious distinction. He did not have too many of them. If nothing else, it was a poem, as he rightly thought, that "cannot be imitated," and he was always to remain secretly proud of it. There was much to be said for treading softly and leaving well enough alone. Except for dropping most of the archaisms in the second edition of the *Lyrical Ballads* (1800), the only important change was to add, in the edition of his poems in 1817, the beautiful gloss in order to flesh out the obtrusive skeletal bones of the supernatural

[2] "Mrs. Barbauld once told me that she admired the "Ancient Mariner" very much, but that there were two faults in it, it was improbable, and had no moral. As for the probability, I owned that that might admit some question; but as to the want of a moral, I told her that in my own judgment the poem had too much; and that the only, or chief fault, if I may say so, was the obtrusion of the moral sentiment so openly on the reader as a principle or cause of action in a work of such pure imagination. It ought to have had no more moral than the Arabian Nights' tale of the merchant's sitting down to eat dates by the side of a well, and throwing the shells inside, and lo! a genie starts up, and says he *must* kill the aforesaid merchant, *because* one of the date shells had, it seems, put out the eye of the genie's son." (*Table-Talk*, May 31, 1830.)

machinery and also to help smooth the flow of the narrative. He also at that time added the epigraph from Thomas Burnet's *Archaeologiae Philosophicae* in order to emphasize his central premise—the mystery surrounding the human soul:

> I can easily believe that there are more invisible than visible beings in the universe. But who will explain to us the nature of them, their ranks, relationships, distinguishing qualities, and functions? What is it they do? Is what places do they dwell? Always about the knowledge of these things the human mind circles, never reaching it . . .

• 2 •

To begin with, this is a poem of exploration and discovery as well as of guilt and partial redemption. The ship that bears the Mariner, after skirting the desolation and strange beauty of the Antarctic, enters a sea that no one else has explored ("We were the *first* that ever burst / Into that silent sea"). So with the Mariner himself as an individual. By thoughtlessly slaying the albatross, which has so gratuitously met and stayed with the ship, he is to come into contact with forces in the universe which lie beyond the experience of ordinary men and of which he would otherwise remain ignorant.[3] The poem is by no means single-minded in its attitude toward this deed. The Mariner has done a guilty thing, and he is certainly punished. Yet had he not done it, his sense of the universe (and ours through him) would be more limited. If he is a guilty man, he is also something of a hero simply because he has gone further in experience than others. In an admittedly qualified way, he is akin to those romantic heroes that were to become so common in nineteenth-century writing—some of them Byronic, others patterned after Faust—who by violating laws acquire a depth of experience that others lack. As a rule one of three things tends to happen. The hero is emancipated by his

[3] Interpretations of the Mariner's act as Coleridge's thoughtless slaying of his own poetic talent not only forget this but violate chronology. The poetic talent is only now beginning to appear—and very successfully. (Nor even in later years did he feel it was thrown away or slain. Depending on his mood, he regarded it as evaporated, suspended, as never having existed anyway, or as subsumed in more important tasks.)

crime, and finds the taboos were groundless; or the crime is simply a frustrated and often tragic expression of revolt against a universe meaningless and cruel; or (as in the case of the Mariner) the hero acquires painfully a knowledge that others lack, though they may pay lip service to it—a knowledge that there really is a moral order in the universe that cannot be violated with impunity.

It is less the simple act of shooting the albatross than it is the Mariner himself that makes us feel that it was so fearful and guilty a deed. The wedding guest, incredulous and appalled by the horror on the Mariner's face, cries out: "God save thee, ancient Mariner . . . *Why looks't thou so?*" And the Mariner answers: "With my cross-bow / I shot the Albatross." We therefore strain needlessly at the poem when we try to rationalize the horror of the act (for example, viewing it too literally as equivalent to the murder of a human being—partly because of the Mariner's own statement that the albatross had come to them out of the fog *"As if* it had been a Christian soul"). We are tempted to do this simply because Coleridge himself is able to make so much out of what would have seemed, as the incident was given him by Wordsworth, to be so limited a symbol. If Coleridge is identified with the Mariner after the crime, he is identified before it, as David Perkins points out, with the albatross itself—that creature with its great wingspread, so awkward-looking, unfamiliar, and above all friendly, which as a gift of nature has appeared on the ship from another world and is then thoughtlessly slain. But the subjective implications are under control and remain only as it were in solution. Moreover it is the Mariner's later story that is of primary importance. The entire episode of the albatross, though naturally indispensable, is confined to only five stanzas—less than a thirtieth of the poem.

An alternative approach interprets the poem in a Wordsworthian way. The Mariner violates the bond of communion between man and the natural world, a bond restored, or partly restored, when the Mariner is able to bless the water-snakes. Much can be said for this interpretation provided we do not try to use it as an exclusive framework. Certainly one of the central premises of the poem, as Robert Penn Warren has shown, is that suggested in the lines of the "Eolian Harp" beginning

> O! the *one Life* within us and abroad,
> Which meets all motion and becomes its soul;

and the shooting of the albatross is the Mariner's offense against the "one Life." Coleridge felt free to make as much as he did of the act simply because the incident, which Wordsworth had suggested to him, was not too obviously extreme. The murder of a human being would have created complications beyond the control of a poem of this length. Sufficient motivation would have had to be shown in some detail unless the Mariner were to appear a monster. And, in any case, *motivation* was not the concern. In fact its presence would have dissolved the potentialities that now seemed open to Coleridge. For months, as we have already noticed, he had been thinking of writing an epic on "The Origin of Evil." The whole subject had begun increasingly to elude as well as intrigue him. For if we postulate a universe pervaded by "one Life," then—as in monistic and pantheistic religions generally—we seem confined to one of two choices in our attempt to understand evil, neither one of which satisfies both the mind and the heart. That is, we must either admit evil as an inevitable part of the fabric and thus qualify our conception of a benevolent God, or else we are encouraged to explain it away as something other than "evil" (i.e., as something not so bad after all). No one knew this better than Coleridge himself, and as the years passed he was to grow even less satisfied with either of these alternatives. But for the moment the poem permitted him to choose what seems to be a version of the second one simply because it was not too terrible a thing, and then through suggestion—especially through the Mariner's own reaction to what he did—to indicate its relevance to more patent and drastic forms of evil. The Mariner's offense against the "one Life"—the act of picking up the cross bow and killing the albatross—is essentially an act of thoughtlessness, of idleness of mind and conscience: an attempt to fill out the moment, to make it pass more intensely, by an idle assertion of will, of selfhood, of sense of power, that will impress both oneself and others.

It is one measure of the poem's success that there is something in the Mariner's act we are afraid of—this sudden impulse to kill something innocent, if different—even if we do not share the Wordsworthian attitude toward the communion of man with nature. This is enough. We need not try to make the chain of events seem more reasonable, more immediately explicable and clear-cut. When things are left indistinct, as Coleridge understood so well, the mind is more likely to continue to return to them and to find further meanings. Certainly the whole conception of the Mariner's act is imaginatively capable of wide extension (to moral if not to other forms of evil). To at least some extent, therefore, we face, in this suggestive, ambiguous act, another expression of what Coleridge wrote to his brother George shortly after finishing the poem: "I believe most stedfastly in original Sin; that from our mothers' wombs our understandings are darkened; and even when our understandings are in the Light, that our organization is depraved, and our volitions imperfect."

• 3 •

It is after the Mariner shoots the albatross that he enters a sea where no one else has been. From here on we realize that we are dealing with the fate of an individual human being rather than that of the crew. In this section of the poem—certainly the most starkly existential lines of the nineteenth century—the theme is the nakedness of man's trembling existence before the vast unknown, an existence made the more vulnerable by what Coleridge in a later poem ("The Pains of Sleep") called "the unfathomable hell within." Hence the relative unimportance of the crew. At first pleased and then displeased by the Mariner's act, they are in either case unaware of the implications. Their dramatic importance is at first as a backdrop, and later in the regret that their fate causes the Mariner.

In the condensed treatment of isolation and guilt that follows we have the most graphic prototype in English poetry—probably in modern European poetry as a whole—of the state of mind that William James described in his famous chapter "The Sick Soul" in *Varieties of Religious Experience.* This becalmed ship is a hell, a desert in the midst of a boundless ocean. To the Mariner there are only heat, thirst, motionlessness, rottenness ("The very deep did *rot*"). The creatures he is later able to see with so different an eye are "slimy things"; and the colors that might in another state of mind seem so beautiful are like the "death-fires" of a witches' sabbath. Then, greeted at first with cruelly deluded hope when it is still only a speck on the horizon, comes the "skeleton ship" of which Coleridge's neighbor, John Cruikshank, had dreamed, its bars flecking the merciless sun. The two figures on the ship, Death and Life-in-Death, cast dice for the Mariner and the ship, and Life-in-Death wins the Mariner. The nightmarelike experience is that also mentioned in the poem "The Pains of Sleep," five years after the "Ancient Mariner" (the "powerless will" paralyzed by guilt and remorse—"Life-stifling fear, Soul-stifling shame") or in the frightening poem "Limbo," written fourteen years later still, with its hell of "positive Negation."

Now that Life-in-Death has won him, while the crew themselves drop dead (their souls whizzing past him "Like the whizz of my cross-bow"), the Mariner is completely alone on the "rotting deck," looking out on the "rotting sea," seeking death for seven days and nights, himself as foul and accursed, to his own mind, as everything else around him. Then slowly, and just as gratuitously as the albatross itself had appeared, the healing process starts. For however paralyzed the world in which he has now found himself, freedom of motion, he learns, still exists somewhere:

> The moving Moon went up the sky,
> And nowhere did abide:
> Softly she was going up,
> And a star or two beside.

Caught up in the beauty and wonder of a motion completely free and on a far vaster scale than the scene of what he has been experiencing, the Mariner himself becomes at least partly freed from the paralysis and prison-house of self. In order to emphasize what has happened, at this turning point of the poem, Coleridge in his revision added the longest and most beautiful of the glosses:

> In his loneliness and fixedness he yearneth toward the journeying Moon, and the stars that still sojourn, yet still move onward; and everywhere the blue sky belongs to them, and is their appointed rest, and their native country and their own natural homes, which they enter unannounced, as lords that are certainly expected and yet there is a silent joy at their arrival.

The moon, as Mr. Warren says, is for Coleridge a constantly recurring symbol of the imagination, partly because its half-light frees the imagination to act, and partly because the very idea of reflected light is associated with reception and response. The Mariner's whole situation begins to change. He is by no means certain, as he tells the story, that this was a *true* transformation (the moonlight at first only "bemocked" the "awful red" of the sea, covering it with an appearance like "April hoar-frost"). So too with the unexpected beauty he now finds in the creatures of the deep that had before seemed so vile. But in any case they are at least known now as "living things"—as "God's creatures of the great calm"; and it is as "living things" that the Mariner, further transcending his loneliness and loathing of self, blesses them "unaware." In this moment of humility and release, he finds that he can pray, and the albatross, which had been hung about his neck by the now dead crew, slips off into the sea.

• 4 •

The tale of the Mariner's redemption then follows. Of primary importance is the fact that his redemption is only partial. The poem is often cited as one of the most vivid modern versions of the archetypal theme of psychological rebirth—of what William James called the "twice-born" soul. This is true, but only up to a point. For the archetypal theme involves the almost total destruction of the old self in order to make room for the new. This was an impossible belief for Coleridge—even in the dark years ahead when he was to hunger very much for that belief. In any case, as he realized, the poem would have been immensely cheapened had the redemption of the Mariner been more than partial. It could easily, in fact, have become rather silly, as is quickly shown by a little speculation about the possible ways of portraying a complete redemption in this context.

Hence the prediction, so ominous because expressed so softly, of the second of the two Polar-Spirits as they discuss the Mariner:

> The other was a softer voice,
> As soft as honey-dew:
> Quoth he, "The man hath penance done,
> And penance more will do."

The continued penance, of course, is that the Mariner is condemned to relive the experience—in a sense to re-enact imaginatively what he has done—by telling it repeatedly, trying to come to terms with it, trying to put it into some context of meaning. It is here that the poem acquires its widest universality, a universality that sustains the final third of the poem which (however brilliant as a *tour de force*) otherwise suffers from an inevitable drop, both in Coleridge's personal involvement and in his inventive freedom. For the brute fact remained that he still had to get the Mariner back to human society, and preferably with some dispatch unless the poem was to drag. Here Wordsworth's help proved invaluable. Coleridge himself was constitutionally loth to bring anything to a neat close. Too many avenues were always opening, too many valuable nuances seen, that would have to be disregarded if a thing were to be brought to a close—too many objections, too many alternatives, that would then have to be left unreconciled. Wordsworth had already suggested that, after the killing of the albatross, the "tutelary Spirits" of the polar regions should take it upon themselves to "avenge the crime." Since a practical problem was faced in returning the ship, he also, he said, "suggested the navigation of the ship by the dead men."

Our symbolic interpretations of the poem, therefore, become

especially vulnerable when we strain with too much subtlety and indirection at what we may call the "machinery of the return." A return was needed, and Wordsworth provided one. Again, with the sudden sinking of the ship when it returns to the English harbor: unless it and the crew of corpses were disposed of, the complications for the story would have been enormous. At the very least they would have suffocated the existential and highly individual theme. The focus is altogether on the Mariner himself as he returns. The Mariner, hoping that the Hermit, who lives in the wood by the harbor, would absolve him of sin, begins his tale with an agony of spirit that seems to depart with the telling. But

> Since then, at an uncertain hour,
> That agony returns:
> And till my ghastly tale is told,
> This heart within me burns.

It follows that the Mariner, even after the passage of so many years, has not yet completely understood what has happened any more than he has been completely "redeemed." Now that his tale is over, he speaks only of his own personal need, after so fearful a loneliness, for the simplest and humblest relationship with others and with God:

> O Wedding-Guest! this soul hath been
> Alone on a wide wide sea:
> So lonely 'twas, that God himself
> Scarce seemed there to be.
>
> O sweeter than the marriage-feast,
> 'Tis sweeter far to me,
> To walk together to the kirk
> With a goodly company! —
>
> To walk together to the kirk,
> And all together pray . . .

And the mention of prayer leads him to add—again in the simplest language—something else that he had learned:

> He prayeth best, who loveth best
> All things both great and small;
> For the dear God who loveth us,
> He made and loveth all.

However else we react to the poem, we radically misread it if we pluck these lines of the Mariner from their dramatic context and view them as a final summing up by the poet himself.[4] The same mistake is often made with the close of Keats's "Ode on a Grecian Urn," and with similar results. The less sophisticated are pleased to have what they conceive to be an authoritative statement of the "theme" from the writer himself. The more sophisticated feel obliged to point out the naïvety of the poet in permitting so simpleminded a conclusion to an otherwise complex poem. But the naïvety is not in the poet but in the diagnosis. It is one of the merits of the poem that, instead of having the Mariner mount the chariot of prophecy, Coleridge to the end "keeps decorum"—to use the traditional classical phrase. The deeply shaken Mariner is no philosopher, no prophet, no leader of men. He has learned a profound and simple truth. But he is not able—he is not even pretending—to explicate the entire mystery of what he has encountered. That continues to elude him. Hence his real message is the tale itself ("it is "my tale I teach"). It is the Mariner's actual story, not his simply worded concluding remarks, for which the "strange power of speech" comes to him, and which he continues to repeat (to himself as much as to others) while he also continues to grope for further meanings. It is left for the reader as well to infer or guess at them from the greatest and certainly the most dramatic of Coleridge's poems.

• 5 •

The realization in two or three months (January or February, 1798) that he was actually completing a work of this magnitude, and in a mode so unfamiliar to him, may have surprised Coleridge himself. Certainly it gave him a confidence he had never had before; and in the wake of the "Mariner" were written at least two, probably three, of the four finest poems he was yet to write

[4] Nor did Coleridge's remark to Mrs. Barbauld about the "obtrusion" of the moral sentiment refer to these few, deliberately prosaic lines, which could have been so easily revised or replaced at any number of times. It is the general moral framework of the last third or half of the poem to which Coleridge refers.

—"Christabel"; the best of the conversation poems, "Frost at Midnight"; and, though the date is disputable, "Kubla Khan."

Yet he could never be of one mind about what he had done or was in the process of doing. As he passed the middle point of the "Ancient Mariner" and began to work toward its predetermined conclusion, qualifications and alternatives started to suggest themselves. Fortunately he was able to exclude them from the "Mariner," and divert them instead into the thought of other poems, particularly "Christabel," in which, as he said later in the *Biographia Literaria,* "I should have more nearly realized my ideal [had they been finished], than I had done in my first attempt." In other poems he would try something analogous but different, at once other and the same. With this thought he seems to have begun "Christabel" by December or January, a month or two before he finished the "Ancient Mariner." Characteristically he drew a new line of distinction in order to affirm his resolve and give himself fresh ground for proceeding. In place of the *supernatural* he would now concern himself more modestly with the *preternatural*—not what is necessarily *above* nature, in other words, but only what is outside the ordinary course of it or inexplicable by ordinary means. Warming to the thought of the distinction, he planned, or later said he planned, to write two essays that would clarify it further, though as was so often the case the essays were never written. The first of the two essays prefixed to the "Ancient Mariner" was to discuss "the uses of the Supernatural in poetry, and the principles which regulate its introduction," while the second, to serve as a preface to "Christabel," would deal with the uses of the "Preternatural."

He would now, he thought, be freer. For to begin with, the "supernatural" imposed a heavier burden of conscience, if not invention. It presupposed a frame of symbolic reference that would inevitably involve his own religious beliefs without his quite knowing yet where he really wanted to step or indeed felt at liberty to step. Moreover, there would be no need this time for "machinery." The obvious "moral," and with it the teasing provision of apparatus that encourages the reader to infer a one-for-one kind of allegory where "this" stands for "that," would be avoided. Instead the interplay—indeed interpenetration—of natural and "preternatural" would be complete. The result would then be of no more rational, of no more patently symbolic or allegorical significance than the tale from the *Arabian Nights* that Coleridge mentioned to Mrs. Barbauld. At the same time, as a beginning gesture of his confidence and his sense of doing something new, he selected a verse form quite different, yet in one important way analogous, to that of the "Mariner." Through it he would once again avoid the great but inhibition-inducing pentameter line that Shakespeare and Milton had so triumphantly used. But this time, instead of employing the ballad form as a basis, he would use a meter that disregarded metrical feet, and, whatever the number of syllables, contented itself simply with four accented beats in a line with a few variations and with interspersed use of rhyme. The concept behind it has interested poets from Scott and Byron to the present day, even inciting a few, especially Gerard Manley Hopkins, to emulate it in one way or another. It was perhaps the most successful part of the poem, as Coleridge himself gradually seems to have felt. There is a certain pathos in the fact that, as the years passed and the poem continued to remain unfinished, he tried increasingly to call attention to the novelty of its meter rather than to its other qualities. This is the aim of the self-defensive, attemptedly casual preface in 1816 that takes the place of the once-planned essay on the "preternatural."

• 6 •

With the escort of a different versification, and with his resolve heartened by a new definition of aim, Coleridge seems to have made rapid progress, possibly writing Part I within a month before he returned to the closing stages of the "Mariner." The setting for this adventure into the "preternatural" is medieval. A few words of summary, however unwelcome in the discussion of narrative generally, may be tolerated when we are confronted with only a fragment. The lady Christabel, living with her widowed father and betrothed to a knight who is far distant, leaves the castle at night to pray for her absent lover. This is the thoughtless courage of innocence, to which a forest at midnight is no more hazardous than the center of a castle. Meanwhile the poem repeatedly suggests that something dire awaits her. She proceeds, makes her prayer, and meets another woman ("Geraldine") who tells of her recent misfortunes (a story that would convince no one except an innocent and rather obtuse maid), implores pity and help, and is then protectively taken back to the castle by Christabel. Geraldine cannot by herself cross the threshold, which has been blessed against evil spirits. (The reader is thus alerted to the fact that she is an evil being.) Christabel, with whom Coleridge-as-habitual-usher is becoming rapidly identified, must lift her over it. But this once done, Christabel is no longer a free agent, and despite warnings to which she is impervious, leads Geraldine to her chamber. As Geraldine disrobes before entering Christabel's bed, she is forced to reveal something terrible to any eye not blinded by her spell: "her bosom, and half her side—A sight to dream of, not to tell." This is probably the withered, scaly bosom and side traditionally attributed to the sorceress.

The character of Geraldine coalesces several things, for the interest there is in the elusiveness and ambiguities of evil, its varied and quickly shifting nature, and above all its need for human welcome and embrace if it is to become completely alive and fulfill itself. In all of these respects the two principle prototypes of Geraldine's character supplement each other. To begin with, she is a sort of vampire—that is to say, a creature partly living through or by means of human beings, and to that extent dependent on them, like evil itself, for what she can be or do. At the same time she is a kind of "lamia," shifting between a mortal and immortal state; and with this is the implication that she *may*—just possibly—be a phantasm, existing immortally merely *in potentia,* able to attain concrete existence only through the mind of a human being. As compared with these more complex considerations, the sexual ambiguity that automatically leaps to the mind of the post-Freudian is perhaps relevant but by no means basic. If we use a little historical imagination, we quickly see that Coleridge's two other alternatives (that is, to make either Geraldine or Christabel a male) would have created impossible complications, and that, by contrast, the idea of Lesbianism—if admitted only by suggestion—was less likely to arouse in the reader a stock response. For a male vampire would not only have lost the mythical "lamia" properties that Geraldine can suggest, but, more important, would have put the poem too grossly on the level of the Gothic "shockers" of the day. Once the male vampire was admitted to Christabel's bedroom for the night (and how, given the whole conception of her character, was she to invite him into it?), there would not be much else to say. On the other hand, to have made Christabel herself a man, meekly succumbing to a female vampire, would have turned Coleridge's main character, already passive enough, into something so jelly-like as to be dangerously close to farce. In short, the practical inevitabilities of the poet in facing a situation should be kept in mind before we hasten to strain at them in other terms. Nor, in this case, does Coleridge make much capital anyway out of the inevitable. The real concern, to repeat, is the multi-sidedness of evil, its mercurial ability, when we think we have pinned it down or defined it, to take almost any shape, and share chameleon-like in any color, and, above all, to derive its strength, to fulfill itself, only through human cooperation. Finally, Geraldine is far from single-minded; she has moments of hesitation and self-misgiving. She is not, in fact, altogether free. As she approaches the maid's bed, "Ah! what a stricken look was hers." She seems to be trying to "lift some weight"; and she "seeks delay."

Implicit in the whole conception of the story, but far less developed, are also the ambiguities of virtue, presumably to be typified by Geraldine's counterpart, Christabel. Innocence, unless it is to be a mere accident within a vacuum, is forced to come close to evil in some way, though in the process it may be destroyed or altered. More specifically, open heartedness—that welcome and interest Coleridge felt himself to offer to all comers, all opinions—will inevitably expose itself and admit (precisely because it is so open) what could harm it.

• 7 •

The central thought, whatever else is involved, is plainly the open admission of evil by innocence. This does not mean we explain this puzzling fragment by relapsing into a reference to the Fall of Man. If Geraldine has some of the properties of the serpent, the castle is far from being an Eden, Christabel is no Eve, and there is no Adam at all. But the idea of the Fall, as so frequently in Coleridge's more serious writing, does exist as a general backdrop. My own guess is that it was originally intended to be a little more than a backdrop, but that personal sympathies and projections, together with limitations of setting and above all the conceptions of the characters, began to conflict with themselves and with Coleridge's need to bring the story into a tolerable cleanliness of outline and get it to the press.

The principal embarrassments were those created by the character of Christabel herself. She was not emerging very clearly. Yet this was to be her story, not Geraldine's. With his usual vicariousness, Coleridge could do more than justice to the complex Geraldine. But his approach to his main character—like himself vulnerable and half-orphaned, benevolent, trustful, and misled—was hopelessly divided. She was to be at once a martyr [5] and at the same time an active participant. The first—the idea of martyrdom—tapped so forceful a well of identification in the writer that it took immediate precedence over the second inter-

[5] "The story of the Christabel," he told James Gillman, "is partly founded on the notion, that the virtuous of this world save the wicked" (*Life of S. T. Coleridge,* [1838], I. 283). The thought is extended in a remark to Thomas Allsop: Crashaw's lines on St. Teresa ("Since 'tis not to be had at home, / She'll travel to a martyrdome. / No home for her confesses she, / But where she may a martyr be") "were ever present to my mind whilst writing the second part of *Christabel;* if, indeed, by some subtle process of mind they did not suggest the first thought of the whole poem" (Allsop, *Letters, Conversations, and Recollections of S. T. Coleridge* [1836], II. 195-196).

est, which was so much more necessary for the narrative. The betrayal of innocent trust and openheartedness was in effect what happened to the albatross, which had come so hospitably to the ship and was then slain. Similarly, this hospitality on the part of the "dove" Christabel is violated. In the second part of the poem, Christabel's father, Sir Leoline, welcomes the new guest, who imposes on his sympathies as she had on those of the daughter, this time by claiming to be the daughter of an old friend of his, Roland de Vaux of Tryermaine, with whom he had quarreled years ago. Here again the thought is that through our virtues—in the case of Christabel's father, the impulse for forgiveness—we become vulnerable.

The story, in short, was exploiting at far greater length one of the things that had personally most appealed to Coleridge when he had begun the "Mariner"—the betrayal of openheartedness. There the demands of the poem—the voyage, the theme of exploration, the need to concentrate on the Mariner himself, Wordsworth's suggestions for the plot, and the stark but helpful fact that even with so unusual a bird one could go only so far without becoming ridiculous—combined to modify this particular form of self-projection, turn it to profit, and hurry him on to other matters. Now, however, the identification with the martyred heart, unhindered from the beginning by external controls, had prematurely, almost self-defensively, solidified into a portrait of such simplicity of virtue, such purity of motive and thought, that he found himself limited to one of two choices, neither of them satisfactory. So passive and restricted a character could be allowed to suffer its martyrdom. But then, as when the albatross was shot, the action would all be one way, with Christabel on the receiving end; and the tale, unless it were to become tedious, would soon be over. The other alternative (unless he began all over again) was to admit into the character of this demure maiden, with her Christ-like name, something other than simple innocence, something that would actually take its own steps, make its own advances. Divided between these alternatives as he quickly wrote the first part of the poem, he moved within a middle ground, sometimes verging toward one side, and sometimes toward the other. He tries to suggest the confinement in which Christabel has lived, and underlines it when he begins the second part by stressing the death-mindedness of her father, who thinks back so obsessively to the loss of his wife when she had given birth to Christabel. There is more than a hint that Christabel, however docile, is naturally restive, understandably receptive to something different. It is presumably without her father's knowledge that she goes at night to the forest to pray. It is she who suggests that Geraldine share her chamber, and who says, even before they enter the castle, that they must move "as if in stealth." The "as if" is merely palliative to her own conscience. She is very much in earnest. The sight of her father's shield on the wall, after they enter, produces only one reaction: "O softly tread, said Christabel, / My father seldom sleepeth well"; and she takes off her shoes in order to move the more quietly.

The effect is not happy. We begin to have the impression of a person who, unless doomed from the start to the role of an automaton, is only too eager to skirt the borderline between security and risk, and, if in danger, is quite capable of subterfuge. This is not at all what was wanted, whatever direction the poem took. If the hope was to dramatize the subtleties of the human will, the inner debates, the tensions and self-betrayals of the open heart that he was trying to understand in himself, we have instead only the portrait of demureness becoming sly—of the mouse softly advancing to the cheese. In short, the whole problem of finding motives and actions for Christabel (in other than her more spotless moments) had imposed an impossible psychological burden on Coleridge, forcing him as it did to re-examine and then drastically oversimplify his own. At the same time he further confronted the technical embarrassment that, with so simple and specialized a conception of virtue as Christabel typifies, any departure or change in her character will necessarily be a descent or falling off—a disintegration rather than a development. The eye, says Bacon, is more pleased by light emerging from a dark background than by darkness from a light ground ("Judge therefore of the pleasure of the heart by the pleasure of the eye"). And Coleridge, in the critical writing of the years ahead, was to be fond of saying much the same thing.

The whole concept of the poem, then, was too great for the vessel of this quasi-Gothic tale, with its admittedly suggestive atmosphere but with its small roster of characters, two of which—Christabel and her father—proved so limited for further development. That Coleridge could see this readily enough is shown by the extraordinary drop in his momentum when he began on the second part. Throughout the next three years, in fitful returns to the poem, he managed to write as much more as he had already written in a month. It is the piecemeal effect of Part II that makes "Christabel" seem to read, as Harold Bloom says, more like "a series of poems" than a single fragment. A final effort is made before the close to revert to the original theme and introduce more complexity into the character of Christabel. But Coleridge brakes his own effort, and the figure, though it rocks, does not otherwise move. He still cannot permit this simple innocence to depart from itself without the excuse of something like hypnosis. If she has so "drunken in" the look of the serpent-like eyes of Geraldine that her own features take on the same expression, it is still only "passively" that they "imitate / That look of dull and treacherous hate." "Her thoughts are gone." Helplessly a prey to inner conflict, she stands (it is twice repeated) "in dizzy trance." The fragment then stops except for a separate "Conclusion" that Coleridge, after still another year, tacked on to Part II: some lines, prompted by thoughts about his infant son Hartley, on the temptation of the parent, in the very excess of his love, to seek relief by rebuking the child with "words of unmeant bitterness" ("Perhaps 'tis pretty to force together / Thoughts so all unlike each other"). What Coleridge is here freer to express, because he is at last free of the story of Christabel herself and can now advance the suggestion in a gentler, more benevolent context, is the thought of the natural perversity, the uneasy and unpredictable contrasts within the human heart. In the excess of devotion we may begin to recoil, as if in some instinctive need for balance, and to rebuke, perhaps even to profane, what we most cherish. We are certainly expected to read the implication back into the whole fragment as one hint of what was afoot.

Admirers of Coleridge are forgivably unwilling to believe that anything but bad luck and acute personal problems prevented him from finishing "Christabel." But they forget Coleridge's immense fluency when he was confident of what he was doing. There was really nothing to prevent him during these three years (not to mention the next fifteen) from finishing the poem—except for the nature of the poem itself. The truth is that, by the close of the second part, the poem had almost completely disintegrated. Our love of Coleridge—and he was a lovable human being—and our admiration for the range of his genius should not prevent us from acknowledging as much. Naturally he talked about finishing the poem, as he often did about projects of which he was least confident (the "Mariner," he knew, could speak for itself). As with most of his unfinished prose works throughout the next thirty years, he tried to give the impression, to himself as much as to others, that the poem had simply been pushed to the back of the stove, and that, when the opportune moment arrived, more would appear than would ever have been expected. Teased to say how the poem would have ended (for he claimed to have it all in his head), he gave two versions that not only throw little light on the themes of the fragment thus far, but sharply conflict with other later remarks, especially the statement about the martyrdom of St. Teresa being present in his mind as he wrote the poem. Wordsworth, who knew the genesis and history of the poem so well, maintained that Coleridge never had any definite idea for the ending.

Meanwhile, Coleridge learned a great deal from "Christabel," more perhaps than from any other poem he ever wrote. It remained a thorn in his flesh, spurring him to consider and reconsider the dramatic development of character, and above all the need, in even the most vital sympathetic identification, for the poet first to "*eloign* himself" from his subject in order afterwards to return to it "with full effect."

• 8 •

The haunting "Kubla Khan," so unlike anything else in English, was also probably written during these months. Because the exact date is so uncertain, we discuss it last.[6] After it was written it was put aside with a reticence unusual in Coleridge, otherwise so ready to speak of his works. Even in his notebooks, intended for no eye but his own, he did not refer to it. Then, almost twenty years later (1816), when he was desperately trying to justify himself and was drawing on whatever capital he had, he printed it. By that time the habit of apology had become even stronger, and he prefixed to the poem an account stressing that it was being published only "as a psychological curiosity." The story, which may have been embellished for the occasion, has become part of the legendry of English literature:

> In the summer of the year 1797, the Author, then in ill health, had retired to a lonely farm-house between Porlock and Linton, on the Exmoor confines of Somerset and Devonshire. In consequence of a slight indisposition, an anodyne had been prescribed, from the effects of which he fell asleep in his chair at the moment that he was reading the following sentence, or words of the same substance, in "Purchas's Pilgrimage": "Here the Khan Kubla commanded a palace to be built, and a stately garden thereunto. And thus ten miles of fertile ground were inclosed with a wall." The Author continued for about three hours in a profound sleep, at least of the external senses, during which time he has the most vivid confidence, that he could not have composed less than from two to three hundred lines.

Waking, he at once wrote down the present fifty-four lines of the poem but was suddenly interrupted by "a person on business from Porlock, and detained by him above an hour." When he returned to the poem, Coleridge found all memory of it fled except for the "general purport" and "eight or ten scattered lines and images."

[6] Coleridge, in his 1816 preface, states it was written in the summer of 1797. An earlier, probably more accurate account gives the date as "the fall of the year," 1797. A third statement (not about the poem but about the retirement to the farmhouse near Linton) suggests May, 1798 (ably argued by Lawrence Hanson, *Coleridge: The Early Years* [1962], pp. 259-60). The date is exhaustively discussed by Elizabeth Schneider, *Coleridge, Opium, and Kubla Khan* (1953), pp. 153-237, and extended, not quite convincingly, to October, 1799, or the following spring.

The "general purport" was never divulged or even hinted at. It is more than possible that what we have is all there was to it. Certainly without Coleridge's note, written so long afterwards, few readers would think "Kubla Khan" a fragment. In its self-sufficiency it differs from all of Coleridge's other poems that we actually know to be fragments. Moreover, how could Coleridge have been carrying with him, on his long walk from Nether Stowey, the huge folio of Purchas? He was certainly not likely to find it in the lonely farmhouse. More probably, he was simply remembering the words he mentions. He wanted the reader, however, to think that the subject had not been much in his mind (for the claim expressed in the poem violated almost every taboo he had about self-assertion) but only accidentally suggested by something he was reading. As for the man on business from Porlock: why should he be seeking out Coleridge, who had so few business dealings, and how, even so, would he have known that Coleridge, who had been seeking seclusion, was staying at this particular place? Indeed, there is no mention of either Purchas or the man from Porlock in the only earlier statement we have, attached to a holograph manuscript of the poem—a statement briefer but more circumstantial (from it we can also infer one of the two possible places where he wrote "Kubla Khan").[7] The poem, he says, was

> composed in a sort of Reverie brought on by two grains of Opium, taken to check a dysentery, at a Farm House between Porlock & Linton, a quarter of a mile from Culbone Church, in the fall of the year, 1797.

The "profound sleep" mentioned in the published account (as

[7] One would be Ash Farm (still standing), exactly a quarter of a mile above Culbone Church. But about thirty years after the poem was written, Coleridge told his nephew he wrote it at a place he picturesquely remembered as "Brimstone Farm" (actually "Broomstreet Farm," two miles from Culbone Church). The specific statement of the earlier account ("a quarter of a mile from Culbone Church") has more of a ring of probability. Names could more easily be confused by Coleridge, especially after several years. There is no reason why the simple "Ash Farm" should have remained permanently engraved on his memory, or even much noticed at the time, whereas the more unusual name of its neighbor, even if heard casually, could have caught his notice and as the years passed become associated with the incident.

contrasted with this mere "Reverie," from a very light dose of opium) had two advantages. It would suggest that he was far from habituated to the drug, that a little of it would go a long way. Moreover, to admit that he was only in a sort of revery was also to admit that the conscious mind was working, that he was at least partly aware of what he was saying. This was not something he at all wished to do: this claim that he—Coleridge himself—might in poetry rival (might even have daydreamed of rivalling) the architectural splendor of an oriental monarch. Least of all could this be permitted to be his thought now, in 1816, after he had long abandoned poetry and was trying, from the wreckage of his life, to begin a very different career.

A note should also be added about the richness of Coleridge's reading distilled in the poem. As in the "Ancient Mariner," and much of "Christabel," the gates of inhibition that Schiller said the self-conscious modern poet is forced to storm were lifted or bypassed. Lowes, in *The Road to Xanadu,* traces most of the relevant reading—Purchas, of course, James Bruce's *Travels to Discover the Source of the Nile,* Thomas Maurice's *History of Hindostan,* and William Bartram's *Travels through North & South Carolina,* together with Herodotus, Strabo, Seneca, *Paradise Lost,* and Burnet's *Sacred Theory of the Earth.* Since the pioneer work of Lowes, the list has been extended. But the pickings among possible verbal parallels tend now to be rather slight. In any case we are still left with the central problems of form and meaning, or, in Coleridgean terms, of form through meaning and meaning through form. Also of interest and stressed by Wylie Sypher is the landscape immediately above Culbone Church—probably the smallest parish church in England. Coming from the east, as Coleridge did from Nether Stowey, one suddenly encounters the long slope, some of it covered with cedar, that slants from a hill into a deep valley; and there are frequent glimpses of the sea. Descending from the area to Culbone Church is one of the steepest ravines in this part of England—heavily forested, rocky, and cavernous.

• 9 •

With none of Coleridge's major poems is less gained by avoiding the obvious. Even a surface interpretation of the "Ancient Mariner"—not to mention "Christabel"—faces difficulties. But in "Kubla Khan" the simplest and most direct interpretation is not only permitted but almost compelled by the poem. If we accept it, we find it immediately capable of further development. If we overlook or forget it, we are left with a more static conception of the poem. And it is very easy to overlook if we are too eager to elucidate some special part or aspect of the poem, or to apply something extraneous about Coleridge's medical or psychological history.

Whether the poem was really an introduction to something else or whether Coleridge had said about all he had to say, "Kubla Khan" falls into a simple, twofold division that was to prove congenial to the greater Romantic lyric, especially some of the odes of Shelley and Keats. To begin with, there is the "odal hymn," which postulates a challenge, ideal, or prototype that the poet hopes to reach or transcend. The second part, proceeding from that challenge, consists of one of those concluding "credos," those personal expressions of hope or ambition, that were to become more common in the later Romantic period (particularly associated with such poems as Shelley's "Ode to the West Wind" or Keats's "Ode to Psyche"). Here, in "Kubla Khan," the poet hopes to match in another way—even exceed, with something more lasting—what the princes of the earth have been able to perform.

The theme, in short, as so often in the Romantic lyrics that take this form, is the hope and precarious achievement of the human imagination itself. The universality of the poem evaporates if we concentrate too myopically on Kubla himself. He has been interpreted as everything from a remorseless Tartar despot (which may enter somewhat into the picture) to a symbol of God himself, whom the poet would hope to emulate in his own way. But Kubla, as Humphry House said, is really "representative man." Moreover, whatever else can be said of him, this princely prototype of the human imagination is sharply dissociated from the religious and sacramental. Any association of the great religious domes of Christianity—of Byzantium and St. Peter's—is aesthetic, relevant only because of magnitude and splendor. (We need not linger with the more desperate equations of the dome with the maternal breast.) The religious censor in Coleridge, even at this stage of his life, is as strong as it was in Johnson. Harold Bloom rightly emphasizes that it encourages him to select a "remote dome in Xanadu," and thus avoid "the issue of the poet's relative sanctity against more than natural verities." A "religious" dome as an image of what the poet hopes to emulate or transcend would be out of the question: the claim is more modest. The need, in fact, is for what we now call "distance" —an image of power and magnificence sharply removed from the religious.[8] Moreover, whatever its splendor, and the apparent reconciliation of opposites that always intrigued Coleridge, precariousness is of the essence of this "sunny pleasure-dome with caves of ice."

• 10 •

Kubla, in other words, is man as he in general would be (including what we can only call the poet in man) placed in an enviable position of power in which he now seems able to gratify his vision—able imperially, if briefly, to "decree" a magnificence, a union or synthesis, to which the human heart aspires. The imagination hopes to keep its paradise secure, and Kubla "girdles" his around with "walls and towers." The whole conception of Kubla is in the vein of those oriental allegories

[8] If anything the dome partly represents those intermediate, less spiritualized attempts of the aspiring mind mentioned by Coleridge in "Religious Musings" (11. 201-210) to raise itself from the primitive through refinement and splendor —that intermediate stage of development in which the imagination begins to "conjure up" a "host of new desires," leading to the arts of luxury ("the soft couch, and many-coloured robe, / The timbrel and *arched dome*"), but in the process stimulating "the inventive arts" that, by degrees, "unsensualized the mind."

(themselves an elaboration of Ecclesiastes) in which the monarch is Everyman, but Everyman given what appears to be every opportunity to fulfill his dream. There is even something of a parallel (though in the "decree" of Kubla Khan the years have been melted down into moments) with Johnson's brooding passage in *Rasselas* on Cheops, the builder of the Great Pyramid, in which this "mighty structure"—the product of "that hunger of imagination which preys incessantly upon life"—is seen as a protest of will and hope against the "insufficiency of human enjoyments." A closer parallel is with Johnson's allegory of Seged, Emperor of Ethiopia (in the *Rambler,* Nos. 204 and 205). Seged ("the monarch of forty nations, the distributor of the waters of the Nile"), who has now ensured peace throughout his domain, resolves to retreat for ten short days to a place from which all trouble will be excluded. There, where "the sun played upon the water," and the grounds are interspersed with gardens, thick groves, and "bubbling fountains," Seged commands a great "house of pleasure, built in an island in the lake Dambea, to be prepared for his reception." But in this house of pleasure, where he hopes to be shut off from "tumult and care," his dreams are troubled by the thought of "deluge and invasion" in his dominions. So with Kubla, who has hoped to withdraw into a lasting present, from which both the ills of the past and the expectations for the future are excluded. But they cannot be excluded. They return in fact together—the past forecasting the future:

> And 'mid this tumult Kubla heard from far
> Ancestral voices prophesying war!

The point, of course, is that in the very commitment of the imagination to its dream, the closed paradise for which it has hoped proves incomplete and ultimately threatened—all the more since Kubla, like Lycius in Keats's "Lamia," seeks to impose his paradise directly into the midst of life and at the same time incorporate life within it. For this is no simple stream docile to the human will on the bank of which Kubla builds his "stately pleasure-dome" and which he boldly thinks to enclose within his grounds. Significantly there was no river in Purchas's account of Xanadu. This was Coleridge's own addition to the landscape of the poem. For at least a couple of years he had been thinking, indeed taking notes and "often moulding my thoughts into verse," of that long philosophical poem, "The Brook," in which he would treat the stream as an extended symbol of life "from its source in the hills" to its final disappearance into the sea. The association of river and life, which he felt no need to avoid as too conventional, had always attracted him.[9] But now, as contrasted with his earlier associations with the symbol, and this would include his prose account of "The Brook," the more placid ones, so congenial to his pliable nature, are condensed into the image of that short ten miles ("meandering in a mazy motion") in which, like Hogarth's famous serpentine or winding "line of beauty," the flow of the stream only appears to be amenable to human uses and aspirations. The real emphasis is on the mystery of the before and after of that deceptive ten miles—the "before" and "after" that Kubla had hoped to exclude: the creative violence of birth and creation, and the mystery of finality with which it sinks into a "sunless sea." Back in his poem "Religious Musings," he had spoken of "the immeasurable fount / Ebullient with creative deity." He had since been struck by a German poem, written by Count F. L. Stolberg, which he translated ("On a Cataract"). The cataract leaps, with "unperishing youth" from its chasms, "ceaseless renewing," "born in a *holy twilight,*" and then descends

> the cliff inaccessible;—
> Thou at once full-born
> Maddenest in thy joyance,
> Whirlest, shatter'st, splitt'st,
> Life invulnerable.

So, in "Kubla Khan," we have the "deep romantic chasm," at once "savage" and yet "holy" as are birth and creation them-

[9] So in the little poem, "Life," written when he was seventeen, the central image is his native river, the Otter ("May this . . . my course through Life portray"). Again, in the Latin ode he translated at Jesus College ("A Wish, Written in Jesus Wood"): he thinks of the course of his own "Life's little day" as he fancies this stream "*meandering* round its native fields," through vales and "green retreats," until it finally "downward flowing with awaken'd speed / Embosoms in the Deep."

selves ("A savage place! as holy and enchanted / As e'er beneath a waning moon was haunted / By woman wailing for her demon lover"). From it emerge the "ceaseless" toil of the river, the fountains, the tossing fragments of rocks:

And from this chasm, with ceaseless turmoil seething,
As if this earth in fast thick pants were breathing,
A mighty fountain momently was forced;
Amid whose swift half-intermitted burst
Huge fragments vaulted like rebounding hail,
Or chaffy grain beneath the thresher's flail.

The end of the river, after the ten miles that Kubla tries to enclose, is equally mysterious as it reaches "caverns measureless to man" and then sinks "in tumult to a lifeless ocean." Despite his hope to control and "girdle round" even a part of this, Kubla hears simultaneously (a "mingled measure") the "tumult" of what came before and more ominously of what is to come. Meanwhile only "the *shadow* of the dome of pleasure" floats "midway on the waves" of the passing river. No other impression on the river, no other control of it, is achieved than the shadow cast by this dome, this "miracle of rare device."

The "credo" then follows. The principal interest is that it is so diffident. The *premise* is bold enough: the poet who will also "build that dome in air" will be like that other inspired orphan and singer, Amphion, who, abandoned as a child and left exposed with his brother on Mount Cithaeron, later proved able —as was no prince or architect—to build the great walls of Thebes with his music. He also echoes the Renaissance theme familiarly associated with Shakespeare's sonnets: "Not marble, nor the gilded monuments / Of princes shall outlive this powerful rhyme . . ." But Coleridge brings in his "credo" only vicariously, through the little five-line vignette of the Abyssinian maid:

A damsel with a dulcimer
In a vision once I saw:
It was an Abyssinian maid,
And on her dulcimer she played,
Singing of Mount Abora.
Could I revive within me
Her symphony and song,
To such a deep delight 'twould win me,

That with music loud and long,
I would build that dome in air . . .

We should resist the temptation to distract ourselves, at this point, by speculations of the crudely biographical sort at which Coleridge himself always laughed (e.g., the Abyssinian maid is Sara Hutchinson, Wordsworth's sister-in-law, while the "woman wailing for her demon lover" is Coleridge's wife). As Coleridge said of the word "stimulus" in medicine, this sort of speculation at most enables us to talk around a subject while giving us a delusive feeling that we are making some sort of headway. The real point of interest is the sudden modesty and indirectness of the Amphion-claim to build something more lasting though "in air." The music that will do so will come from him—if it comes at all—because he has heard the song of another ("in vision *once*"). And why an "Abyssinian maid"? Because, as the first version of the poem said, she was really singing of Mount *Amara,* which is actually in Abyssinia, that alternative seat of Paradise cited by Milton in Book IV of *Paradise Lost* ("Mount *Amara,* though this by some supposed / True Paradise under the Ethiop Line, / By Nilus head . . ."). Coleridge's own religious censor had naturally demanded that the song of paradise that he heard—the song the poet is inspired to emulate—should not be a song of the true Eden, just as it had demanded that Kubla's dome be secular, however splendid. But "Mount Amara," while resolving this difficulty, introduced another. To the devout it suggested a *"false* paradise," and however modestly he was hedging his credo, he was not saying that he wanted to draw his inspiration from an admittedly "false" paradise. Worse still, "Mount Amara" could suggest that the author was thinking of an "alternative" paradise, almost as good, perhaps better, at least for the purposes of art. The change to "Mount *Abora*" disposed of the problem.

• 11 •

What was Coleridge to do with this boastful assertion? For assertion it was, if not of deliberate intention, at least of unconscious desire. However muted and indirect the "credo," the self-involved challenge was there for himself and others to see (the poet reviving the "dome in air," while those that hear him close their eyes "in holy dread"). What greater contrast with the apologetic, deliberately relaxed mode of poetry in which he habitually walked? Here, in fact, the "Abyssinian maid," conceived as a vicarious, indirect contact with the source of inspiration, suddenly usurped his own habitual role. It was she who was serving as usher—and to the poet himself. One thinks ahead to the long-promised chapter in the *Biographia Literaria* (on the Imagination "or Esemplastic Power"), where he has been introducing himself in another way. Then, when the moment comes, he substitutes a long letter, ostensibly from another person, telling himself to wait: this is not the proper time.

The poem was put aside. It could so easily be misinterpreted as an expression of the writer's own hope. Of course it was not that! It was simply a fanciful embroidery of something he had read—in fact (as he implied in his account so many years later) a fanciful devlopment of something he had been actually reading at that very moment—*Purchas his Pilgrimage* (that weighty folio which had somehow found its way to this lonely farmhouse). The years passed, including the terrible period from 1801 to 1816, until he was forty-four. Timidly, as he tried to get some practical use out of what he had written earlier, he escorted it, as he was to escort so much by that time, with a cloud of apology. He had been urged to publish it at the request "of a poet of great and deserved celebrity," Lord Byron, now at the height of his fame. Coleridge himself had finally agreed to publish it, but "rather as a psychological curiosity, than on the ground of any supposed *poetic* merits."

V

Germany and the Move to Keswick; Opium; "Dejection"

WHILE COLERIDGE WAS WRITING "The Ancient Mariner," the Unitarian ministership at Shrewsbury became open, and he was invited to preach a sermon there in January, 1798, "preparatory to an offer." He had been warmly recommended by his friend John Estlin, the Unitarian minister at Bristol, and the position was obviously his if he wanted it. He would be paid £150 a year, given a house for himself and his family, and have some leisure to write. Sarah's patience was wearing thin, and his scruples about preaching for pay were beginning to seem a little subjective. If it were solely a matter of self-sacrifice, it would be different. But how much of a virtue was the continued sacrifice of others for one's own ideals? Of course he would try for the position! With that resolve he turned down a gift of £100 just sent him by Josiah and Thomas Wedgwood, sons of the famous potter. They had come to know Coleridge through Tom Poole, and had heard from Poole that Coleridge would soon be forced to sacrifice his career as a writer and look for salaried employment. Coleridge understandably replied that, if he accepted the gift, he would only be deferring the day of need.

He then hurried to Shrewsbury, eager to put his best foot forward. One of the most vivid accounts we have of any of the great English poets is of Coleridge at this moment, at the age of twenty-five. For the young William Hazlitt, whose father served as Unitarian minister in the nearby village of Wem, went to Shrewsbury to hear the Coleridge he had admired from afar. We can quote only a few sentences from his memorable essay, written twenty-five years later ("My First Acquaintance with Poets"):

> When I got there, the organ was playing the 100th psalm, and, when it was done, Mr. Coleridge rose and gave out his text, "And he went up into the mountain to pray, HIMSELF, ALONE." As he gave out his text, his voice "rose like a steam of rich distilled perfumes," and when he came to the two last words, which he pronounced loud, deep, and distinct, it seemed to me, who was then young, as if the sounds had echoed from the bottom of the human heart, and as if that prayer might have floated in solemn silence through the universe. The idea of St. John came into mind, "of one crying in the wilderness, who had his loins girt about, and whose food was locusts and wild honey." The preacher then launched into his subject, like an eagle dallying with the wind. The sermon was upon peace and war; upon church and state—not their alliance, but their separation—on the spirit of the world and the spirit of Christianity, not as the same, but as opposed to one another. . . . Truth and Genius had embraced, under the eye and with the sanction of Religion. This was even beyond my hopes.

Invited by Hazlitt's father for the Tuesday afterward, Coleridge appeared at Wem, and Hazlitt describes him at length: the "voluptuous, open, eloquent" mouth; the "good-humoured" chin; the nose ("the rudder of the face, the index of the will, was small, feeble"); the projecting eyebrows and eyes "with darkened lustre"; the "undulating" walk; the range of his conversation, in which he seemed to touch upon every interest that Hazlitt himself had.

While staying at the Hazlitts', Coleridge suddenly received another offer from the Wedgwood brothers, this time of a lifetime annuity of £150. The Wedgwoods had reconsidered the matter, had learned more about him from his friends, and had concluded that this was one of the best uses to which they could turn their fortune. In a flurry of gratitude and relief, but also feeling something close to guilt at receiving so easily what amounted to a perpetual fellowship, Coleridge immediately wrote to his friends. The calm, completely reliable Poole reassured him. To accept this annuity was right in every way. Could he not, for that matter, do as much for the "Christian religion" in this new freedom as he could as a Unitarian minister? "You don't think Christianity more pure by coming from the mouth or pen of a hired man? You are not shackled. Your independence of mind is *part of the bond.* You are to give mankind that which you think they most want."

During the excited month that followed, the momentum of his work on the "Mariner" and the newly begun "Christabel" continued, and he wrote on the side the fine conversation poem, "Frost at Midnight" and the somewhat declamatory "France: an Ode" (called at this time "Recantation" because in it he recanted the idealistic expectations of the French Revolution betrayed by the course that events had since taken). In April, by which time he had completed the "Mariner," he wrote two more poems, "The Nightingale" and "Fears in Solitude," in the conversation mode. These were almost the last in that vein. Thereafter he might revert to it incidentally, out of old habit (although once, three years later, with a power of expression that lifted it to another plane, he went back to this form for the great ode, "Dejection"). His active career as a poet was almost at its end.

• 2 •

The Wedgwood annuity, while it freed him from the need of salaried employment, soon began to impose a heavy burden on his conscience (or release a burden always ready to descend but thus far kept in suspension). He now had no obvious excuse for delay in proceeding with his work. But what *was* his work? Certainly not that of a poet, however good he might be at it in moments. Political writing for the newspapers and journals? This was hardly what the Wedgwoods had in mind: their gift was expected to "free" him from these things. Nor was it what he himself really wanted to do. No, the general expectation—even his own self-command—was clear enough: a career devoted to the espousal and further understanding of the Christian religion. But though he had talked so persuasively to Poole, the Wedgwoods, the Unitarian congregations to which he preached, did he really know where he stood? He seemed at every half-year to be discovering more avenues to this all-important subject. Was it because he was really open-minded or because he lacked some essential firmness of character in his own nature?

In the meantime he began to suffer from what we can only call floating anxiety. Lacking external needs to blame, he became sensitive to minor difficulties as a distraction from the greater uneasiness. In a thoughtless moment, for example, he had written and sent to the *Monthly Magazine* three mock sonnets (under the name of Nehemiah Higginbottom) in which he parodied the style of himself, Charles Lamb, and Charles Lloyd. The sensitive, at times half-crazy, Lloyd sought revenge by doing what he could to create ill-feeling between Coleridge and Lamb (a cruel stroke was to show Lamb a letter in which Coleridge, contrasting genius with talent, had cited himself as an example of the former and Lamb of the latter). Lloyd also published a novel, *Edmund Oliver,* in which he mercilessly satirized Coleridge—his sloth, his pretensions, his use of opium. These incidents, magnified out of all proportion by Coleridge's restless imagination, preoccupied far too many of his hours in the spring of 1798. He was crushed that friends—people he had considered friends—could be thinking of him thus. He had moments of sudden illness, when, as Wordsworth said, he would have to stop on their walks and lie on the ground in agony. One of his notes speaks of his need, after the shock of Lloyd's novel, to retreat to a farm between Linton and Porlock when, because of his distress, he had his "first recourse" to opium (this is the basis for the argument that "Kubla Khan" was written then). If his image of himself was shaken by this sudden revelation of the way others could look at him, it was because he was so completely without inner resources, without conviction how to proceed, as he faced what he felt was the most decisive step of his remaining life.

• 3 •

There was a possible—and the more he thought of it, a more than possible—answer. Throughout the spring of 1798 his thoughts turned increasingly to Germany. There, in this land of universities, was an intellectual ferment unequalled anywhere else in Europe. Why not try to learn at firsthand what these gifted Germans seemed almost unique in possessing at this time?—an ability to combine a frank recognition of what modern science and scholarship were rapidly accumulating with a power of generality in thinking and an eagerness to find philosophic meaning. In other countries the men who welcomed modern science seemed to have no philosophical stand except a loose skepticism or a militantly childish mechanism, while those of wider philosophical background were beginning to become defensively anti-modern, with the inevitable thinness and stridency that mere defense so often produces.

He would be disrupting his personal life, of course. For after a little reflection it seemed out of the question for Sarah and the two children to go (a second son, Berkeley, was born May 14). Nor was Sarah interested in doing so. To emigrate to the Susquehanna with the whole Fricker family and Southey (how admirable a man her brother-in-law was!) may have attracted her at one time. But the Frickers would not be going to Germany; there would be no Southey; she now had children to think about; and the difference in language alone was enough to repel her. Not that she was opposed to Coleridge himself going away for a while. She had an immense respect for Poole—she knew how highly he was regarded—and Poole thought this a good thing. To Coleridge the knowledge that such a trip would interrupt his domestic life was by no means a serious disadvantage. But it could be a source of embarrassment to his friends and possibly to his new benefactors, the Wedgwoods, who would be subsidizing this trip. He did not want to go alone. Not that he was shy before the strangeness of the adventure: he always delighted in these things, and could strike up conversation with anyone, even if his knowledge of the language was uncertain. No, it was simply that there would be something openly irresponsible in an expedition of this sort if carried out alone. He needed the escort of respectability, and not only for its impression on others but also for his own sake, as a help in his resolve to make this a serious effort.

He therefore turned all his powers of persuasion on Wordsworth and Dorothy (Poole could not come; he was tied by his business to Stowey). Wordsworth slowly warmed up to the idea. Coleridge had given him so many valuable ideas; could he not be right here? Wordsworth had the means, if the trip was done cheaply; and Alfoxden, because of the trouble over Thelwall, was not subject to further lease. Yes, he and Dorothy would come. To the trio a fourth was added at his own firm request: a native of Stowey, John Chester, described by Hazlitt, who had visited the Coleridges in the spring, as "one of those who were attracted to Coleridge's discourse as flies are to honey, or bees in swarming-time to the sound of a brass pan." Short, bowlegged, with a drag in his walk like a drover, he would trot by the side of Coleridge like a dog or like a footman running beside a coach. Coleridge was never much aware of him since the man rarely spoke. Chester desired to come along in order to study German agriculture—he appears to have known little of agriculture at home.

Wordsworth meanwhile began negotiations with Joseph Cottle for the publication of the *Lyrical Ballads*. Coleridge, excited by the prospect of the trip, was glad to leave the details of the book to Wordsworth. He viewed himself as the lesser partner anyway. This was to be primarily Wordsworth's book. Included of Coleridge's own work were only the "Mariner," "The Nightingale," and (a strangely self-effacing choice) two scenes from the ill-fated play *Osorio,* though, because of the length of the "Mariner," Coleridge's contribution to the volume still filled a third of it. The book was published a few days before they sailed. The reception, of which they were not to learn for some time, was tepid. The reviews, uneven about the Wordsworth poems, had nothing favorable to say of the "Ancient Mariner." Among them was one by Southey (in the October number of the *Critical Review*). It was not, of course, signed by his name, though his friends soon learned who had written it. His grudging, mixed reaction to the Wordsworth poems does not concern us, but his pompous dismissal of the "Ancient Mariner" as "a poem of little merit" does. For it helps to explain something of the *milieu* in which Coleridge had been living and was later to live. (Mrs. Coleridge and the Fricker family generally took Southey's opinions as gospel.) Southey's heavy attempt to sneer at the poem—"a Dutch attempt at German sublimity"—is kept alive by the grotesque inapplicability of the remark, and by the delightful self-revelation, as in a Dickens character, of his own limitations and his pride in feeling that he had shown epigrammatic power. "German," of course, dismisses all the philosophical implications of the poem, particularly the Neoplatonic elements and the use of the various spirits; while "Dutch" (as in the Dutch "realistic" paintings) possibly suggests for him the piecemeal, mechanical method of copying from which he is trying laboriously to free himself. The review produced very different reactions in the two poets when they read it: stern anger on Wordsworth's part, and hurt bewilderment on Coleridge's. In fact Coleridge went out of the way to seek a reconciliation with Southey when he returned to England. Perhaps, in a way, Southey was right. How much Coleridge admired these firm and confident people who could act as they believed and, without self-division, do "one thing at a time"! He himself could think of many things that could be said against the poem.

• 4 •

They left Yarmouth for Hamburg on September 16 in a crossing recounted by Coleridge in his "Satyrane's Letters" (later added to the *Biographia*). On the boat Coleridge fell into conversation with a Dane who invited him to drink with his party. Together the group drank, sang, and danced reels on the deck. Here, felt the others, was a philosopher after their own heart. "Vat imagination!" said Coleridge's new friend, "vat language! vat vast science! and vat eyes!" It was soon plain that they were mistaking him for a deist or freethinker. Becoming uneasy (what would the Wordsworths think? and even so he must begin this trip in the right spirit), Coleridge concluded that he had to disabuse them. The stern self-righteousness with which he says that he did so is neither attractive nor probable.

At Hamburg Coleridge and Wordsworth interviewed the venerable German poet, F. G. Klopstock, now seventy-four, his legs swollen with dropsy, but cheerful, kind, and eager to talk. ("My eyes," said Coleridge, "felt as if a tear were swelling into them.") Then the Wordsworths and Coleridge thought it sensible to part company, at least for a while. Wordsworth, though hoping to learn some German, wanted principally to work on his poetry. Coleridge was determined to learn the language as well as he could and then to have some experience of university life. Followed by the doglike Chester he settled in the town of Ratzeburg at the home of a pastor to whom he had been given a letter of introduction. Daily accompanying the pastor from cellar to roof, from the garden to the street, and spending some time also with the children, he learned the colloquial language while he read as widely in German as he could.

Feeling after four months that he had acquired a good general grasp of the language, he left for Göttingen and in middle February enrolled at the university. He attended in the morning the lectures on physiology and in the evening those on natural history of the famous J. F. Blumenbach, whose work in anthropology helped to lay the foundations of the modern study of the subject. Almost immediately Coleridge became personally acquainted not only with the convivial and learned Blumenbach but also with J. G. Eichhorn, one of the principal early scholars in the history of German Biblical criticism, though, not wanting to dispute with the rationalistic Eichhorn, Coleridge stayed away from his lectures on the New Testament and studied the notes of a fellow-student. But his main effort was to ground himself as thoroughly as he could in the history of German language and literature. He even studied Gothic and "Theotiscan" (what we now call Old High German) under the supervision of the Orientalist, T. C. Tychsen, whose special field was Near Eastern philology but whose learning extended to most of the Indo-European languages of which anything at all was known. It tells us something about Coleridge that he should have so quickly aroused the personal interest of such men. For it could always be said that hitherto he had lacked acquaintances of this sort, and could only too easily shine by contrast. Equally interesting, if not at the moment at least in the future, is the psychological effect on him of the German ideal of erudition they typified. True, he might write to Poole: "I find being learned is a mighty easy thing," and a "miserable poet must he be, and a despicable metaphysician, whose acquirements have not cost him" more effort than all the learning of "Tooke, Porson, and Parr united." Sheer learning, especially when one has "the advantage of a great library," is "a sad excuse for being idle." But he was a little on the defensive here, or affectedly casual. The magical appeal of erudition, always strong for him, was being heightened. He had not known before that men with this range of competence existed in these numbers—at least a dozen of them at each of the major German universities. What psychologists would now call his "body-image"—his sense of identity, of himself—was to incorporate some of these ideals more firmly in the years after his return.

Meanwhile he was caught up with the thought of a special project (an interim and relatively small one, while he was grounding himself for larger efforts). This would be a life of Lessing, who had done as much as anyone to lift modern German literature to its new plane. Lessing, as he studied him further, fascinated Coleridge. He seemed exactly like himself—in endowment, in general character of mind—with the difference that Lessing went ahead and did things with more confidence. ("His eyes," said Coleridge, speaking of a portrait of Lessing, "were uncommonly like mine, rather larger and more prominent.") Looking ahead six years to Friedrich Schlegel's brilliant essay on

Lessing (1804), we could feel that we are reading a discussion of the later Coleridge. Schlegel stresses his "boldly combining mind," and the fertile use of wide knowledge and interests in which "new chemical connections and *interpenetrations* take place" (and it is exactly this that we most prize in the later writings of Coleridge). But in those forms of writing that "are especially a product of imagination, Lessing was never able to satisfy himself and bring forth something worthy of him." If any of his faculties—imagination, philosophical reasoning, sheer knowledge—were "isolated" from each other, "he became less than himself. Art and imagination," in their more specialized senses, are not "his proper fields; and also in [abstract philosophical] speculation properly so called, many may excel him." The real greatness of Lessing lay in the "mingling and *interpenetration* of reason and imagination."

Relaxing moments with some of the English students at Göttingen are recorded by Clement Carlyon, who held a traveling scholarship from Cambridge. Of more interest than his other details is his remark, after speaking of the sloppiness of Coleridge's dress: "But I have heard him say, fixing his prominent eyes upon himself (as he was wont to do whenever there was a mirror in the room), with a singularly coxcomical expression of countenance, that his dress was sure to be lost sight of the moment he began to talk." If Coleridge's eye strayed to the mirror, it was less from vanity than with the despairing check of those who chronically dislike their appearance and are resigned to hoping that it is becoming no worse than before. What bothered him about the "ugly arrangement of features, with which Nature has distinguished me" was not the ugliness *per se,* if there was any, but the particular form it took: the "idiotic" and adenoidal expression, with the heavy, open lips; the "fat vacuity of face" (a "carcase of a face," as he said in his stoical description of himself to Thelwall). It was only too symbolic of what he disliked most in himself generally—like the suction sounds he feared he made while eating, or like his first name, "Samuel." He preferred the brisk, businesslike designation "S. T. C.," and so addressed himself in his notebooks (typically Mrs. Coleridge insisted on calling him "Samuel"). From his earliest years, he told Southey, he had a feeling of "disgust" for his Christian name: "such a vile short plumpness, such a dull abortive smartness," in that first syllable, Sam, followed by the "obscurity and indefiniteness" of the vowel *u* and "the feebleness of the uncovered liquid [el] with which it ends, the wabble it makes, & staggering between a diss- and a tri-syllable. . . . Altogether, it is, perhaps, the worst combination of which vowels and consonants are susceptible." The defense, after the despondent check in the mirror, was an old one—and justified: that his appearance was irrelevant anyway as soon as he began to talk. But it is forgivably becoming a little more self-conscious. Throughout the next thirty years the uncertain Coleridge is increasingly tempted to assume a role, as he was as a child when he became, he thought, a "character" to the people at Ottery. We should recognize this form of defense for what it is, without exaggerating it or misusing it in the psychological haste with which we are eager to reduce greatness to the lowest common denominator. The identification with the role of talker, of talking sage, was one way—though only one of several—by which the chain of personal associations and inhibitions could be forgotten, cut, or transcended. It could even be described as a form of vicariousness, though in this case the identification is not with another individual but with an imaginary person—a potential, more purified self or "body-image."

In April he learned that the baby Berkeley, his second son, had died (February 10). Poole had wanted to keep this secret as long as he could: why distress Coleridge at this time, and what could Coleridge do to help anyway? Poole and Mrs. Coleridge at last decided they had to tell him. They could not hide the news forever. Distressed, feeling guilty without cause, Coleridge replied at length. He had been writing homesick letters anyway, and was eager to return, or at least he thought it necessary to try to feel that he was. With Carlyon, four other Englishmen, and a son of Professor Blumenbach, he took a short tour of the Harz mountains (May 11–16). He talked brilliantly throughout the trip. This, he knew, was to be the end of his short *Wanderjahr*. After a few weeks he left for England. Professor Blumenbach gave him a farewell dinner. Coleridge had meanwhile bought a large trunkful of metaphysical works "with a view to the one work, to which I hope to dedicate in silence the prime of my life."

• 5 •

When he returned to Nether Stowey in July, it was with a heavy burden of self-expectation, and the next fifteen years of his life are a history of his wrestle with it. The day had come when he must at last begin. But naturally he must first find a good place in which to work. The cottage at Stowey—the "old hovel" as he later called it—was out of the question. Nor was anything else around Stowey quite satisfactory. To return to it, especially with the Wordsworths now gone, was a terrible anticlimax after the years abroad. Poole's company was a great asset. But the prospect of life with Sarah, of picking up all the old threads of it, depressed him. According to her sister, her violent temper as a girl had been a trial to the rest of the Fricker family. There is no reason to suppose it had greatly moderated after her marriage, which had proved so disappointing. But of course Coleridge, so quick to feel guilty about his own habits and so eager to take where possible the most benevolent and respectable view of his relations, could not allow himself to think of it in this way. No, it was simply a matter of finding a convenient place to work—quiet, but with stimulating company.

In September he had a rheumatic attack more painful than any "since my Rheumatic fever at school." Efforts were meanwhile made at a reconciliation with Southey, and he acquired a new friend at Bristol, the brilliant young chemist, Humphry Davy. News that Wordsworth was unwell (there was nothing seriously wrong) gave Coleridge an excuse for hurrying North with Joseph Cottle. Wordsworth was at Sockburn, the home of the Hutchinson family in Durham, drawn there especially by Mary Hutchinson, who was to become his wife in 1802. Coleridge at once captivated the Hutchinson family, and was in turn delighted by them, especially by Mary's sister, Sara (a spelling he much preferred; it helped to distinguish her from Sarah Fricker; and when his own daughter was born, in December, 1802, she was named "Sara"). What a contrast this family was with the Frickers, and needless to say, what a contrast was this Sara—thoughtful, warm, full of practical good sense and humor—with "Sarah." The parallel with the earlier situation can hardly fail to strike us. The virtuous Southey had married one Fricker and Coleridge another; and now Wordsworth, a better man than Southey, was attracted to one Hutchinson sister and Coleridge—again following—to another. There were two differences: a qualitative one (as Wordsworth was to Southey, so was this Sara to "Sarah") and the fact that some compulsion had been used on him with the first Sarah, whereas now there was not only no compulsion but a barrier because of his marriage. Throughout the next few months, indeed the next two years (for this was one of the two matters—the other being his "serious" work—in which he never moved rapidly, perhaps because the more he cared the more self-doubtful he became), he was to fall increasingly in love with Sara Hutchinson.

Since Wordsworth was now well there was no need for Coleridge to continue to absent himself from home and the claims of work. He could hardly in conscience linger at the Hutchinson farm. Wordsworth's suggestion that they make a short tour of the Lake Country was welcome. This could be done in a good cause: Wordsworth was looking for a place to settle. While on the trip, Coleridge received a proposal from Daniel Stuart of the *Morning Post* to come to London and write political articles for the newspaper. Now this, of course, was not what he had been intending to do, nor what the Wedgwoods had expected. But could it not be viewed as a short effort, helpful while he got his bearings? He had overdrawn his account while in Germany. Moreover a part of the Wedgwood "fellowship" was always having to be sent to the dragonlike Mrs. Fricker (Sara Hutchinson's mother was dead). There would be no harm in a short flirtation with political journalism, especially since he would also have time to begin his real work.

Hurrying to London (Stuart paid the expenses), Coleridge took lodgings in Buckingham Street, the Strand (November 27), and Mrs. Coleridge and Hartley soon joined him. He spent his afternoons and evenings writing for Stuart at what was then good pay (four or five guineas a week), his articles strongly anti-Pitt and in favor of peace. The article on Pitt himself, March 19, 1800, is one of the classics of political journalism. Indeed much of what he wrote for Stuart is of high quality. If we do not linger on it here, it is because, in so short an essay on his life and work, we must naturally concentrate on his major interests. But we could say of him as we could of Samuel Johnson that, when he turned to anything in which his inhibitions were not an opponent, he wrote fluently and well, far above the level of mediocrity in men who had made a lifetime profession of a particular field of interest.

He had expected to devote his mornings to his other work. But the thought of even the *Life of Lessing*—itself a preliminary work—was beginning to take on the association of duty. Why not, as merely a temporary job, take up a proposal from the publisher Longman to translate Schiller's dramatic trilogy, *Wallenstein,* or at least the last two parts? Freed from inhibition, since here he was only serving as escort to a deserving writer, he rapidly translated the last two plays of the Wallenstein trilogy from a manuscript provided by Schiller. Considering the length of time he spent on it—free hours in the morning throughout a period of six or eight weeks—the translation is remarkably good. But it was only a side effort. That it fell flat—and only because interest in German tragedy generally was waning—did not greatly bother him. He had expected it. Nor did the hostile reviews of the *Lyrical Ballads,* though Mrs. Coleridge had been so much impressed by Southey's unfavorable opinion of the volume. If Southey thought the "Ancient Mariner" a poor thing, this settled the matter for her. What could Coleridge say in return? Better to forget it—better to forget poetry itself. How far away those months seemed when he wrote the "Mariner"!

He could not live in London forever as a hack political journalist. The Wedgwoods, indeed all his friends, he himself, were expecting something different. But where to go in order to make the new beginning? There was probably only one place: the North, where Wordsworth was settling. It was not simply that he needed to be around Wordsworth. Rather Wordsworth needed him. And this could also be a way of making a really fresh start. There would be no temptation to fiddle away at journalistic articles (how could they be written in so remote and rural a place?). There in beautiful countryside, starting afresh, he could do what he could not amid the distractions of London life and the kind of minor project with which one is tempted when one is easily accessible to publishers. But he wavered. Was he really ready to make this plunge? He would miss Poole and other friends. Of course, Sara Hutchinson would not be far away. Meanwhile, since he had told the Wordsworths how much he wished to be near them, they had been looking for a place. He could hardly tell them differently now after Dorothy had found him an excellent place on surprisingly lenient terms.

• 6 •

In July, 1800, the Coleridge family moved to Greta Hall, Keswick. The building still stands as part of a school. Here he began the unhappiest decade of his life. For during the next two years one thing after another seemed to coalesce—ill health, laudanum, financial worries, loneliness, domestic trouble, and, above all, guilt at being unable to progress with anything he felt really important. Naturally, as soon as he arrived at Keswick he had thrown himself enthusiastically into his new life, praising the beauties of the place as much to himself as to others, and in a half-playful gesture named his third baby, born September 14, Derwent after the nearby lake. Within the first two months he also wrote the second part of "Christabel." But the cold and damp of the northern winter came as a shock. By January he was spending much of his time in bed, and even in April, said Dorothy, he was "ill all over, back, and stomach and limbs, and so weak that he changed colour whenever he exerted himself." Mrs. Coleridge did not care for the new home. Her family was in the South. She missed chatting with the neighbors in Nether Stowey. Neither the celebrated beauties of the Lake Country nor the Wordsworths meant much to her. In fact she had long since come to dislike the Wordsworths, whose company her husband so obviously preferred to her own. Coleridge knew this and felt all the guiltier for having moved.

For that matter, he himself missed Poole, who had been only next door to him in Stowey, whereas Wordsworth was now fifteen miles away in Grasmere, happily absorbed both in his own native surroundings and also his work. And where was Coleridge's home? There had really never been one, and in any case it was certainly not here. He had drifted northward to this place only because of Wordsworth. And what was his own work? Not poetry, though he wrote at least some verse in the next three years.[1] No, as he had told a friend soon after he came north (December 19, 1800), Wordsworth "is a great, a true Poet—I am only a kind of metaphysician." He kept repeating this to others as well as to himself. He is studying not only metaphysics, he tells Thelwall, but philology—the early German and Celtic languages; but as for poetry "I have abandoned it, being convinced that I never had the essentials of poetic Genius, & that I mistook a strong desire for original power." The failure of his halfhearted efforts to continue "Christabel" confirmed this belief. And a short time afterwards he wrote William Godwin: "If I die, and the Booksellers will give you any Thing for my Life, be sure to say—'Wordsworth descended on him like the Γνῶθι σεαυτόν ["Know Thyself"] from Heaven; by shewing to him what true Poetry was, he made him know, that he himself was no Poet.' "

Yes, he had another task. But to get to it involved some care, some preparation; and he was certainly reading philosophy more closely than ever before. He was still only twenty-eight when he

[1] Aside from "Dejection: an Ode" (April, 1802) and "The Pains of Sleep" (September, 1803), anthologists occasionally include the lines to Sara Hutchinson ("To Asra," 1801), "The Picture, or the Lover's Resolution" (1802), and the "Hymn Before Sunrise in the Vale of Chamouni" (1802)—an expansion, in part translation, of Friederika Brun's ode, *Chamouny beym Sonnenaufgange*. In addition he wrote about twenty minor pieces, most of them consciously ephemeral.

had come north. But people were expecting results—or at least so he felt—and largely because of his own effervescent way of talking about projects. They had too much faith in him: he had somehow struck people from the beginning, from the days at Ottery and then at Christ's Hospital, as being so much better than he feared he really was. True, he could talk well—conversation, as he said, "suspends the terror that haunts my mind." Was that why he got into situations where so much was always being expected? Why did he then meet these situations with still further promises, thus heaping up the pile of expectation by outlining one project after another? To live this far from a city, without the nuisances, the daily distractions and excuses he had been used to, was an immense gain if the track before you was clear, as it apparently was to Wordsworth. But otherwise it could force you back further on yourself in a way that simply inhibited effort.

• 7 •

The letters, always eloquent in their record of his physical sufferings, become more so now. Throughout the spring of 1801 he is afflicted, in fact forced to go to bed because of it for ten days at a time, with a kind of "gout": his knees swell, his stomach is nauseous, even his fingers are "knotty" and rheumatic. He is subject to profuse sweats at night. With these troubles and his "dizzy head," he is becoming an "object of moral disgust to my own mind." He is also afflicted with violently irregular bowels—diarrhea alternating with constipation.

All of these complaints, when they occur in combination, are among the classic symptoms of the opium addict. We should remember how little was known about opium in Coleridge's youth—how freely it was prescribed, even for babies, usually in the liquid form called "laudanum" in which it was mixed with alcohol. No real stigma was attached to it. This makes Coleridge's uneasiness, guilt, and comparative secrecy in using it especially fascinating. He was partly aware, with that brilliant self-consciousness of his, of some of the complications to which continued use of opium could lead. Yet, to repeat, it was still widely considered a medicine as well as an anodyne. Until Sir Astley Cooper's famous article in 1824, comparatively little was known of what we now call "withdrawal symptoms." The sweats, the swelling of limbs, the rise in blood pressure and temperature, the irregularity of the bowels, that followed the use of opium, were often assumed to mark the recurrence or a new development of the disease that the drug had been used to alleviate if not to cure. To the patient there naturally seemed no recourse but to revert again to the drug.

For the next fifteen years at least, Coleridge was to suffer painfully from these symptoms, together with the psychological complications of guilt, fear, and uncertainty that might be expected. Because there was so much loose talk during the Victorian period and the first part of the twentieth century about the disastrous effect of opium on Coleridge's later career, our own generation has tended to discount it. We like to feel we are psychologically more acute. If there were difficulties ahead (the self-doubts, the guilt, the unfinished works, the constant planning of projects never even begun), the situation, we say, would have been much the same anyway: the use of opium was only a "symptom." We could in fact go further and describe much of the illness that encouraged him to resort to opium as what we now call "psychosomatic." To a nature so ebullient and outgoing—as he could be even during his unhappiest years—and so quick to sympathize with others, the word "hypochondria," with its usual suggestion of self-centered concentration, does not seem to fit. We put the matter more accurately if we say that he was immensely susceptible to it, or rather to one form of it—that to which the mind can resort when it seeks retreat or excuse before overwhelming self-demand. He was susceptible to it and struggled, often heroically, against it. But the situation was at the same time intensified by a further complication: the proneness to psychosomatic illness when a powerful sense of guilt—self-conscious distaste for the self, for every part of the self—tends not only to solidify and objectify itself in the body but also to impose its own crippling punishment.

He was at least partly aware of both tendencies in himself, of the former more than the latter. "What I keep out of my mind," he wrote in a letter of 1811, "or rather *keep down* in a state of under-consciousness, is sure to act meanwhile with its whole power . . . on my body." "The Body & Senses," as he said in another letter about the same time, "are the means of *sheathing* & shielding the Soul," drawing off emotional and other "Disharmonies" as a protection to the mind. We should note, by the way, that it was Coleridge himself who coined the term "psychosomatic" a century before it was generally adopted by the medical world, and a fragmentary essay on the emotions (about 1812-1815) specifically refers to what he there calls "my Psycho-somatic Ology [or science]."

Even so he asked, before he died, that an autopsy be performed, as if in hope that it might explain to others some of the physical suffering of his life and thus, by implication, what he feared were some of his failures. The kindly James Gillman, eager to excuse his friend, asserted that the autopsy showed Coleridge had suffered from a disease that began "nearly 40 years before his death," involving pain so constant that it amply explained his lifelong recourse to narcotics. Coleridge's daughter Sara, on the other hand, wrote to a friend (Mrs. Plummer, October, 1834):

> His body was opened, according to his own earnest request—the causes of his death were sufficiently manifest in the state of the vital parts; but that internal pain from which he suffered more or less during his whole life was not to be explained, or only by that which medical men call nervous sympathy.[2]

The truth seems to lie somewhere between these two remarks—perhaps more closely to Sara's statement until Coleridge reached his late forties. For the report of the autopsy, which is only now being printed,[3] establishes that he had never had anything like

[2] *Memoirs and Letters of Sara Coleridge* (1874), p. 99. Gillman's account was printed by his granddaughter, Lucy Watson, in *The Times,* June 8, 1895.

[3] By Professor E. L. Griggs in the *Letters,* VI. 992-993 (App. A), printing from the copy in the possession of the Coleridge family. The library of the Michael Reese Hospital, Chicago, contains another copy, with insignificant variants, from which Dr. Louis Zetzel and Dr. Lincoln Clark kindly made for me the analyses I summarize. Since the report is to be given in full by Professor Griggs, I simply paraphrase or quote the crucial remarks (from the Chicago copy). In the thorax, the right pleura was strongly adherent. A cyst between it and the cartilages of the fifth to seventh ribs contained half a pint

"rheumatic fever" (the valves of the heart, even at sixty-two, were still in good condition) nor in all probability anything else that would *organically* explain protracted physical suffering as a boy or a young man. We may more profitably speak of the autopsy report at this point than at the close of our final chapter. It is from here on, rather than after the story of his life is finished, that we need to know what can be gleaned from the report, and to clear the ground of useless speculation. The principal interests of the report are two: (1) Coleridge in his later years suffered from hypertensive heart disease resulting in congestive failure. But if he had been severely afflicted with anything like this in his twenties and thirties—which would have been unusual—he would hardly have lived to the age he did. (2) The findings in the lungs could be (a) dismissed as one of the classical symptoms of congestive heart failure, or (b) construed as a result of some chronic disease in the past (in particular, tuberculosis) that had been arrested. The latter may be more probable than the former.[4] If so, the period of active infection when Coleridge was a youth could have resulted in sharp, localized pains in the chest. Probably something like this happened. But it did not result in a long-drawn-out discomfort. Coleridge, always so ready to talk about his symptoms, does not

---

of bloody serum. In addition "the cavity on the right side contained at least 3 quarts of bloody serum. Right lung gorged with serous fluid. . . . The air-tubes throughout exhibited marks of former inflammation." The left lung and bronchial tubes were in fairly healthy condition. The heart, heavy with fat, was half again as large as normal. "Dilatation of both ventricles and hypertrophy of the left—valves healthy. Deposit of a caseous matter, not quite amounting in hardness to cartilage, under the lining membrane of the aorta." In the abdomen: "Liver pale—of exceeding softness so as to break down on the least pressure—Gall bladder enormously distended with pale coloured bile." The lining of the stomach was inflamed, with "patches of ulceration," and the intestines are described as "natural," with "some congestion of the coats of caput coli but hardly amounting to inflammation. Other viscera healthy." In reading the report, the layman may need to be reminded that some of the details that seem so lurid are the product of natural aging and that others (particularly the condition of the liver, the result of normal autolysis) are to be explained by the fact that the autopsy was made thirty-six hours after death.

[4] The fluid, if it resulted from congestive heart failure, would probably have been more evenly spread throughout the chest. But it is the right lung that is especially affected, which would suggest the earlier infection mentioned above.

mention pain in the right side of the chest or thorax until his later years. Then (January 12, 1828), he tells a friend, Dr. Joseph Green, that for the previous six or seven years—i.e., since 1821—he has suffered "every morning" from "pain across my body just below the thorax." In short, from 1821 on, an old infection of the right lung may have begun to produce the results inferred from the autopsy report, especially in combination with progressive hypertensive heart disease. Significantly Coleridge, during these later years, does not dwell on particular symptoms with the same particularity and anguish that he did thirty years earlier. His mind, by that time, is too much preoccupied with other matters.

Having glanced ahead, as we should at this point, we return to the matter of psychosomatic illness, or, to put it more exactly, a tendency to a strong psychosomatic *intensification* of physical ills. We should remember that we are dealing with a psychological intelligence to which we cannot condescend without absurdity—a man who, as we noted above, gave us the very term "psychosomatic." We should also try to be as sophisticated medically as we think we are psychologically (the latter usually meaning that we are interested in and mechanically look for only the more indirect and hidden motives). His long struggle with what he himself suspected to be a tendency to imaginary ills would have been vastly easier if he had not also been forced so often to face the frightful withdrawal symptoms of opium, in particular without knowing for certain that they were withdrawal symptoms. Like other drugs that produce a strong physical dependence, opium inhibits the production of enzymes. In compensation the enzyme synthesis is increased (hence "tolerance" to the drug), and then, when the suppressive effect of opium is withdrawn, this marked excess in enzymatic activity produces hallucinations, violent irregularity of the bowels, nausea, cramp, tremor, gooseflesh, sweats, tears, rises in blood pressure and temperature, and difficulty in breathing. The Chinese laborers imported to work on the Panama Railway in 1854, accustomed to opium and then suddenly deprived of it when a self-righteous group brought pressure to have a U.S. law applied (Panama was not at this time under U.S. jurisdiction), hanged themselves by the score. Even today, when so much is known about withdrawal symptoms, few addicts can cure themselves by their own unsupervised efforts. When we try to remember what is involved, we should also keep in mind what it can mean, to a powerful and guilt-ridden imagination, to be so uncertain as it tries to pull itself into coherence, action, manageability. To an imagination far less active than Coleridge's, the withdrawal symptoms alone—never understood clearly for what they were—could provide abundant raw material to be meshed with the other ills, psychosomatic or purely physical, that were soon to make up so much of the daily experience of living.

• 8 •

With every month Coleridge's relations with his wife were becoming less happy. Yet neither wished an open break, Sarah because she was concerned with proprieties and kept hoping that her husband might in time show financial proof of the talents others said he had; and Coleridge because he too was concerned with proprieties—almost as much as Sarah—but also because a part of him sympathized and understood what she felt.

Always inclined to shrink from open quarrel, his tendency was increasingly to drift elsewhere. In July, 1801, a year after they had moved north, he went to Durham in order to borrow books from the cathedral library, especially the works of Duns Scotus, but also in order to visit the Hutchinsons (his relations with "Asra," as he now referred to Sara Hutchinson, were always to remain on a conventionally approvable plane). Meanwhile the thought of a second northern winter preyed on him. He toyed with the idea of going to the Azores or even the West Indies. He settled for London, for which he left on November 10, got lodging at a tailor's in Covent Garden, read philosophy, and did some work for the *Morning Post.* Returning in the early spring, he stopped at the Wordsworths' in Grasmere. Wordsworth, while Coleridge was there, wrote the opening part of his great "Immortality Ode." Caught sympathetically by both the example and the general thought of what Wordsworth had written, Coleridge—though he had made such a gesture of putting poetry aside—began (April 4) the long epistolary-conversation poem to Sara Hutchinson from which the ode "Dejection" was later condensed. The most naked and vulnerable of his major poems, "Dejection" is naturally prized more highly by the Coleridgean than by other readers. Wordsworth's "Immortality Ode" or Keats's "Ode on a Grecian Urn" may lead us to wish to know more about Wordsworth and Keats. "Dejection" interests especially the reader who has already been led to Coleridge through other works and now wishes to discover more about the writer.

Like most of the greater lyrics of the Romantic period, "Dejection" enacts a drama of intellectual discovery. It is this that makes the poem as good as it is. But it is a drama in which the discovery is pushed aside, half buried, almost denied. The opening stanzas that Wordsworth had just written for what was later to become the "Immortality Ode" had ended with the wistful, brooding question:

> Whither is fled the visionary gleam?
> Where is it now, the glory and the dream?

And "Dejection" begins in the same vein, though otherwise the poems were to become very different. Here too the poet feels a loss of response. But it is put far more drastically: not as a mere decline of joy, of the feeling of wonder and freshness, but as a "grief" so pervasive that the heart itself has become almost empty. The setting is also more specialized. Significantly the poet in "Dejection" (clairvoyant to his own future) is witnessing the shift of light and shade, feeling the change of atmosphere, before the rise of a storm. How will he respond to that coming challenge? Will what is almost dead in him now—"this dull pain," this blank eye gazing without response at the splendor of green light and cloud in the west—become replaced by anything more alive?

In this more personal context, "Dejection" develops dramatically through two stages followed by a sort of coda that has by now become expected and stylized. They are the more interesting because Coleridge is here consciously unscrambling, cutting, and rearranging the verse-letter from which "Dejection" was made. First, there is the recognition, so difficult to absorb, that

> We *receive* but what we *give,*
> And in *our life alone* does nature live:
> *Ours* is her wedding garment, *ours* her shroud!

This is no triumphant assertion of the "creative imagination." (He was not for another decade or more to work his way through to that.) It is a cry of despair. The corollary is that "nature will not give to us." In the earlier poems, man could be thought of as partly on the receiving end. Nature could meet us more than half-way. So the loving wind had fingered the "Eolian Harp" into music; the sunlight, in "This Lime-Tree Bower My Prison," could touch with beauty anything to which the receptive eye was opened; the frost, in "Frost at Midnight," symbolized the "ministry" of nature. Or in the "Ancient Mariner" the albatross could come through the fearful ice and fog to the mariner. This is the nature that "ne'er deserts the wise and pure," the nature through which God molds and teaches the human spirit, and "by *giving* make[s] it *ask.*" But now (he has been studying Kant) there is a new premise. We cannot hope

> from *outward* forms to win
> The passion and the life, whose fountains are *within.*

The burden, in short, is wholly upon the naked self. It is we ourselves—the vulnerable human spirit—that, in "wedding nature," must bestow whatever "dower" is then returned to us.

But what if the heart is empty and there is nothing to give in the first place? At this crucial second stage in the development of the theme the poem staggers a little, admits a dramatic counterpart to what it goes on to say, and then leaves it to dominate the scene. "Joy"—the confident reaching out of the spirit—has evaporated; and "each visitation" of affliction and grief

> Suspends what nature gave me at my birth,
> My shaping spirit of imagination.

Accordingly he has turned for solace to "abstruse research," as if hoping in this way to steal "From my own nature all the natural man." These lines are by no means the heart of the poem they are sometimes thought to be. In the powerful seventh stanza that follows, the imagination turns out to be far from dead or suspended. It is only too active. If joy is creative, the poem exemplifies that dejection can be equally so. The wind, as the poet listens to it, becomes something mad, raving, even devilish as it evokes from the Eolian lute (as if in grotesque parody of the earlier poem, "The Eolian Harp") "a scream / Of agony by torture lengthened out." In the wind the poet hears groans, shuddering, the frightened scream of a lost child.

Whatever the ostensible theme, it is plain that the imagination can only too easily bestow on nature (in that "dower" afterwards returned to us) images of horror. But Coleridge never admits this aspect of the imagination explicitly. Rarely in the poems and never in the later theoretical writing is there an openly acknowledged *fear* of the imagination. Here we perhaps touch on one of the many possible causes of the brief, hampered range of Coleridge's poetry. In "Dejection" the wind becomes the image of a bold and "mighty Poet" as it tells of "the rushing of an host in rout / With groans, of trampled men . . ." It is of course his own imagination that finds these "tragic sounds" in the wind. In his own formal stance as a poet, the point of view is never permitted to be tragic, except to some extent in the "Ancient Mariner." There is always the hope that somehow the imagination may be discovered to be in touch with ultimate truth, and that the ultimate truth will turn out to be a benevolent rather than a tragic truth. Later, through Schelling, he was to find a way of believing this, but only when we put the problem in special epistemological terms. The craving now, as later, was to recapture the belief that man's active, restless mind could prove an advantage rather than a curse—a means of reaching out to a reality with which we can be harmoniously reconciled. Meanwhile the seventh stanza of "Dejection" reveals both the release of "imagination" (in a way not wanted) and, as he suddenly drops the subject in mid-air, his headlong flight from its implications.

This is the true end of the poem. For what follows, in the brief third and final transition, is not a development but only an exit bow in the habitual usherlike gesture of the conversation poems. Rest, security, a good conscience, must be assured someone. Let these things and all that come with them, as the poet writes alone at midnight, "Visit *her* [Sara Hutchinson] . . . Joy lift *her* spirit." The blessing is possible, more than possible, but it is not for him.

VI

The Dark Years: Malta, *The Friend*, Lectures, the *Biographia*; the Problem of Coleridge's Plagiarisms; the Move to Highgate

He could still joke a little about the situation. Particularly delightful is his self-image as a kind of bird—one of the more awkward, less attractive species. Back in the "Ancient Mariner" we had (only in part, of course, for this is a richly complex poem) Coleridge-as-albatross, and we are soon to have Coleridge-as-ostrich: "I lay too many Eggs in the hot Sands with Ostrich carelessness & ostrich oblivion"; and there is that other picture of himself, which we noticed before, as an ostrich among poets, unable to fly but with wings "that give me the *feeling* of flight," running along the plain and looking up at the skylark and eagle. Meanwhile "I am a Starling self-encaged," as he writes Godwin, "& always in the Moult, & my whole Note is, Tomorrow, & tomorrow, & tomorrow." Pursuing the thought, he tells William Sotheby that "when I wished to write a poem . . . instead of a Covey of poetic Partridges with whirring wings of music, or wild Ducks *shaping* their rapid flight in forms always regular . . . up came a metaphysical Bustard, urging its slow, heavy, laborious earth-skimming Flight, over dreary & level Wastes." But he was far less jaunty at heart than he pretended in these playful moments. He was franker when he told Poole that he hoped "Philosophy and Poetry will not neutralize each other, and leave me an inert mass."

The truth is that now, and for the next dozen years, almost everything was converging to produce paralysis of hope and effort. His personal habits were catching up with him, the long habits of retreat and withdrawal, of benevolence and yielding, of hypochondriacal guilt and self-blame, and, above all, the use of opium. Interrelating with these were the embarrassments that snowed down, as in a perpetual December, on his hope to win his way out of the woods philosophically and arrive at a unity of thinking that could serve as a "friend"—a rescuer—to every aspect of thought, in art, science, psychology, theology, morals. This is what he most cared about; and yet he was finding, with every year, that the habit of welcome, in which he so much believed, could clog not only the entrance hall but the whole palace of thought. Meanwhile, during his three years in the North (1800-1803), several small or middle-sized projects occurred to him and were sometimes mentioned as if in the process of being prepared: the essays on the "Preternatural" and on meter, a volume of "Letters from Germany," a book on the philosophy of Hobbes, Locke, and Hume, a critique of Chaucer, a series of essays on contemporary poets, a treatise on church establishment, a schoolbook on geography, a general critical work "Concerning Poetry and the Nature of the Pleasures Derived from It," a "History of English Prose," and, far larger, a scheme for a "Bibliotheca Britannica" dealing with every branch of learning. ("You spawn plans like a herring," said Southey.) He also thought of setting up a small chemical laboratory at Greta Hall, and wrote for advice to his friend Humphry Davy. In particular he continued his reading in metaphysics, became especially interested in Giordano Bruno, recaptured his earlier interest in Neoplatonism, and seriously began his long study of Kant.

The listing of projects, including phantom works almost "ready for the press," was to become stronger as a habit in the years ahead and, as with most habits that become controlling, there was more than one motivation. In part, of course, he was assuring others: he was promising, as he had always promised, to do what they expected—or rather what he *thought* they expected, since the rest of the world is far less tortured by our inadequacies than we imagine. He was also, more importantly, setting a mark for himself, a challenge. If he said a thing was "about to go to the press," then surely he would now have to live up to what he said unless he was to make himself completely ridiculous. And more often than not he had really thought about the subject, had talked about it brilliantly. All that was needed was to face that small, foolishly intimidating object, the sheet of paper waiting to be filled. The trouble with the empty sheet of paper, as contrasted with mere conversation, is that the immediate audience present in conversation now exists only as an abstraction. Into that large blank all the self-censors, the fears of criticism, the inhibitions, begin to move and tower above one. Even the fluent speaker then finds himself weighing every word; invention is paralyzed; one word at a time is jotted down, crossed out, replaced. Of course he could write fluently at times, and had done so. But it was one thing to turn out sentimental or routine verse for the magazines back in his early twenties, and another now that he was trying to work at a higher, more demanding level. So much must be known, subsumed, and reconciled to other considerations. And here he was, stranded in the North. How much at home Wordsworth seemed there! But Wordsworth was writing poetry, slowly and massively assimilating ideas Coleridge himself had given him. Coleridge, condemned to do something so different, must learn to do "one thing at a time."

Years ago, when he was a child at Ottery, there had been that nightmare after reading the story in the *Arabian Nights* of a man "compelled" to search for a completely pure virgin. And he was at last starting on that search now as he began preparations for the long promised *magnum opus.* The irony was that as more and more was discovered that needed to be reconciled to Christianity—Hartley, Berkeley, the Neoplatonists, Spinoza, and now Kant—his conception of the Christian religion itself was also changing. His former Unitarian base, so open and welcome to new insights, was being replaced by something else. As a part of him moved left to science, German epistemology, even a modified pantheism (though he would never have admitted the word), another part of him, with equal openness, was discovering new reasons for moving conservatively from Unitarianism to more traditional theologies. Surely a reconciliation was possible, though it would take time—more reading, more thinking. He could be slapdash about other matters. He could not about this. Or was a reconciliation possible? No one else seemed to think so. In any case the result might be far from "purity," which implies single-mindedness—doing not only "one thing at a time" but the same thing each time. This was one of the many troubles with "Christabel," which he could not seem to get around to finishing. Her static, "pure" character could do and be only one thing. Any development of it, any dramatic interplay, led from purity and single-mindedness into complexity. It should be the other way around, in a work of art or in philosophy: you should start with the honest recognition of complexity and then bring it *into* unity. Well, that was what he was trying to do now. Certainly his sympathies were centrifugally moving in every direction: Spinoza, then Kant, then empirical science generally, then the Neoplatonists, then Christian theology and the medieval schoolmen, then back again. There was so much to bring together as potential friends of each other. But the burden seemed so great, the need for delay and thought so necessary, the situation so unfavorable—up north in Keswick, with a sour and grudging wife, with no one to talk to unless he walked over to Grasmere to see Wordsworth—Wordsworth so single-mindedly at work on his poetry.

• 2 •

As the summer of 1802 drew to its end, with the promise of another hopeless winter, Coleridge again arranged to go south, this time in order to travel with Thomas Wedgwood and his sister through Wales. This could be presented to himself, his wife, and his friends as a natural favor to one of his benefactors.

While the Wedgwoods and he went from one country house to

another, Coleridge's spirits and health improved immensely. He charmed almost everyone. Later, in London, Humphry Davy noted that, when Coleridge could lose himself through sympathetic contagion in groups of people, he became "the image of power and activity. His eloquence is unimpaired; perhaps it is softer and stronger." But Davy also felt that "his will is probably less than ever commensurate with his ability." Feeling so much better, and touched by the birth of his daughter Sara in December, Coleridge in the meantime resolved to forget past quarrels at home, and in a burst of Micawberlike rhetoric, wrote Southey (February 17, 1803):

> In an evil Day for me did I first pay attentions to Mrs. Coleridge; in an evil day for me did I marry her; but it shall be my care & my passion, that it shall not be an evil day for her; & that whatever I may be, or may be represented, as a Husband, I may yet be unexceptionable, as her Protector & Friend.

But when in April he returned to the North and stopped at Grasmere, he was already, said Dorothy Wordsworth, "ill with rheumatic fever," and in the two months that followed he had to spend half of his time in bed. By midsummer the three of them—Wordsworth, Dorothy, and Coleridge—decided to take a trip north into Scotland. It would be like the days they had roamed together back in Somerset, when Coleridge had planned his poem "The Brook" and with Wordsworth had begun the "Ancient Mariner." But when they set off on August 15, the wet and cold, the need for laudanum (Coleridge had apparently carried only a little with him) made the trip almost intolerable. Uneasy himself, he became annoyed with what he called Wordsworth's "hypochondriacal feelings," into which Wordsworth retreated "silent and self-centred." After two weeks they agreed to part, and with a pathetic hope of breaking his dependence on laudanum, Coleridge walked home. Always accident-prone, he encountered any number of difficulties. He was briefly arrested at Fort Augustus on suspicion of being a spy, and he burned through his shoes in an attempt to dry them. Still, he forced himself to walk a full 263 miles in eight days.

That long walk of almost thirty-five miles a day, over very rough country, was a desperate effort. But it was not enough by itself. The difficulties, as he tried to shake himself and his life into manageability, were too multiple, too closely intertwined. Something of the horror of this period—"Life-stifling fear, soul-stifling shame," "the guilt, the powerless Will," the "unfathomable hell within"—is mentioned in the lines called "The Pains of Sleep" (September, 1803). Ill, fatigued, frightened, he finally turned with relief to laudanum. Never before, as he wrote in a notebook, had it been such a comfort as it was now to "sink down the waters, thro' Seas & Seas." Meanwhile the Southeys had arrived at Greta Hall at first only for a visit but actually for the rest of their lives, during which they shared the house with the Coleridge family. Southey had for months been reconsidering his own reactions to Coleridge. He had been—was to continue to be—self-righteously stern. But to see Coleridge so changed, so lacking now in self-confidence, shook even Southey's "perpendicular virtue." If he could tell William Taylor that Coleridge had become completely "palsied by a total want of moral strength," he could also add that "all other men whom I have ever known are children to him." The whole thing seemed so strange to Southey's own methodical way of living. He could not explain it to himself. And later he wrote again to Taylor that "Coleridge only talks," and yet

> It provokes me when I hear a set of puppies yelping at him, upon whom he, a great, good-natured mastiff, if he came up to them, would just lift a leg and pass on. It vexes and grieves me to the heart, that when he is gone, as go he will, nobody will believe what a mind goes with him,—how infinitely and ten-thousand-thousand-fold the mightiest of his generation.

On October 19, 1803, as Coleridge faced his third year in the North, he wrote in a notebook:

> My very heart dies!—this *year* has been one painful Dream/ I have done nothing!—O for God's sake, let me whip & spur, so that Christmas may not pass without some thing having been done/—at all events to finish The Men & the Times, & to collect them and all my Newspaper Essays into one Volume/ to collect all my poems, finishing the Vision of the Maid of Orleans, & the Dark Ladie, & make a second Volume/ & to finish Christabel.

About a month later, shortly after his thirty-first birthday:

> With a deep groan from the Innermost of my Heart, in the feeling of self-humiliation, & a lively sense of my own weakness . . . I yet write down the names of the Works I have planned . . . with a fervent prayer that I may build up in my Being enough of manly Strength & Perseverance to do one thing at a time.

Then follows a list of eight works, including a *History of Logic* and a *History of Metaphysics in Germany*.

But the thought of the long months ahead terrified him—the cold and damp, the confinement and quarrels at home, the inability to talk with others in a way that would allow him to forget all this. Yes, he must go south—to Madeira or Sicily—if he could do it without inflicting any hardship on his family. John Stoddart (Hazlitt's brother-in-law, just appointed King's Advocate at Malta) persuaded him to go to Malta, at least as a beginning point. Most of the Continent was closed to an Englishman because of the war. At Malta, still in English hands, help in the administrative offices was always welcome. This might indeed be a good start. Doing a radically different kind of work, in that warm climate, he could break not only the habit of laudanum but the whole chain of association and inhibition. Meanwhile, in a symbolic gesture that expressed his resolve to begin a new life, he had all the children baptized (November) in the Church of England.

Stopping at Grasmere (December 20) to say good-bye to the Wordsworths, he became very ill, probably from an overdose of narcotics taken to buttress him in this decisive step he was making. For almost a month he stayed there, suffering with repressed guilt, and then, after an "elastic" return of health, went to London to arrange the trip. Wordsworth lent him £105, and Coleridge hoped to raise more from his brothers, though this proved unnecessary when Wordsworth's friend, Sir George Beaumont, gave him another £100. The whole of the Wedgwood annuity could thus be left for Mrs. Coleridge. He stayed in London longer than he had expected. Merchant ships were unwilling to sail into the Mediterranean except in convoy. He filled out the weeks by seeing Lamb and other friends and made some new acquaintances. His portrait—one of the best of Coleridge—was painted by James Northcote.

Finally the boat on which he had found passage, the *Speedwell,* was able to set sail from Portsmouth (April 9, 1804). There was a stop of five days at Gibraltar, where Coleridge climbed the rocks and saw the monkeys. During the trip he made some changes and additions to the "Ancient Mariner."

• 3 •

In Malta, where he was to stay for almost fifteen months, he quickly delighted the governor, Sir Alexander Ball, for whom in July he became private secretary and later acting Public Secretary until the man appointed to the post should return. Meanwhile he took a three-month holiday in Sicily, climbed Mount Etna twice, saved money, sent his wife £110, and for a while improved in health. Freed from the burden of feeling he had to write, he spontaneously turned to his notebooks (some of his finest observations there date from the Malta period).

But as the months passed his conscience began to bother him. Everyone at home—Coleridge himself—had thought of this trip as something of six or eight months. By January 1805, he had been absent from Keswick for a year. His health declined as his feeling of guilt increased. Two months later, hearing at a party for Lady Ball of the death of Wordsworth's brother John, he staggered, struck his head in falling, and took to his bed for two weeks. Yes, he must make plans to return. But it was not until September that he left.

His circuitous return to England, which took another eleven months, is only partly explained by the wartime conditions. He could have sailed directly back past Gibraltar. Instead he went to Naples and then, hoping to find a way of returning through Germany, spent some months in Rome, where he became a friend of the American painter Washington Allston, who painted a fine unfinished portrait of him, and met Wilhelm von Humboldt and

Ludwig Tieck. Urged to flee Rome since he was on Napoleon's blacklist because of political articles he had earlier written in the *Morning Post* (naturally he later exaggerated, possibly invented this as a way of explaining the obstacles that interfered with his return), he went north to Florence and Leghorn. As he came closer to home his health became more uneven and for two weeks he suffered from what he was sure was a paralytic stroke. At Leghorn he met the young captain, named Derkheim, of an American ship. Derkheim had "never heard anything like" Coleridge's talk since he had "left Niagara." He at once did everything he could to secure a passport for Coleridge, even to swearing (Coleridge at this pretended that he was shocked, that he himself would "never" have permitted it, however terrible the consequences otherwise) that Coleridge was an American, and that Derkheim knew both his parents, who lived just outside New York on the road to Boston. Finally, on June 23, the unwilling Coleridge set sail from Leghorn. It was an unpleasant and anxious voyage for everyone on the boat, but especially for Coleridge, who was ill most of the time.

• 4 •

When he landed at Stangate Creek in Kent (August 17, 1806), he was a shattered man. What money he had brought with him from Malta was gone. His dependence on laudanum had increased. Reaching the Bell Inn in London, he got hold of Lamb, informed Wordsworth and Southey he had arrived, and, after three weeks of hesitation, wrote his wife that he was on his way home. One thing after another caused him to delay, always explained with apology and more than half-feigned indignation at the interruptions. By degrees he finally went north. The Wordsworths and Sara Hutchinson were distressed at the change in his appearance. "His fatness," said Dorothy, "is more like the flesh of a person in a dropsy than in health," and "the divine expression of his countenance" had disappeared.

He now openly admitted his horror of remaining with his wife.

A separation of sorts was effected. He would take care of the education of the two boys, and their holidays could be spent with Sarah. Taking Hartley with him, he went to the country house of Sir George Beaumont at Coleorton, where the Wordsworths were also visiting. He was ill much of the time. His guilt and self-condemnation multiplied as he sought relief in laudanum and brandy and then found himself becoming even more helpless. A symptom of his general deterioration and growing self-distrust was his foolish jealousy of what he considered a budding affection on Sara Hutchinson's part for Wordsworth and a drop of interest in himself. Fear that something would happen to the Wedgwood annuity also haunted him. Thomas Wedgwood had died in July, 1805. Josiah had expected that Coleridge would help prepare a biographical introduction to an edition of Thomas's works. Coleridge seemed almost paralyzed before this trifling task, and Josiah, as time passed, naturally became annoyed.

Throughout 1807 he moved about, staying with Poole and other friends. The year produced only one work, the lines "To William Wordsworth," written after Wordsworth, throughout several evenings in January, read to him from "The Prelude"—the great poem that was to be dedicated to Coleridge. Humbled and deeply moved, Coleridge tried to make some response in kind. Coleridge's poem—the last of the conversation poems—begins with a brilliant, condensed outline and interpretation of "The Prelude." Faced with this major achievement, mostly carried out while he himself was in Malta, Coleridge's response follows a predictable pattern as celebration of Wordsworth quickly gives way to his sense of his own failure and waste. At once, however, he wrenches himself free through the outgoing gesture of love so familiar to readers of his poetry, and then comes the further gesture of self-renunciation as Coleridge affirms his passive responsiveness ("like a devout child") before the wisdom and power of Wordsworth's poem. The self-abnegation concludes with a sense of achieved peace and with reminders of consolation. If the promise of his own genius has come to nothing, there still remain to him the love of his friends and his own religious faith. And with touching indirectness the broken Coleridge still allows himself to whisper in the timidity of a questioning parenthesis his reviving aspiration and resolve. The poem begins with the word "Friend" and ends with the word "prayer." These were, at this time, his mainstays against despair; but though Coleridge will hardly acknowledge it, the prayer probably includes a prayer to rival the friend.

• 5 •

In August he met the young admirer of himself and Wordsworth, Thomas De Quincey, who arranged through Joseph Cottle for Coleridge to be presented with a gift of £300 from a donor who wished to remain anonymous. Most or all of the money was used by Coleridge to repay friends who had been helping him.

With every month his self-distrust deepened into paralysis. For some time, as he confided to Humphry Davy (September 9),

> I have not only not answered my letters—God help me, I have been afraid even to open them . . . Within a few minutes after having read a painful Letter my heart has begun beating with such violence . . . I have literally felt *pain* as from blows from within—& this has ended with an action on my bowels that . . . bore no slight resemblance of a cholera morbus.

Through the efforts of Davy an invitation to lecture at the Royal Institution, which Coleridge had earlier turned down because he had felt too helpless to carry it out, was renewed. This time he accepted it, and chose as his general subject the "principles of poetry" as exemplified in English poets from Shakespeare to the present. The series began on January 15, 1808. He often felt too ill to leave his bed. Twice in February he failed to show up at all. Attendance naturally dropped. His appearance, said De Quincey,

> was generally that of a person struggling with pain and overmastering illness. His lips were baked with feverish heat, and often black in colour; and, in spite of the water which he continued drinking through the whole course of his lecture, he often seemed to labour under an almost paralytic inability to raise the upper jaw from the lower.

By June he decided he had to end the broken course of lectures—he had given eighteen in all. He stayed for a while with his friends Thomas and Catherine Clarkson in Bury St. Edmunds, and then at the end of the summer went north to Grasmere. Here at Allan Bank, the house to which the Wordsworths had moved, he was to remain off and on for the next year and a half.

Hoping to begin all over again, he planned a new periodical, *The Friend: a Literary, Moral, and Political Weekly Paper.* Time was passing rapidly. He was now thirty-six. There would be no more of that "Ostrich carelessness and ostrich oblivion" with which he had laid eggs in the past. "Most of them indeed have been crushed underfoot—yet not a few have crawled forth into Light to furnish Feathers for the Caps of others, and some too to plume the shafts in the Quivers of my Enemies." With what was for Coleridge a Herculean effort, twenty-eight numbers of *The Friend* were brought out (June 1, 1809 to March 15, 1810). But even more went wrong with the management and distribution of *The Friend* than had happened with the ill-fated *Watchman* twelve years before. The methods he fell into for the publication, even printing, were so impractical as to verge on the crazy. As we go over the details and Coleridge's long explanations of his woes, we suspect something deeply self-defeating in the whole concept of the thing. The style, richly echoing the seventeenth-century English sermonists, and the subject matter, so often philosophically analytic, were almost calculated to frighten off readers. There were still plenty of people in England who could have read *The Friend* with interest. But a naked new journal, issued from the rural North with so little knowledge of how to reach such an audience, naturally remained unnoticed.

Yet *The Friend,* in its uneven way, is a remarkable effort. If in writing it he was purblind to the function and needs of a new periodical, this was partly because he was trying so hard, however belatedly, to do something else: to live up to the expectation of his friends, his helpers. He dragged himself to work on it against immense inner opposition and self-doubt. Dictating to Sara Hutchinson, he would complete an issue or two and then fall back into paralysis. Dorothy Wordsworth wrote to Mrs. Clarkson, describing the final weeks of *The Friend:*

> His whole time and thoughts (except when he is reading and he reads a great deal) are employed in deceiving himself, and seeking to deceive others. He will tell me that he has been writing, that he has written, half a Friend; when I *know* that he has not written a single line. This Habit pervades all his words and actions.

Worse, Coleridge—and this for the first time—has begun to shut himself off from others. This formerly gregarious man will now stay in bed till noon or later. After he rises, he "never walks out" —even "the finest spring day does not tempt him":

> He never leaves his own parlour except at dinner and tea, and sometimes supper, and then always seems impatient to get back to his solitude. He goes the moment his food is swallowed, and when he does talk it is always upon subjects as far aloof from himself, or his friends, as possible.

• 6 •

The list of subscribers for *The Friend* had included far too many people who, when approached, had said only that they might be interested in it. Still others became disappointed after a few issues. Payments came in slowly if at all. Far from making money, *The Friend* ran a substantial loss. Meanwhile Sara Hutchinson, who had been taking down most of the essays from Coleridge's dictation and who was not very well at the time, decided to join a brother who lived in Wales. However kind her feelings toward Coleridge, she had naturally begun to weary of this position as amanuensis and nurse. Nor did the Wordsworths feel it was good for her.

After the last issue (March 15)—an account of Sir Alexander Ball typically ends "To be concluded in the next number"—Coleridge lingered for some months in the North, uncertain what to do. But to continue to stay in the North was out of the question (the dream of the *magnum opus* now seemed very remote). Of course he had to go to London. Where else could he get any kind of employment for what he could do? How many times he had gone there, since he had first left Ottery for Christ's Hospital, in order to start afresh! To do so now represented another defeat. He was at last, as he had always dreaded becoming, a true waif. He talked a little about going to Edinburgh instead and consulting a physician there. But he may not have meant it seriously.

At this point Wordsworth's brisk and bustling friend, Basil Montagu, who was returning to London with his third wife after a visit to Wordsworth, offered to take Coleridge along in his coach and put him up for a while in his London house in Frith Street, Soho. Montagu, in fact, was sure that he could help Coleridge—if only by his own example of energy and quickness of decision—to acquire new habits almost overnight. His wife was equally confident that anyone, even a genius, could be rapidly straightened out by her decisive new husband. Wordsworth, however, knew both men only too well. The clear-cut directness of Montagu, his almost mechanical tendency to leap from one thing to another, went psychologically hand-in-hand with a flighty nature. Whatever his virtues, he was one of the least meditative of souls. Nuance, complexity of motive, shades of right and wrong, were beyond him. The arrangement would quickly prove intolerable to both. Unable to dissuade Montagu, Wordsworth at last told him in some detail of Coleridge's habits. But Montagu went ahead with his plan, and Coleridge, not knowing what else to do, passively accepted. Later, at Montagu's house in London, a disagreement arose. Without heat but with a blithe directness he thought both honest and practical, Montagu informed him of Wordsworth's warning. Whatever Wordsworth had really said, the upshot in Coleridge's imagination can be pieced together from the following incomplete remarks. Montagu, he told John Morgan (March 27, 1812), "prefaced his discourse with the words, 'Nay but Wordsworth has *commissioned* me to tell you, first that he has no hope of you, etc., etc.,'' and "declared me a nuisance, an absolute nuisance—and this to such a creature as Montagu." To Crabb Robinson, Coleridge apparently said much the same thing, adding that Wordsworth had also described him as a "rotten drunkard" who had been "rotting out his entrails by intemperance." [1]

Wordsworth's remarks, at least as Coleridge's own imagination conceived them at third hand already strained through Montagu, brought into focus all the self-dissatisfaction, the readiness to guilt, that he had always felt but especially during the ten years since he had returned from Germany. Those firm backs on which he had leaned—his father, his brother George, Southey, Poole, Wordsworth—that *approval* he had always hoped to find from the respectable, the moral, the clean-cut (those men who could do "one thing at a time")—all this was suddenly swept away. In his heart he had always known this would someday happen. And if the breach with Wordsworth was so long drawn out (in a sense almost permanent), it was because the indictment was really a self-indictment. He was unable to leave the subject alone. This almost superstitious veneration he had given Wordsworth for fifteen years (he kept saying): see how it is repaid. Months afterwards he was to stumble into Charles Lamb's house, saying brokenly to Mary Lamb, "Wordsworth, Wordsworth has given me up." Nor later, when he went north, would he stop and see the Wordsworths, but turned his face the other way as the coach passed their house. It was not until the spring of 1812, a year and a half after the incident, that the breach was partly healed.

Meanwhile he immediately left Montagu's house, and, not knowing where else to go, took a room in Covent Garden at a place called Hudson's Hotel. Here he tried to pull himself into shape. His friend John Morgan, hearing about the quarrel with

[1] Robinson, seeking to make peace, questioned Wordsworth on Coleridge's behalf. Wordsworth, he said "denies ever having used such a phrase as *rotten drunkard;* such an expression he could not, as a man of taste, merely, have made use of." Nor "did he ever say that Coleridge *had been a nuisance in his family*. He might, in the course of conversation, and in reference to certain particular habits, have used the word 'nuisance.' . . . And with respect to the phrase 'rotting out his entrails by intemperance,' he does not think he used such an expression, but the idea might be conveyed in what he said." Least of all had he given Montagu any "commission." He spoke to Montagu only because "he knew that such an intimacy would be broken as soon as it was formed, and lead to very painful consequences." (*Henry Crabb Robinson on Books and Their Writers,* ed. E. J. Morley, 1938, I. 74-75.)

Wordsworth and Coleridge's distress, carried him off to his house in Hammersmith (7 Portland Place). There the Morgans tried to cut down his use of opium, which according to Southey—who probably exaggerated—now amounted to a full pint of laudanum a day. Coleridge soon left voluntarily, drifting from one lodging to another, but frequently returning to Hammersmith. Throughout part of 1811 (April to September) he wrote miscellaneous pieces for the *Courier* and then, in desperation rousing himself, gave his famous second course of lectures (on Shakespeare and Milton) from November 18, 1811 to January 17, 1812 at Scot's Corporation Hall off Fetter Lane. The lectures are among the classics of English criticism, and they fortunately survive in almost complete form because of the shorthand reports for the arrangement of which Southey was partly responsible. Moreover they quickly attracted attention. Coleridge, said Byron who himself went to some of the lectures, is a "kind of rage at present." In some of what Coleridge said, particularly in his distinction between classic and romantic drama, he drew on the German critic A. W. Schlegel, though he later tried to minimize his debt.

Encouraged by the interest, Coleridge gave another course of lectures, this time on the drama generally, at a place (Willis's Rooms) where he hoped to attract a more aristocratic group of listeners (May 19 to June 5, 1812). But this course of lectures was not a financial success; nor do we know much about it. He also revised the play he had written fourteen years before, *Osorio,* when he was twenty-five, retitling it *Remorse.* To his relief it was accepted at Drury Lane in October; and when it was performed the following January, it ran for twenty nights and reached three editions when published. Still another course of lectures was begun (November 3, 1812 to January 26, 1813), this time at the Surrey Institution, where, giving up hope of an aristocratic audience, he tried now to reach an "evangelical" one.

• 7 •

Meanwhile the Wedgwood annuity (£150) he had been receiving all these years was cut in half. Thomas Wedgwood's share (£75) had been provided for in his will. But owing to the war the Wedgwood losses had been very heavy—over £120,000—and Josiah Wedgwood's expenses had for some time exceeded his income. Josiah informed Coleridge of this (November, 1812) and Coleridge naturally and graciously released him at once from any further obligation. If it was the blow it is often said to be, Coleridge—always so transparent, so quick to communicate and expain to others—never showed it. My own feeling is that it was something of a relief. He might have worried back in 1807 about the imaginary loss of the annuity because he felt unable to do even the trifling task that Josiah expected. But now there was no personal disapproval. Coleridge was simply absolving from his promise a generous man who had done much for him in the past and was now in difficulties. It was a pleasure to be a little generous in return.

It was especially a pleasure when he could be generous by merely stepping aside, or by foregoing something, rather than by always having to perform, always having to justify and live up to expectation. The demand—most of it, of course, self-demand—to live up to the burden of expectation was something he had been living with since the boyhood days of Ottery. Everything in him, if only because of the sheer monotony, the fatigue of constant pressure at one point and for one kind of thing, had long since begun to rebel against it. Of course he tried fitfully to live up to it, and promised, and set goals for himself, and said things were almost finished. But the inner recoil was too strong. Years before, almost as far back as his second or third year at Cambridge and far more after he had returned from Germany, he had found himself becoming half-anesthetized before challenge or demand when it continued to press for one kind of achievement. By now, as he told Crabb Robinson, it seemed as though "Moral obligation is to me so very strong a Stimulant, that in 9 cases out of ten it acts as a Narcotic. The Blow that should rouse, *stuns* me."

Well, he had been trying to get himself into shape now. He had given these courses of lectures and had a play performed, though it was written some time ago. He went to Bristol (October, 1813) where he hoped to repeat his success as a lecturer in London during the winter of 1811–12. Here (October 28 to November 23, 1813) he gave six lectures on Shakespeare and two general lectures on education. Other lectures were advertised and sometimes given. But one illness after another plagued him. By early December he seemed close to death, struggling hourly with the desire to embrace it and have done with this misery. During these weeks he entered a deeper hell than he had ever known. Finally, after what seemed a partial recovery or respite, he wrote (December 19):

> The terrors of the Almighty have been around and against me—and tho' driven up and down for seven dreadful Days by restless Pain, like a Leopard in a Den, yet the anguish & remorse of Mind was worse than the pain of the whole Body. — O I have had a new world opened to me, in the infinity of my own Spirit! — Woe be to me, if this last Warning be not taken.

But the months that followed were almost as terrible. He was afraid or ashamed to visit Tom Poole, who lived so near. If only he could find the money, he would place himself in a private lunatic asylum. His old friend, Joseph Cottle, who had been relatively unaware of what had been happening to Coleridge, was horrified at the change. Coleridge replying (April 26, 1814) to Cottle's appeal, frankly confessed his helplessness and especially

> the conscience of my GUILT WORSE, far far worse than all!—I have prayed with drops of agony on my Brow, trembling not only before the Justice of my Maker, but even before the Mercy of my Redeemer. 'I gave thee so many Talents. What hast thou done with them'? . . . Had I but a few hundred Pounds, but 200£, half to send to Mrs Coleridge, & half to place myself in a private madhouse, where I could procure nothing but what a Physician thought proper, & where a medical attendant could be constantly with me for two or three months (in less than that time Life or Death would be determined) then there might be Hope. . . . My Case is a species of madness, only that it is a derangement, an utter impotence of the *Volition,* & not of the intellectual Faculties—You bid me rouse myself—go, bid a man paralytic in both arms rub them briskly together, & that will cure him. Alas! (he would reply) that I cannot move my arms in my Complaint & my misery.

Meanwhile he turned to a Dr. Henry Daniel for help and himself suggested that a man be employed to watch him constantly and prevent him from getting laudanum. An elderly clerk named

Hatherfield was hired for this purpose. Of course the frantic Coleridge was soon devising ways of tricking his poor keeper, and of course he was ashamed of doing so. As he wrote to John Morgan (May 14, 1814):

> I have in this one dirty business of Laudanum an hundred times deceived, tricked, nay, actually & consciously LIED—And yet *all* these vices are so opposite to my nature, that but for this *free-agency-annihilating* Poison, I verily believe that I should have suffered myself to have been cut to pieces rather than have committed any one of them.

In the summer of 1814 he briefly roused himself to write one of his finest short critical works, the group of three essays entitled "On the Principles of Genial Criticism Concerning the Fine Arts." He would never have done so had it not been as a favor to someone else. An exhibition of the paintings of Washington Allston, whom he had met in Rome, was being held at Bristol. Hoping to draw attention to the paintings, Coleridge volunteered to write this short series, which was published in Felix Farley's *Bristol Journal* (August and September). It is typical that these essays, unexcelled in kind in the English critical writing of the period, should have appeared in so unlikely a place. It is also typical that he quickly forgot Allston and began to discuss the arts at the highest level of generality. This sort of effort could be made for a friend. But when it came to finding money for his son Hartley, now ready to enter college, he was helpless. An essay or two—an entire book—would be of no use. Overwhelmed with shame at his complete impotence to do anything, he could not even bring himself to reply when Southey, who had taken the Coleridge family at Greta Hall into a kind of receivership, wrote and asked him whether he could help. Southey therefore went ahead and collected a fund for the purpose from Coleridge's friends and relatives, to the embarrassed relief of Coleridge. Negotiations were meanwhile begun and then dropped with the publisher John Murray, who had been looking for someone to translate Goethe's *Faust*. Murray's offer of £100 seemed to Coleridge "humiliatingly low." But Coleridge's heart was not in it anyway. The work, whatever its genius, indeed because of its genius, unquestionably disturbed him. Even in the form in which it then was, there was far more to *Faust* than the superficial reader thought, something almost pagan to the true Christian. No, Coleridge had sinned enough, had squandered his talents, had betrayed every resolve, every new self-dedication. But he had done it by neglect. Should he now not merely drift but deliberately swim away from that large current of religious thought he wished so deeply to enter? Moreover at this very time, in this period of need, he was beginning once again to rethink the whole concept of the *magnum opus*. Here at least, however messy his own life, he could justify himself to some extent. And he was thinking of it now in more specifically religious terms. He would start with Scripture itself—with five treatises "on the LOGOS, or the communicative intelligence in nature and in man," followed by a detailed "Commentary on the Gospel of St. John."

• 8 •

From Bristol he went to the country town of Calne, in Wiltshire, where for most of the next year he stayed with the Morgans, who once again did their best to restrict his consumption of opium. He made a few new friends and Hartley visited him during the vacation. Though resolving to start afresh in every way, he also thought it sensible to draw first on what capital he had, and to issue a new edition of his poems (more, if he exerted himself, might be added), and also to prefix to them a preface or apologia. Afterwards he would turn to other works.

It is this preface that within a mere three months (July to September, 1815) turned into the famous *Biographia Literaria*, certainly one of the half-dozen most seminal works in the entire history of criticism. Naturally this "immethodical miscellany," as he frankly called it, is uneven. One is surprised, considering the circumstances, that it is not more so, or indeed that it appeared at all. Desperately resolving to diminish—if possible destroy once and for all—his dependence on opium, he began to dictate his "preface" to John Morgan, who besides keeping a close watch on

Coleridge's use of laudanum, was eager to help him in any other way. Freed from the terror of seeing before him the blank page waiting to be filled, reassured by the daily presence and help of so selfless a friend and dreading to disappoint him, Coleridge went on, from paragraph to paragraph. He worked from eleven in the morning until four in the afternoon, and again from six in the evening until ten. One brilliant section followed another as he went through the first few chapters, constantly interspersing mention of his early life with reflective consideration of literature.

Midway through what was to be the first of two volumes, autobiography begins to recede. It is of special psychological interest that the poems of Coleridge that interest us most are not discussed and "Kubla Khan" not even mentioned. Instead he turns vicariously to Southey and especially Wordsworth. After Coleridge's return from Germany, autobiography almost completely disappears. Naturally he had no desire to speak of the terrible years that followed. Replacing autobiography at this point are the philosophical and theoretical chapters, followed again by a second discussion of Wordsworth's poetry (so much is Wordsworth on his mind). Here the book ended. Later, because the printer needed more to fill out the second volume, he put together two chapters from writing he had already done (the "Satyrane's Letters" about the trip to Germany, published before in *The Friend,* and a series of letters he had recently written for the *Courier* on C. R Maturin's play *Bertram).*

• 9 •

Nothing so reveals Coleridge's lack of confidence in himself, when he dictated the *Biographia,* as his use without acknowledgement of German sources. By this is meant not merely paraphrase nor the unacknowledged use of materials[2] but straight translation. In particular, a good portion of Chapter XII of the *Biographia Literaria* is lifted directly from Schelling.

[2] Some of his history of the "associationist" psychology, for example, follows Johann G. E. Maass, *Versuch über die Einbildungskraft* (1792).

At this point we may linger for a moment on the general subject of Coleridge's "plagiarisms," since Chapter XII is by far the principal example in any work Coleridge himself published. At least two reasons justify more than a page. There is the biographical interest in what it tells us of Coleridge himself. At the same time the matter has been needlessly complicated by the tangled emotions with which it has been approached. This was true even at the beginning, when Thomas De Quincey, a few weeks after Coleridge's death, brought out his articles in *Tait's Magazine,* the first of which dealt in some detail with "plagiarisms" from Schelling that had apparently for years been preying on De Quincey's mind. Naturally De Quincey could justify what he said: he wished, as he said later, to prevent an unfriendly person from using this evidence in a harsher spirit. But De Quincey, one of the arch-plagiarists of modern times, had a more personal motive.[3]

Since De Quincey, subjective emotions have continued to clutter the picture. There is the *Schadenfreude* that the great or even merely prominent inevitably face. Scholars who habitually paraphrase others in their own lectures, or even in their published writings, can become as intent as hawks when a sentence or paragraph, in a fragment Coleridge himself did not publish, is suspected to be a translation or paraphrase. At the opposite extreme are those who dismiss or minimize the matter because of national or cultural jingoism (less common now than in the late nineteenth century); or sympathetic identification with Coleridge, and the understandable reluctance to believe that a man so gifted needed to line his pockets in this way; or the resolve of students of

[3] The amount of material he himself lifted or summarized may be conservatively estimated as at least twentyfold that of Coleridge (Albert Goldman, *The Mine and the Mint* [1965], p. 159, goes so far as to estimate that De Quincey is "dependent to a greater or less degree on literary source materials in something like sixty percent of his writings.") By calling attention to Coleridge's borrowings (which incidentally reinforced De Quincey's own reputation as an erudite journalist), and by then implying that they were not very important anyway, De Quincey—already known throughout the English-speaking world for the *Confessions of an English Opium Eater*—was attempting to insure himself against the future. His hope was to point the way, in any future discovery of his own use of sources, to the excuse that shakiness of memory and confusion in the use of materials could be both expected and pardoned in the opium addict.

Coleridge, after investigating at least some of the charges of direct plagiarism and finding them overstated, to go ahead with what they have to say about Coleridge without wading through volumes of untranslated works in the expectation of finding all the parallels they are told they might confront.

This confusing interplay of exaggeration and dismissal has been possible only because of the peculiar state of German studies in the English-speaking world. Before the 1920's, a close knowledge of German could be expected among scholars. But there was little serious interest in the theory of literature. Now, however, our intellectual interests have shifted. Yet owing to the two World Wars, familiarity with even the German language has declined among literary scholars and critics, and above all familiarity with the great critical and intellectual prose of the period from 1780 to 1830. This very fact has swept into the subject a third complication. Those acquainted with that rich treasury of speculation, enraged to find Coleridge eulogized by English-speaking readers for observations commonplace in the German critical thinking of the time, keep the pot boiling with periodic but general charges of the "derivative" nature of Coleridge's thought ("most of" this or that work "is paraphrased from . . ."). What they really want to say is something very different: that it is a disgrace, at a time when we pride ourselves on our new interest in the philosophy of literature, to neglect a body of critical thinking that went so profoundly into the whole subject. They are justified in what they at bottom want to say. But in using Coleridge as their lightning rod, they have complicated this particular problem without advancing their cause. Their strategic error lies in a militant, heady refusal to distinguish between "plagiarism" in any ordinary sense of the word and Coleridge's general use of ideas, premises, concepts, vocabulary, from German writers of the time. The latter may be taken for granted. It is in fact much to Coleridge's credit. It is the former that we find so puzzling and of which we are speaking now.

Of Coleridge's now published work, which aside from his letters would fill at least a dozen large volumes, about seventy pages seem to consist of direct translation or close paraphrase, principally from two writers, A. W. Schlegel (in the Shakespeare lectures) and Schelling. If we are especially querulous, we might be able to collect together another fifteen or twenty. Once again: we are not speaking here of a general use of the ideas of others. If we did, then, as Goethe says, we should remember that we are all naked and helpless, especially the more detective-minded scholars who build in coral accretion on each other. We should also remember that, when we speak of Coleridge's "works," we are talking about much he would never have dreamed of publishing, and should face the fact that most of his critics are not this subject to the remorseless scrutiny of others. Of the pages of which we are speaking (so small a fraction of what he wrote) only a third appear in a work designed for publication, the *Biographia,* written in such distress of spirit. Another third appear in the four series of Shakespeare lectures, from 1808 to 1818. The bulk of the remaining third appear in the lecture "On Poesy or Art" and in the *Theory of Life*—the discussion he tried to put together as a help to James Gillman.[4]

• 10 •

The subject of Coleridge's "plagiarisms" is psychologically fascinating. There is nothing like it in any other writer, major or

[4] From Schlegel, in the Shakespeare lectures, there are about twenty-five pages. Breaking them down according to the particular lecture series, we have, for the lectures of 1808, two pages; for 1811-12, six; for 1813-14, three; for 1818, thirteen to fourteen. These are carefully documented by A. A. Helmholz (*University of Wisconsin Philology and Literature Series,* III [1907], 279-370) and in the notes of T. M. Raysor's edition of *Coleridge's Shakespearean Criticism* (1930). From Schelling the principal borrowings are in the *Biographia* (about twenty pages, mainly in Chapter XII) and the lecture "On Poesy or Art," in the latter of which he drew on Schelling's *Über das Verhältnis der bildende Künste zu der Natur* (1807). The charge that the entire *Theory of Life* is a mere pastiche of Schelling and his pupil Henrik Steffens is one of those accusations that, when once made, are repeated without examination. Some of the general ideas are quite Schellingian. But directly taken from Schelling are only three-and-a-half pages describing a laboratory experiment in magnetism (from Schelling's *Zeitschrift für spekulative Physik* [1800], I.8) and another six or seven pages translated or closely paraphrased from Steffens (particularly from the *Beyträge zur innern Naturgeschichte der Erde* [1801], pp. 283, 287-292, 302, 309, 314-16).

minor, whose life is reasonably well known. By this is not meant that the amount he lifted was uniquely large. The interest lies in the bizarre combination of the following facts: (1) The ease with which this articulate man could (we should think) have altered the phrasing of any passage he adopted, as is habitually done by hundreds of writers in every generation, endowed with a fraction of his verbal readiness—scholars, critics, reviewers, journalists of every description—or, as every teacher knows, by thousands of students every month. Why, in the relatively few pages he lifts from the Germans, does Coleridge collapse—no other word will do—into an almost *verbatim* translation? (2) The grotesque unevenness, in importance or style, of what he appropriates. Over half the time it not only adds nothing to his particular argument, but it is either commonplace in thought and sentiment or pedestrian in phrasing. De Quincey is right in comparing much of it to the miscellaneous and trifling contents of a child's pocket. These two points alone, before proceeding to others, confirm the explanation that, in lecturing or dictating from notes made years before, Coleridge was often hazy about their source, uncertain whether they were really translated excerpts of what had struck him at the time, or a combination of mere summary with his own observations. My own belief is that this amply explains most of the shorter, more routine "plagiarisms"—this and his retentive verbal memory, however shaky his memory in other ways.[5] But it is probably not enough to explain other borrowings—some of the brief but central passages in the Shakespeare lectures, taken from Schlegel, and constantly quoted as Coleridge's own, to the fury of the Germanist; nor does it at all explain Chapter XII of the *Biographia,* the word-for-word translations in the *Theory of Life,* or the close paraphrase of Schelling in "On Poesy or Art." (3) Then there is Coleridge's common tendency (at least in these middle years) to speak sharply of other thinkers who "derive" this or that in their philosophy

[5] He could repeat at college, as we know, an entire pamphlet of Burke after one reading. The gift was by no means lost at the time we are now discussing. On a visit to Littlehampton (September, 1817), he made the acquaintance of the Reverend H. F. Cary, whose translation of Dante he quickly read. The next day, said Cary's son, during a walk they took together, Coleridge recited entire pages of the translation, comparing them with the original.

from others. Usually so gentle, he can be rather caustic on this one point. The obvious inference is justified, his own uneasy conscience. (4) His almost self-destructive way of calling attention to the matter, notably in the *Biographia*. A happier plagiarist would either have left his source unmentioned or would have thrown himself into the usual hatchet job of the summarizer who wishes to dispose of those to whom he is indebted. But the guilt-laden Coleridge keeps throwing out hints, as if wishing to be discovered, saying that a "genial coincidence" may be found between him and Schelling. Let anything in the *Biographia* "or any future work of mind, that resembles, or coincides with, the doctrines of my German predecessor, though contemporary, be wholly attributed to *him*." Granted Coleridge's attempt to mislead when he says this. The suggestion is that there may be some over-all similarity, not several pages taken verbatim. But the fact remains that the unhappy Coleridge has put us on the track and that he need not have done so. Adding to what we can only call the general craziness of the situation—the word, even to a sympathetic admirer, is justified—is the uselessness of the whole thing, with its surrounding apparatus of guilt, apology, deception, and semi-confession. Chapter XII is far from necessary to the *Biographia*. It is in fact something of an excrescence, and it is rather dull reading, far from Schelling at his best.

What we are encountering is, first of all, the immense fatigue of spirit and self-doubt into which even the most creative intelligence can fall when almost everything in its personal life has been stripped from it, not once but repeatedly, while at the same time it feels condemned on one occasion after another to be fertile, brilliant, suggestive, and in the very way in which it has become least confident. No major writer whose life we know well has been so reduced, for so long a period or at so crucial a time in his life, as Coleridge was in the fifteen years from 1801 to 1816, from the age of twenty-nine to forty-four. It is common in such circumstances for even an articulate man to sink to the same level of paralysis into which most human beings, unaccustomed to writing or speaking, fall when they know that they must address a large group or that their remarks will be published. To say this should be no shock to those willing to consult their own experience. We could go further. It is more than possible to sink below this level—as the eye, fatigued with one color, begins to see the opposite color on the retina when it closes, or as circus performers, after straining too hard to walk the high wire, feel an overwhelming temptation to let go. In expressing even the most commonplace thought, in work written constantly against the grain, another's phrasing—however pedestrian—may be desperately grasped at in order to get us over the next hump. (We could see this, if we wished, in any number of other writers of every sort, except that we are less interested in them.) Secondly, there is the treacherous effect of habit. A few excerpts had been used from Schlegel (about eleven pages) in the three series of desperately assembled lectures on Shakespeare before Coleridge turned to the *Biographia*. Now, when he was really trying to justify himself, and against immense odds, the temptation—already yielded to in the past—was stronger. Thirdly, there is the long affliction of opium, with all that this can mean to anyone addicted to it and especially to Coleridge, for whom it was so complicated by the fatigues of constant self-distrust and guilt. (He could not, despite the relative ignorance of the time about it, be even mildly conscience-free about it as De Quincey was able to be.)

Lastly there was his long impasse in facing up to the *magnum opus*. So much that had seemed to him for years to offer a hopeful solution was tabooed by his religious conscience. This was the quasi-pantheistic philosophy of organicism that was now being so profoundly explored in the German world. It could—almost—answer everything. But could he himself follow it completely? Did not the reservations of the religious conscience have to be answered first? Significantly, in all of the serious "plagiarisms" (A. W. Schlegel, Schelling, Steffens) he is presenting arguments or details that might support an organic, almost monistic interpretation of life and art to which orthodox Christianity could not seem to be reconciled in any way that he had yet discovered. As he sought to assemble his ideas, his old habit of vicariousness, of serving as usher for what he could not feel completely free to advance himself, reasserted itself more strongly, though now in a distorted, almost somnambulistic way. He instinctively reached out for another to take his place, as if to say to his inner censor that it was not he but Schelling, or someone else he happened to be reading, who was speaking thus (as it was not he who was voicing those claims in "Kubla Khan," which he is at last to publish in a few months—that was only a curious dream suggested by a book he had been reading). Yes, better even to let the world think he might be echoing passages, though only for a special momentary purpose (and was he not inserting clues?) from writers of a pantheistic tinge—better this than, in his own voice, to say confidently what they were saying. He was not yet ready, in this all important matter, to surrender himself completely to their premises.[6] But he might be; he would know soon; and he could then more than repay the debt (and he was not sure how much of a debt it was anyway). One of the effects of opium was to distort his sense of time—of what was almost ready to put to paper or would soon be. As he talked out his ideas so brilliantly (in conversation he was not pinned down—could stress what appealed to him most and neglect what did not), he could feel that the chore-work he was doing now—the lectures on Shakespeare given in order to make ends meet, the hastily written *Biographia*—were mere interim skirmishes. They would be quickly superseded once he got himself in hand. All would then be made right.

• 11 •

During the hours when he was not dictating the *Biographia,* Coleridge put together his volume of poems, and at the end of the summer (1815) sent them off to Bristol to be printed under the title of *Sibylline Leaves.* Neither "Kubla Khan" nor the unfinished "Christabel" was included.

Back in March, as he had thought over the difficulties of finding a London publisher, his heart sank. He had always been

[6] See the discussion of the *magnum opus,* pp. 183–203.

ineffective in handling arrangements of this sort. He would probably be more so now, and at a time when it was especially important that he not be. Following a suggestion of W. L. Bowles, he had written a letter of self-introduction to Lord Byron and asked his help. Would Byron look at his poems and, if he thinks them good enough, "recommend them to some respectable Publisher"? The letter, obsequious and self-deprecating, is still embarrassing to read. But then, as Coleridge said in it, "anxiety makes us all ceremonious." Byron generously agreed to do what he could, and also suggested that another dramatic tragedy like *Remorse* would find an audience. Since Byron was involved in the management of Drury Lane, the desperate Coleridge grasped at that suggestion and continued to think about it during the summer that he dictated the *Biographia* and assembled the poems. Now, in October, Coleridge reopened the correspondence. He was forwarding to Byron the newly printed copy of the poems with the hope Byron might approve and recommend them to a good London publisher. He also snatched the opportunity to say that "All my leisure Hours I have devoted to the Drama, encouraged by your Lordship's advice and favourable opinion." He has in fact several dramatic projects in mind, which he lists, and in particular a tragedy far better than *Remorse*. It would be finished in less than two months (December 12). Would it be possible to have it produced within a few weeks after he submitted it? He was also at work on a dramatic "entertainment," loosely based on *The Winter's Tale*. This was the strange retrenchment from drama called *Zapolya,* which he at once began to dictate to Morgan.

The thought of the other projects on which he had supposedly been at work, especially the tragedy to be finished by December 12, began immediately to prey on his mind. Why did he get himself into these situations? Why, in this eagerness to reaffirm his resolve, did he always allow for so little time in what he promised? Was it for fear he might otherwise never even start? He became ill. He was obviously turning again to laudanum. Meanwhile Byron asked why the famous, still unprinted "Christabel"—he had heard part of it recited by Walter Scott—was not among the poems

Coleridge had sent him. Coleridge replied that there was still much left to write. The poem was to extend to no less than five books. But he forwarded what he had of it to Byron, who strongly commended it to the publisher John Murray. Since Coleridge had said his work on the tragedy was delayed by his need to "earn the week's food by the week's Labor for the Newspapers & the like," Byron sent him a present of £100.

Coleridge was plainly in deep psychological distress. He could not afford to fail now. This was the last chance. It was with this realization that the *Biographia* had been dictated a few months ago, in a desperate effort to make a new start. He could not let that new momentum die away—not after all these wasted years. Ill, frightened, slipping increasingly back to opium, he went on dictating *Zapolya,* ashamed and guilty that it was not the tragedy he had promised Byron.

At last in March (1816) he decided he had to go to London, ostensibly to see whether he could make arrangements at Covent Garden for a production of *Zapolya.* Probably the real reason was a hope of somehow finding a physician who might really be able to control Coleridge's use of opium. It could be no more than a hope. For how could Coleridge repay any such help, at least for a while?

• 12 •

In London he took lodgings above an apothecary's shop at 43 Norfolk Street, the Strand. It may have been the instinct of the homing pigeon, as Charles Lamb implies, that led him to "take up his abode at a Chemist's Laboratory . . . God keep him inviolate among the traps and pitfalls." But an additional motive, conscious or not, would be the chance of having medical advice of sorts if anything happened.

Something did happen, and very quickly. As if there were not enough already to worry about, the faithful Morgan, who had for years been troubled with financial probems, was now being hounded by his creditors. Suffering sympathetically—all the more because Morgan, after doing so much for him, had still taken time to escort him to London—Coleridge, already frightened enough at the dark uncertainties of the future, turned to laudanum at once for relief, and collapsed within a mere three days after he arrived. It may have been half-deliberate—a final signal of need that might or might not be noticed by the right people, whoever they might be. At all events, the apothecary below was alarmed. A physician, Dr. Joseph Adams, was summoned. Fortunately for Coleridge he was a good and observant man. He got Coleridge partly on his feet. Within a few days Coleridge called on Byron. During that meeting, probably at Byron's inquiry whether there were still other poems, Coleridge recited "Kubla Khan." Byron was naturally impressed, and passed the word to John Murray. Murray called on Coleridge above the apothecary's shop, and offered £70 for "Christabel" and £20 for "Kubla Khan." Arrangements were made to publish in May, as a small volume, these two poems together with "The Pains of Sleep."

Studying his unusual patient, Dr. Adams was convinced that something could be done if Coleridge could be really sequestered. Adams turned to a young surgeon, James Gillman, who lived and practiced out at Highgate, which was still semi-rural. Gillman, reluctant to take on such an obligation, agreed at least to talk with Coleridge. The interview, said Gillman years later, left him "spellbound." He had never met anyone of comparable powers. They quickly agreed that Coleridge should come to Highgate, in fact the very next day. If Coleridge did not leave his place above the apothecary's shop the next day but two days afterwards, it was not because he hesitated or needed an unusually heavy dose of laudanum to support him. He wanted to present to Gillman a frank, considered letter of resolve. No period of more than sixty hours has passed, he tells Gillman, though he does not say for how long, without his taking opium. His whole nature detests dishonesty. But he needs to be watched.

When he showed up at Highgate, it was assumed he would stay for only a few months, but he stayed for the remaining eighteen years of his life. Now at last he was in a harbor of sorts, and in quick succession appeared a series of works that mark the transition of his thought from his middle to his later years.

We may stop at this point and consider him briefly as a critic. To do so appears to violate chronology only if we demand that a biographical account should finish its mention of the external circumstances of a writer's life, throughout however long a period, before we discuss the works or ideas of that period of his life. True, Coleridge continued during his first three years at Highgate to write and lecture as a critic of literature, and some of his finest insights date from those three years. But he is there drawing on a capital of thought that had been accumulating since the trip to Germany or even before. We could in fact go back for its start to the years at Christ's Hospital when he proved so gifted in interpreting literature that it probably intimidated—as his brother George said—Coleridge's own development as a poet. Certainly his mature thought as a critic begins not later than 1800, when he was twenty-eight, especially if we use—as we do—the letters and the notebooks to help us understand it. In the nineteen years that follow, 1816 is a convenient point at which to pause. If he continues for a while to write and interpret as a critic after *Biographia,* he is also beginning the third and final period of both his intellectual career and his inner life generally.

VII

Coleridge as a Critic; the Function of Literature; the Imagination

HOWEVER DISTRESSING HIS YEARS from thirty to forty-three, Coleridge emerges from them and from the next three years at Highgate as at least one of the half-dozen greatest critical interpreters in the history of literature. Reservations based on the incompleteness of his work or his use of the insights of other men have had no serious effect. If he is vulnerable in ways that most critics are not, he transcends them in other, more important respects; and if he exposes himself more, it is partly because he attempts more.

His resources—intellectual, imaginative, emotional—were enormous. What makes him almost unique is the active union of qualities usually found only separately or in smaller combination. To begin with, in philosophic profundity he excels every other English critic. For anything really comparable we are forced to turn almost exclusively to the seminal reinterpretation of literature and art begun in late eighteenth-century Germany, to which, like Coleridge, we ourselves owe so much but to which—again like Coleridge—we are forgetful or cavalier about acknowledging our debts. At the same time Coleridge possesses what is so rare in the general theorist of art: the close practical grasp of form and style, the direct perception of the thing as it appears in the concrete, for which English empirical criticism, whatever its theoretical weaknesses, is unrivalled. He is one of the foremost in the long line of Engish poet-critics for which no other literature offers a counterpart, and which extends from Sir Philip Sidney through Ben Jonson, Dryden, Addison, Johnson, Wordsworth, Shelley, and Arnold, to Eliot. And the point to be stressed is that these two ordinarily diverse interests or gifts not only reinforce and extend each other but together form something greater than the mere sum of the parts—something different (to use one of Coleridge's favorite distinctions) in "kind" as well as "degree": the informed tact, the coalescence, into habitual feeling, of knowledge, imaginative insight, and reflection that he himself had in mind when he wrote to William Sotheby (July, 1802) that

> A great Poet must be, implicitè if not explicitè, a profound Metaphysician. He may not have it in logical coherence, in his Brain & Tongue; but he must have it by *Tact*. For all sounds & forms of human nature he must have the *ear* of a wild Arab listening in the silent Desart, the eye of a North American Indian tracing the footsteps of an Enemy upon the Leaves that strew the Forest—; the *Touch* of a Blind Man feeling the face of a darling child.

Thirdly, there is the range of Coleridge's intellectual curiosity, the wealth of his reading in so many fields of learning outside literature and philosophy—something in which, among modern critics of literature, only Johnson in England and Goethe and perhaps the two Schlegels in Germany compare with him. And as Bacon said in the *Advancement of Learning*, no discovery "can be made on a flat or level; neither is it possible to discover the more remote and deeper parts of any science, if you stand but upon the level of the same science."

We should add two qualities of character that certainly inhibited his other work but were here of the highest value—though only, of course, because they could now be rescued for use and exploited by genuine intellectual and imaginative gifts. One is his pliable and vicarious nature, his habitual and eager openness in surrendering himself to the achievement or cause of another. (This may help to explain why in the critical prose a power of phrase, a metaphoric brilliance, is often released that far exceeds anything we find in most of his poetry.) The second is the fact that like Johnson he was so deeply divided a soul—and in so many different respects. The two qualities, however closely related in Coleridge himself, are not usually found together. In fact, self-division only too often tends to work against the openness and generosities of empathy, inducing self-defensive rigidities, as we see in the schizoid. This is another reason for inferring that in Coleridge the self-division is more a result of the vicariousness than vice-versa. The result for Coleridge was a still broader psychic raw material, so to speak, from which to proceed—a more fertile ground of experience and sympathy. No critic so sophisticated in literary technique, at the same time so familiar with the deeper philosophical reflections on the nature of art, has been so open to the homely, the simple, the uninvolved. No one who has written on literature—or for that matter the arts generally—has more directly and emotionally felt, and philosophically understood, the claims of the subjective (whether of the idealistic or the British-empirical variety) and at the same time retained so firm a grip on the philosophically objective, the specific, or the claims of the technical. The classical and the romantic, the ideal and the concrete process, reason and feeling, symbol and direct statement, form and mimesis—the list could easily be extended—are equally meaningful. And always, within the theater of his mind, the drama of speculation is one that seeks to combine them—to conceive them as they exist in active interplay and assimilation.

Lastly, in confronting daily in himself, as we see in the notebooks and the letters, so diverse an array of insights, interests, admirations and sympathies, and self-recriminations for his own failure to attain the standards he valued; and in trying to pull himself together into action and unity of insight, while at the same time retaining both philosophical amplitude and direct emotional openness of heart, he also acquired a psychological clairvoyance about the nature of the creative mind that no other writer has attained or at least has left any record of which we know.

• 2 •

In approaching a mind at once so many-sided and yet at all times pervaded—indeed possessed and haunted—by the ideal of unity, any avenue is potentially as good as another, provided only that we keep it open. One premise, value, insight ultimately leads in Coleridge to most of the others. But there are myopias of affection as well as hostility, and it is easy to overlook the centrality of his thought because of our delight in its suburbs. He says so much at different levels and from apparently different points of view, that of no other critic are we so tempted to use his works as a treasure house from which to appropriate whatever mirrors or supports our own interests.

We can face this rich body of speculative thought most directly, as well as most in its own spirit, if we begin with the central interest to which he himself is always returning: the aim and function of art. He adopts without question the great classical premise that art is at once an *imitator* of nature—a means of catching, transcribing, reproducing reality, of whatever kind—and, in addition, a *communicator* of what it has found and has tried to duplicate. In exploring every aspect of experience, in trying to communicate it through words, as in literature, or through sounds, as in music, or through visual lines and forms, art is not only an "imitator" of nature or reality but also a "mediatress between, and reconciler of, nature and man." Here, in this conception of art as a potential bond of union—a uniter, a reconciler or "friend"—we have the essence of his critical thought and the aspiration if not the achievement of his thought generally.

Typically, as he takes over this traditional classical premise, his aim is to re-animate it, to rescue it into further meaning, by helping it to open its own arms and bring into its embrace much of the modern movement in the arts, superficially assumed to be not only unclassical but anti-classical. At the same time his hope is to rescue the modern movement from its self-imposed orphanage, its burly self-exile, its floundering helplessness and pride in its new isolation. With the instinct he always had to divide or distinguish in order later to reunite—to grant and argue for every claim for individuality and difference and then seek for a deeper ground of union—he took over, as one of his own stock premises, the distinction between classic and romantic (or modern) that is one of the many contributions of German critical thought at this time, and with which we especially associate the Schlegel brothers, August Wilhelm and Friedrich. Classical art reveals the rational harmony inherent in ordered nature. It distingushes carefully in the objects it presents. It is concerned with classes and types; and, in subduing its objects to a proper decorum, it tends to circumscribe them as "fixed" and "self-sufficient." The romantic or modern spirit is more restless. Its goal is less to depict the fixed and formal quality of the object than to suggest a dynamic fluctuation which lies beneath exterior distinctions. Neglecting clear-cut boundaries and "self-existent perfection," it penetrates at once, as A. W. Schlegel said, to the fluid reality of nature, "is perpetually striving after new and marvellous births," and hence "approaches more to the secret of the universe." Art achieves a profounder, more essential truth if it presents life, not in its "simple, clear . . . self-sufficient" aspects—which Schlegel considered the aim of classicism—but as a vital evolving of process. So with Coleridge. The ancient or classical dramatist, for example, because of his hope to capture the "universal," portrays "fixed" or set types of character. Shakespeare—"romantic" or modern—presents "our *inward* nature, the working of the passions in their most retired recesses."

The modern spirit at its best is closer to the concrete *process*. "The artist must imitate that which is *within* the thing, that which is active *through* form and figure." "They and they only," Coleridge wrote in the *Biographia,*

> can acquire the philosophic imagination, the sacred power of self-intuition, who within themselves can interpret and understand the symbol, that the wings of the air-sylph are forming within the skin of the caterpillar; those only who feel in their own spirits the same instinct which impels the chrysalis of the horned fly to leave room in its involucrum for antennae yet to come. They know and feel that the *potential* works *in* them, even as the *actual* works on them!

And both the ideal of the organic and the active direct sense of interconnection are constantly present in him as in no other English critic before or since. Even in Germany, admittedly the intellectual home of the ideal of the organic, it is hard to find a counterpart. The Schlegels and Schelling, not to mention others, preceded him and went further—Schelling especially—in developing the idea of organicism in the *theory* of art. Still, even with Germany in mind, we could argue that Coleridge is the first major writer to apply the concept of organicism concretely, in a thoroughgoing way, throughout an extensive practical criticism of style, expresion, and thought.

The concept of organicism pervades every aspect of his practical criticism—language, idiom, metaphor, semantics, larger problems of form and genre; the psychology of the "creative imagination," of taste, of sensibility; the relation, in the drama, of expression to character and of both to over-all structure; and in all these respects he has proved the most fertile of pioneers for a swarm of twentieth-century specialisms in critical gymnastics. From this abundance we may select just one example from the practical criticism—his treatment of Shakespeare's characters. Far from exemplifying mere "types" of the classical sort, they emerge in a vital verisimilitude with their various qualities as an inherent part or outgrowth of them. Even in the comic characters that come closest to burlesque, their features are never more than an "exquisitely characteristic" part of them:

> however awry, disproportionate, and laughable, yet like his Bardolph's nose [they are] still features. But Jonson's [characters] are either a man with a huge wen, having a circulation of its own, and which we might conceive amputated, and the patient thereby losing all his character; or they are mere wens instead of men—wens personified.

Similarly, when Shakespeare lays bare the working of a given passion or reaction in one of his characters, we have not a mere abstraction, description, or even presentation of that passion as a passion, as we do in the run-of-the-mill neoclassic dramatist, but rather the living fluctuation of feeling taking its natural outlets, so that we see not the passion but the actual man. An example would be Capulet's anger when Tybalt prepares to challenge

Romeo for coming to the celebration at Capulet's house. After bidding him without success to drop the matter, Capulet's anger rises at having his authority flouted in his own house. Then, observing that the lights are burning dimly, he breaks off suddenly, and his anger is shifted upon the servants. In this transition of his anger to another object,

> we see that no one passion is so predominant, but that it includes all the parts of the character, and the reader never has a mere abstract of a passion, as of wrath or ambition, but the whole man is presented to him—the one predominant passion acting, if I may so say, as the leader of the band to the rest.

• 3 •

While Coleridge more than shares the modern interest in the concretely vital and organic—and we have hardly begun to suggest the extent—his critical writing also shows a repeated struggle to combine its values (formal, stylistic, mimetic, psychological) with the classical ideals of universality. He adopts "with full faith the principle of Aristotle, that poetry . . . is essentially *ideal* . . . that its apparent individualities . . . must be representative of a class." Coleridge would go even further. He has in mind nothing less than the Platonic ideal of absolute univerality. Poetry, the arts generally in so far as they are a truly *noetic* medium—a form of real knowledge and not an expression of something else less essential—will reflect and share in the ultimate forms or universals of nature itself. These are not to be confused, as Locke and the empiricists confuse them, with the mere generalizations the mind constructs on the basis of experience, but are grasped by a higher faculty of mind (reason) than discursive generalization. They are the formative aim and guide of the concrete process we have been stressing, the particular existing merely as the "organ" of the universal, "as the lungs in relation to the atmosphere, the eye to light, crystal to fluid, figure to space." But if the particular is meaningless except as it is seen to reveal the universal—its self-sufficiency being only "a framework which the human imagination forms by its own limits, as the foot measures itself on the snow"—the universal, on the other hand, is comprehensible only through the particular. It is, in ordinary human terms, "without character" in the sense that "water is purest when without taste"; and art, in order to make it realizable, must show it as "the substance capable of endless modifications," working in and through the particulars with which human reaction is familiar.

In doing so, art presents an "abridgement" of reality itself. For "universal" and "particular" are mutually dependent in nature. Reality, that is, consists in the manner in which value or form becomes definite and emergent in the particular: reality is the bridge between concreteness and value. Value becomes *real* at the same point where the concrete exemplifies the *ideal*. In this sense, therefore, the *ideal* and the *real* are one and the same, and "Idealism" is at the same time "the truest and most binding realism." This conception is crucial for the whole of Coleridge's thought. If his critical writings generally have a rather puzzling, hieroglyphic quality, this fundamental standpoint, when completely understood, can be used as something of a Rosetta stone, by the aid of which other principles and assumptions are seen to fall into place. Yet it is also at this decisive point that one is even more tempted than usual to echo Johnson's sentiments about that shadowy member of his household menagerie, Poll Carmichael: "I had some hopes for her at first, but . . . she was wiggle-waggle, and I could never persuade her to be categorical." For in a broad sense, Coleridge's premise is simply a repetition of Aristotle's basic thesis that universal and particular, form and matter, exist only through each other. Yet we find Coleridge, in his famous distinction between "Platonists" and "Aristotelians," using the terms as a division between the sheep and the goats; his point being that for Plato—and hence Coleridge, as one of the sheep—the universals are inherent and "constitutive," while for Aristotle they are only "regulative." The difference is that, for Coleridge, Aristotle did not go far enough by regarding form and matter as simply two sides of reality, without separate existence except through artificial abstraction; whereas Coleridge himself wished to emphasize that such a union of form and matter presupposes a prior existence of form. His apparent inconsistency rests largely on loose terminology. The universals exist independently, but they become "real"—that is, they attain fulfillment and thus a higher degree of being—only as they are emergent in the particular. It is as though one took Plotinus's conception of universality as being both transcendent and yet immanent within individuality, and then maintained that the universal achieves a "higher reality"—that is, a fuller manifestation—through becoming immanent. It is here that the Neoplatonism of Jakob Boehme could appeal so much to Coleridge. Universality, for Boehme, presupposes immanence for its fulfillment: unity, for example may exist as a universal, but it also achieves its complete realization only when there is "opposition" to be unified. In its full value, it exists as *process*: it should then be thought of as "unifying" rather than as "unity."

Similarly, for Coleridge the realization of the universal might be better expressed by the active participle than by the noun. Hence his emphasis on thinking in terms of "an *act,* instead of a *thing* or a *substance*"—a statement which is misinterpreted if it is connected simply with a vague organic vitalism. Coleridge seems generally to use the word "universal" when he is speaking of a principle existing separately ("unity"), and to apply the term "idea" to the "act" ("unifying") in which the universal becomes manifest. Accordingly, he refers to "ideas" as "real," "living," "seminal," and the like. The universal, then, as he uses the term, is not a "mere abstraction" of the mind; it has objective existence. But it becomes an "idea" only as it executes its function of a controlling and formative principle, and such a principle is not controlling unless there is something being controlled. It is therefore necessarily immanent in concrete individuality, the "controlling" and the "being controlled" substantiating and fulfilling each other in and through the same act. Hence Coleridge describes the "idea" as "the universal *in* the individual, *or the individuality itself*—the glance and exponent of the indwelling power." Similarly, in art, "the ideal consists in the happy balance of the generic with the individual," since "nothing *lives* or is *real,* but as definite and individual."

The focal point for the artist, therefore, is neither the "universal " nor the "particular" as such, but a process of union which sustains and fulfills both. It is the "germ" of universal potentiality in the particular itself which biases and directs the particular to its own "self-exposition," and thus creates individuality, while at the same time it "elaborates essence into existence" by exhibiting value at the point where it attains reality. It is this basic premise that underlies his criticism of Shakespeare, whose dramas, like nature itself, have "a vitality which grows and evolves from within." In fact, it is because he so habitually turns to Shakespeare as the grand exposition of his entire aesthetic theory that we begin to feel, in reading Coleridge's criticism, that Shakespeare is almost the only poet, and Coleridge is his prophet. For it was the prerogative of Shakespeare

> to have the *universal* which is potentially in each particular, opened out to him . . . not as an abstraction of observation from a variety of men, but as the substance capable of endless modifications, of which his own personal existence was but one, and to use *this one* as the eye that beheld the other, and as the tongue that could convey the discovery.

In this sense, Shakespeare himself might be viewed as a particular "modification" through which the universal is declared! His disclosure of the active thread of connection that binds the specific with the general is thus opposed, for example, to the pseudo-universality of dramatists like Beaumont and Fletcher, who portray only "what could be put together and represented to the eye." Far from grasping the living potentiality inherent in the particular, they viewed the particular *ab extra,* and constructed a piecemeal synthesis on the basis of their empirical observation. It is as though one

> might fit together a quarter of an orange, a quarter of an apple, and the like of a lemon and a pomegranate, and make it look like one round diverse colored fruit. But nature, who *works from within by evolution and assimilation* according to a law, cannot do it. Nor could Shakespeare, for he too worked in the spirit of nature, *by*

> *evolving the germ within by the imaginative power according to an idea.*

Art, as it achieves this aim, is accordingly viewed as analogous to the fulfillment of religion itself. For religion, as he says in *The Statesman's Manual,* acts "by a contraction of universal truths into individual duties, such contraction being the only form in which those truths can attain life and reality." As the universal revealed concretely, religion

> is the echo of the *voice of the Lord God walking in the garden*. Hence in all ages and countries of civilization religion has been the parent and fosterer of the fine arts . . . the common essence of which consists in a similar union of the universal and the individual.

• 4 •

If reality consists in the "evolution and assimilation" of the particular and the universal, beauty, in Coleridge's aesthetic theory, may be described as a means by which this reality can be comprehended by the "total" mind. Beauty, that is, is not itself the character or meaning of nature; it is not truth. It is a quality that sustains the peculiarly human conception or awareness of that reality. Only to this extent is it subjective. For far from being a mere pleasant feeling which arises when one's personal associations are agreeably stirred by whatever happens to appeal to one as an individual, beauty—which may even involve "the rupture of association"—is present only when what is being conceived is the objective truth of the dynamic and vital taking universal form and value. "The BEAUTIFUL is thus at once distinguished both from the AGREEABLE, which is beneath it, and from the GOOD, which is above it." Since it is a means rather than the ultimate object of the act, it is not the good. Beauty is a process of *approaching* the good, and hence is subservient to it. Similarly, since beauty is ultimately directed to the good and the true, it is not merely the agreeable.

Agreeableness, of course, accompanies the beautiful. But beauty is not beauty because it happens to please. Rather, it pleases *be-*

cause it is beautiful. This is an elementary fact of experience that seems to elude the run-of-the-mill psychological relativist. Priding himself on his analytic rigor, with which he has confused simple reductionism, the relativist lumps together everything that "pleases" from a haunch of venison at dinner to classical statuary. In his hurry to reduce to a common denominator, he forgets that "pleasure" is not itself a specific "emotion" or "motive" but only a loose term applied to a result of radically different *kinds* of experience. Some pleasures arise when an experience applies to a very limited part of the mind, even a mere sensation. If venison "pleases," it is because it appeals to the senses of taste and smell during the short time in which it is eaten. Other pleasures may arise when we have a far more complex range of experience, in which many facets of the mind are aroused and brought into harmony. In the word "pleasure" (or any of its equivalents) we have a Serbonian Bog to which the reductionist is always heading. This is the central theme of Coleridge's "Essays on the Principles of Genial Criticism." "Beauty" in art "pleases us *because* it is beautiful."

Thus, as art itself is the mediator between nature and man, "Beauty," says Coleridge, "is the shorthand hieroglyphic of Truth —the mediator between Truth and Feeling, the Head and the Heart." Beauty, in other words, though it is not truth itself, is something which can make truth immediately realizable. As such, it imitates the reality of nature by presenting a "reduction of many to one" in symbols familiar and meaningful *ad hominem.* "It is, in the abstract, the unity of the manifold, the coalescence of the diverse; in the concrete [that is, in a work of art], it is the union of the shapely (*formosum*) with the vital." Thus Coleridge praises Raphael's Galatea as showing, he says, the balance and reconciliation "effected between these two conflicting principles of the FREE LIFE, and of the confining FORM! How entirely is the stiffness . . . of the latter, *fused* and almost *volatized* by the interpenetration and electrical flashes of the former." Using an illustration common in eighteenth-century aesthetics, Coleridge cites how, among simple visual forms, "rectilineal" lines exemplify the rigidity of pure form as such, "determined *ab extra*"; while, in the *curved* line, the restraining form is met and modified by the inner movement of a "self-justifying" vitality:

> The beautiful in the object may be referred to two elements . . . the first belonging to the shapely . . . and in this, to the law, and the reason, and the second, to the lively, the free, the spontaneous, and the self-justifying. As to lines, the rectilineal are in themselves the lifeless, the determined *ab extra* . . . The curve line is a modification of the force from without by the force from within, or the spontaneous. These are not arbitrary symbols but the language of nature, universal and intuitive.

In the balance and reconciliation of "these two conflicting principles," form and content embody each other, as a crystal contains and gives shape to light and yet is lost within it:

> Something there must be to realize the form, something in and by which the *forma informans* reveals itself . . . An illustrative hint may be taken from a pure crystal, as compared with an opaque, semi-opaque, or clouded mass, on the one hand, and with a perfectly transparent body, such as the air, on the other. The crystal is lost in the light, which yet it contains, embodies, and gives a shape to; but which passes shapeless through the air, and, in the ruder body, is either quenched or dissipated.

Yet the simile is insufficient. For the balance desired is not static, but dynamic and emergent. Reconciliation, by its very nature, implies process, a movement *into* unity. It is this active progression, then, and not the final unity itself, which constitutes beauty. Accordingly, art attempts not to suggest "the apex only," but to present, as he says, "a harmonized chaos." For "harmony"—Coleridge is here echoing Jakob Boehme and Schelling—becomes manifest only as it opposes and subdues "chaos": it presupposes, that is, something that is *being* harmonized. "Virtue consists not simply in the absence of vices, but in the overcoming of them. So it is in beauty. The sight of what is subordinated and conquered . . . should be exhibited by the artist either inclusively in his figure, or . . . beside it to act by way of supplement and contrast."

Such a "fusion to force many into one" may characterize the unfolding of an entire drama. In the form of a "feeling . . . made to modify many others" it may also be shown in a particular character, as when the anguish of Lear "spreads the feeling of ingratitude and cruelty over the very elements of heaven." Or, in a single image, it may produce "out of many things, as they would have appeared in the description of an ordinary mind, described slowly and in unimpassioned succession, a oneness"; and Coleridge cites from Shakespeare the flight of Adonis from Venus in the dusk of evening, where, as he says, the brightness of Adonis, the rapidity of his flight, the hopeless yearning of Venus, together with "a shadowy ideal character thrown over the whole," are all united:

> Look! how a bright star shooteth from the sky,
> So glides he in the night from Venus' eye.

This principle of reduction into unity is so intrinsic and pervasive in beauty that it is also echoed in the emergence of likeness from difference—"the coalescence of the diverse"—when an original is imitated in a given medium of art. Like Kames, Adam Smith, and other writers of the century before, Coleridge points out, for example, our lack of response when the resemblance between original and imitation is too obvious and close. For in this case the sense of unity and likeness does not emerge through and replace that of difference. Rather, it comes first, with patent flatness, and is followed by the disappointing, anticlimactic notation of differences. The progression, that is to say, is not from difference to likeness but from likeness to difference. Thus, in seeing wax figures, we at first almost mistake them for men and women; and then,

> not finding the motion and the life which we expected, we are shocked as by a falsehood, every circumstance of detail, which before induced us to be interested, making the distance from the truth more palpable. You set out with a supposed reality and are disappointed and disgusted with the deception; whilst, in respect to a work of genuine imitation, you begin with an acknowledged total difference, and then every touch of nature gives you the pleasure of an approximation to truth.

Art, then, imitates what is essential in nature—the reconciliation of universal and particular—by presenting, within its own given medium, a similarly active progression of "multëity into unity," and of difference into likeness. The symbols which it employs, therefore, are themselves an active repetition of "the germinal causes in Nature" and may be distinguished from mere "copying," which produces "masks only, not forms breathing life." It is thus that one should interpret the statement that the "symbol," as distinct from "allegory," "always partakes of the reality that it renders intelligible." Coleridge's use of A. W. Schlegel's distinction between "organic" and "mechanical" form falls into place as a further ramification of this standpoint; nor can it be understood otherwise. Form is mechanical when it is superimposed instead of "arising out of the properties of the material": when, that is to say, a work of art—the unfolding of a plot, the revelation of a character, an image, a symbol—does not offer, within its *own* medium, an organic progression in which unity issues through and by means of a given multëity. But "organic" form proceeds directly and intrinsically from such a multëity. It will be remembered that the "idea" is "the universal *in* the individual," the universal become active and formative. It therefore evolves the particular, while, as a controlling principle, it fulfills itself through the very act of controlling. Similarly, "organic" form in art "shapes [its material at the same time] as it develops itself from within." It thus symbolically duplicates nature, "the prime genial artist," in which form is also "the physiognomy of the being within, the true image reflected and thrown out of the concave mirror."

As distinct from truth or the good, therefore, beauty is a means rather than an end. It offers in symbols which are apprehensible and persuasive to man a living "abridgement of nature," a "shorthand hieroglyphic of truth," and thus, in its function of mediating between nature and man, is at once a transcriber and a conveyor or admitter. "As light to the eye, even such is beauty to the mind . . . Hence the Greeks called a beautiful object . . . [a] *calling on* the soul."

• 5 •

No other aspect of Coleridge's criticism has so interested the modern reader as his psychology of art, especially his theory of the imagination. Because his remarks on the subject are so fragmentary, they have the attraction of allowing us to turn them into anything we want, if we take them up in isolation. That is a legitimate use of his insights. Where we err is in trying to construct from them a general theory that we then attribute to Coleridge. If the latter is our concern, we get a better perspective if we approach his theory of the imagination as a corollary to the more basic conceptions just summarized.

The cornerstone of his psychology, aesthetic or otherwise, is his distinction between "reason" and "understanding" developed first from his reading of Kant and then coalesced with traditional Platonic rationalism.[1] The understanding (Kant's *Verstand*) is directed to the concrete world, subsuming and proceeding from the impressions the senses receive from the world of phenomena. It projects on them the categories inherent in its own subjective structure that Kant describes in the *Critique of Pure Reason*. But man also possesses, through *reason,* a direct insight into those universal and transcendent forms in and through which the concrete process of nature works or fulfills itself. "Reason" is indeed, in man, a mental counterpart or analogue of these persisting forms, sharing with them a "common ground."

Hence, in order to explain how we conceive not only the concrete world of process but also the universal forms of nature, Coleridge postulates two distinct functions of mind, "understanding" and "reason." But this very distinction, left by itself, violated his own organic conception of nature. For reality, as he had emphasized, is to be found in neither the universal nor the particular as such, but in the process of fulfillment where each declares the other; and value and concreteness, the "ideal" and the "real," become one in mutual substantiation. If the human mind is to grasp and share in this reality, it could be only through some capacity which brings together and coalesces what each of these two aspects of mind provide. Following the lead of Schelling, he turned (at least until his later religious writing) to the "imagination" as what he called a "completing power" in and through which the diverse functions of all that we call mind are united.

[1] See p. 185.

Such a process of awareness would duplicate the creative impulse of nature itself. It could in this sense be described as "a repetition in the finite mind of the eternal act of creation," and would serve as "the living Power and prime agent of all human Perception." For if the concrete world has, in the human mind, a counterpart in the form of the senses and the understanding, and if the universal possesses its counterpart in man's reason, in a similar way the energizing creativity of nature, which unites the universal and the particular, is matched by the imaginative capacity, which welds the insights of reason with the impressions and conceptions drawn from the concrete. Thus, as reality itself is the bridge, the point of meeting and emergence between concreteness and value, the imagination is a similar bridge between the various faculties of the mind. It is "the spirit of unity, that blends, and (as it were) *fuses,* each into each," revealing itself in "the balance of sameness, with difference; of the general, with the concrete; the idea, with the image; the individual, with the representative." Accordingly, in what is perhaps his most specific single definition (in *The Statesman's Manual*), Coleridge describes the imagination as

> that reconciling and mediatory power, which incorporating the reason in images of the sense, and organizing (as it were) the flux of the senses by the permanent and self-circling energies of the reason, gives birth to a system of symbols, harmonious in themselves, and consubstantial with the truths of which they are the conductors.

The imagination, then, is less a "faculty" than it is a *process* of realization by which the products and insights of two distinct aspects of mind become transmuted and funneled into a single stream of awareness. On the one hand, it is turned to the images and objects of the concrete world, which, since they are rendered by the senses and the understanding, appear "fixed and dead." But by sensing the dynamic potentiality inherent in these particulars and behind the static "masks" they seem to have, it volatilizes the impressions of them and the conceptions to which they give rise; it charges and lifts them, as it were, to a state of fusible intensity. At the same time it draws down the forms, the universals, which reason has descried, converting them into a similarly vital response. At this point of active fulfillment, universal conceptions become "ideas"; and it is in this sense that Coleridge defines an "idea" as an "educt of the imagination actuated by pure reason." In the reconciling centrality of the imagination, therefore, both the form and the concrete potentiality become *processed* into each other as they are in nature, the imagination thus serving as "the laboratory in which thought elaborates essence into existence." Art, in its highest function, is a repetition and expression of such a process as it is translated into the terms of a given medium: hence the statement that Shakespeare evolved "the germ within by the imaginative power according to an idea." Similarly, in the response to art, "taste," as one mode of the imagination, "connects the active with the passive powers of our nature, the intellect with the senses," and involves the ability "to elevate the *images* of the latter, while it realizes the *ideas* of the former."

At least the broad outlines of Coleridge's conception of the imagination may thus be ascertained if it is viewed, in his own phrase, as a "completing power," which he assumed as a concluding synthesis to more basic principles and assumptions. Indeed, it is doubtful whether one can approach it profitably in any other way. His specific remarks on the imagination itself are surprisingly few. Least of all should one take as a starting point the definition of the imagination that concludes chapter XIII of the *Biographia Literaria.* Coleridge had planned for this place, he tells us, an analysis of the subject which would not "amount to so little as an hundred pages"; and the chapter bears the promising title, "On the Imagination, or Esemplastic power"—he has coined the word "esemplastic" from the Greek, "to shape into one." But then, instead of the hundred-page discussion of the imagination, he inserts a letter to himself from himself, though said to be from a "judicious" friend, congratulating him on the work but stating that "to *unprepared* minds" his "speculations on the esemplastic power would be utterly unintelligible." Coleridge has therefore decided to defer the discussion until he could supplement it with others in a "future publication."

Obviously the treatise on the "esemplastic power" was never

written at all. The explanation is that here again he was blocked by his religious censor, not that he lacked ideas, even though he was dictating the *Biographia*, as we have seen, at a difficult time. For he was preparing to treat the subject in the vein of Schelling, except that he would be claiming even more for the imagination as an organ of insight into ultimate truth. This would bring him very close to the semi-pantheistic monism to which a part of him was so attracted but from which another part of him was already trying to disengage itself.[2] In any case, he prints only the following general remarks as a suggestion of what he had been planning to say:

> The primary IMAGINATION I hold to be the living Power and prime Agent of all human Perception, and as a repetition in the finite mind of the eternal act of creation in the infinite I AM. The secondary Imagination I consider as an echo of the former, co-existing with the conscious will, yet still as identical with the primary in the *kind* of its agency, and differing only in *degree*, and in the *mode* of its operation. It dissolves, diffuses, dissipates, in order to recreate; or where this process is rendered impossible, yet still at all events it struggles to idealize and to unify. It is essentially *vital*, even as all objects (*as* objects) are essentially fixed and dead.

This distinction between "primary" and "secondary" imagination seems to be a development of Schelling's. The "primary" imagination refers to the unconscious unifying involved in perception and common to all mankind. The "secondary" imagination refers to the more conscious, restricted use of the imagination in art, to the same creative and energizing power as it is directed to the world of material phenomena—of "objects," which, as they appear to sense and the understanding, are "essentially fixed and dead"; and these objects it "struggles to idealize and unify." In its twofold aspect, the imagination would thus draw upon nature in its totality and present an analogous synthesis. Coleridge then adds another distinction, between "Imagination" and "Fancy," developed from a distinction already half-established in English, especially in Scottish critical writing during the previous fifty years: [3]

[2] See p. 191.

[3] In particular by William Duff and Dugald Stewart. For more discussion of the background of the distinction, see *Modern Language Notes*, LX, 8-15.

> FANCY, on the contrary, has no other counters to play with, but fixities and definites. The Fancy is indeed no other than a mode of Memory emancipated from the order of time and space . . . But equally with the ordinary memory the Fancy must receive all its materials ready made from the law of association.

This famous distinction is simply a means of underlining the unique function he is assigning to the imagination. He wanted to cut off the word "imagination" from any associations it still had with a mere "image-making" faculty which reproduces, separates, or joins together images derived from sensation. The mind possesses such a faculty, of course. There is an obvious form or mode of memory, that is, which can retain or repeat sensations without being limited by their original contexts, and which is to this extent "emancipated from the order of time and space." It can transpose, divide, and combine impressions of "fixities and definites" according to the various laws of association. To this ability Coleridge gave the name "fancy" in order to distinguish it from both the power of organic fusion and the total exertion of mind, including reason, which enter into creation of art.

• 6 •

As an energizing capacity, immanent throughout all the faculties of the mind, the imagination not only unites reason with sense and understanding; its reach also extends to the most basic emotional impulses of human nature, through appealing to which it achieves a heightened awareness and a more formative realization. For it is in this substratum of response that human motivation is actualized and secured, and not in the mechanical jostling of what the associationists call "ideas" or impressions. Indeed, association itself (as Coleridge wrote in a letter to Southey, August 7, 1803)

> depends in much greater degree on the recurrence of resembling states of feeling than on trains of ideas . . . a metaphysical solution, that does not instantly *tell* you something in the heart is grievously to be suspected as apocryphal. I amost think that ideas *never* recall ideas, as far as they are ideas, any more than leaves in a forest create each other's motion. The breeze it is that runs through them . . . the state of feeling.

The imagination is thus not only the synthesizing and creative insight into truth; but, as a corollary to this function, it also transmutes that insight into beauty, "the mediator between Truth and Feeling." The corollary process ideally follows as the inevitable accompaniment of the former. Hence the remark that, in Shakespeare's nondramatic poems, the "intellectual energy," which conceives the original conception, and the "creative power," which renders this conception into symbols *ad hominem,* "wrestle as in a war embrace. Each in its excess of strength seems to threaten the existence of the other. At length in the DRAMA they were reconciled, and fought each with its shield before the breast of the other."

In such a process, therefore, the transmutation of the conception into the "mediating" form of beauty is not accompanied by loss or intrinsic change. The original insight, being the unique achievement of the imagination itself, remains present, with formative and ready effect, in the continuing imaginative process which, as a natural and automatic supplement, translates its conception into terms or symbols persuasive to human feelings. The symbol or resultant product thus evolves with inevitable and organic derivation, remaining "consubstantial" with the original conception. This is the significance of the remark in *The Statesman's Manual* that, in organizing "the flux of the senses by the permanent and self-circling energies of the reason," the imagination

> gives birth to a system of symbols, harmonious in themselves and consubstantial with the truths of which they are the conductors. These are the *wheels* which Ezekiel beheld, when the hand of the Lord was upon him . . . *Whithersoever the Spirit was to go the wheels went, and thither was their spirit to go:—for the spirit of the living creature was in the* wheels *also.*

It is this standpoint and not romantic subjectivism, then, that underlies the occasionally misinterpreted statement that the artist "must out of his own mind create forms according to the severe laws of the intellect, in order to generate in himself that coordination of freedom and law . . . which assimilates him to nature, and enables him to understand her." By evolving derivatively from an objective conception, the symbol, as its "conductor," thus retains an appeal to the total mind. Coleridge's distinction between "allegory" and "symbol" is primarily a means of emphasizing just this point. The appeal of allegory is restricted to sense and to a given mode of the "understanding." It is merely a "translation of abstract notions into a picture language, which is itself nothing but an abstraction from objects of the senses." The symbol, however, as the "wheel" conveying truth to feeling, renders what is meaningful, on the one hand, to sense and understanding, portraying what is specifically individual in the particular, at the same time revealing to the reason what is truly "universal" in the generality that the understanding forms or descries. This seems to be the point of the needlessly involved remark, again from *The Statesman's Manual,* that the symbol should be

> characterized by a translucence of the special in the individual, or of the general in the special, or of the universal in the general; above all by the translucence of the eternal through and in the temporal.

By stressing the objective appeal of the true "symbol," Coleridge is by no means in conflict with the spirit of Aristotle's belief that poetry should offer an *imitation* of an original rather than symbolic representations. Aristotle's attitude is explained by his assumption that symbols rely upon what we now call "convention"; and conventions, of course, change. But symbolism does not necessarily imply complete relativism, either local or personal, unless one adopts subjectivistic premises that would equally restrict any other theory of communication. Eighteenth-century associationism, which virtually created our modern theoretical interest in symbols, had emphasized their value in proportion as they rise above the "local and temporary" and appeal to universal principles of human nature. Coleridge's standpoint involves this much and more. He is not speaking of symbols that arbitrarily rest upon conventions alone, or, least of all, private association and subjective emotion, but of something not far from "imitation" in the broadest sense of that word. He is speaking, that is, of objective conception transmitted into terms of feeling—the "union and reconciliation of that which is nature with that which is exclusively human."

Even so, it is significant that in the later writing Coleridge should turn increasingly to this word "symbol," which he did so much to popularize. Not that he wanted a real substitute for the classical concept of art as "imitation" but rather a *supplement,* or, as he might say, an "active co-partner" in terminology. The truth is that, after having done as much as he could to open the classical idea of "imitation" and to the point where it could theoretically embrace almost everything in the range of experience, he still wanted a more malleable word. "Symbol," relatively new as a critical term, had that advantage. It was less tied to our stock notions of *natura naturata,* however Coleridge himself, in another of his favorite distinctions, might try to dissociate "imitation" and "copy." "Symbol" could also admit a freer play of mind and emotion. But as he moved more to the subjective, in using this more flexible word, his second thought is to qualify it, through his distinction between "symbol" and "allegory," and so move back to a center in which objective and subjective, classical and modern, can meet.

• 7 •

Coleridge's emphasis on feeling as a necessary element in genuine insight has thus nothing in common with the romantic-primitivistic trust in sheer instinct or impulse ("On such meagre diet as feelings, evaporated embryos in their progress to *birth,* no moral being ever becomes healthy"). However impulsively benevolent himself, he distrusted as a moral guide what he called the "sentimental pro-virtues." This applies as much to art as morality. He has no more patience than Goethe, Hazlitt, or Keats, with the thought so common at the time, and one which proved to be the most dubious legacy of the Romantics to later art, that our principal interest in art should be in the expression of merely private, subjective feelings in their "original," primitive state. This, for Coleridge, was a dead-end street in art as in life generally.

Whatever his psychological clairvoyance as he explores the

subjective self, his ultimate standpoint is by no means unclassical. Feeling, by itself, is blind and helpless. It may offer the distinctively human content to complete realization; but prior to the imaginative inducement of that realization, the significance of feeling is only potential, like clay waiting to be molded. What Coleridge says of the mind in general is especially applicable to feeling: "Events and images . . . are like light, and air, and moisture," without which it "would else rot and perish," and it must "assimilate and digest the food which it thus receives from without."

Far from being an organ of insight, therefore, feeling is merely a process of response, neutral in aim, which is peculiar and inevitable to our physical being: it is passive in being dependent for direction on what is outside it, and active in responding to what it has received. In this sense, "Our notions resemble the index and hand of the dial; our feelings are the hidden springs which impel the machine, with this difference, that notions and feelings react on each other reciprocally." Art, as the rendering of truth *ad hominem,* exploits and develops this interaction. In one of its functions, therefore, it incites an expectant tension; but it does so only for the purpose of increased receptivity. The use of meter in poetry would be one example. Meter "tends to increase the vivacity and susceptibility both of the general feelings and of the attention," but only as a means. Its effects, however pervasive, should not themselves be "objects of distinct consciousness," but should act "as a medicated atmosphere, or as wine during animated conversation":

> Where, therefore, correspondent food and appropriate matter are not provided for the attention and feelings thus roused, there must needs be a disappointment felt; like that of leaping in the dark from the last step of a stair-case, when we had prepared our muscles for a leap of three or four.

Similarly, in the creation of art, "sensibility" is a necessary accompaniment of genius. But, as he adds in the *Biographia,*

> It is not less an essential mark of true genius, that its sensibility is excited by any other cause more powerfully than by its own personal

> interests; for this plain reason, that the man of genius lives most in the ideal world . . . and because his feelings have been habitually associated with thoughts and images, to the number, clearness, and vivacity of which the sensation of *self* is always in inverse proportion.

Consequently, "A poet's heart and intellect should be *combined,* intimately combined and unified with the great appearances of nature."

Sensibility finds its fulfillment, that is, in sympathy. The importance of sympathetic identification is one of the most marked characteristics of English romanticism, and Coleridge's statements on the subject may be viewed as one extension of this characteristic, though he takes it for granted that sympathy is not an inherent guide but a product or result formed and developed through the imagination. Still, the potential aspiration of feeling, dependent as it is on what it "receives from without," is toward sympathy, as though the "body" itself were "but striving to become mind." It is for this reason that what is originally "the same feeling" becomes modified and altered in the conception of different forms. For example: "The Heaven lifts up my soul, the sight of the ocean seems to widen it." The difference of feeling, in each case, is that which

> we should feel in actual travelling horizontally or in direct ascent . . . For what are our feelings of this kind but a motion imagined, [together] with the feelings that would accompany that motion, [but] less distinguished, more blended, more rapid, more confused, and, thereby, coadunated? Just as white is the emblem of one in being the confusion of all.

Feeling, then, achieves value and becomes the handmaiden to realization to the degree that it is developed outward, through the imagination, into sympathy, and is modified by what it absorbs. It is through this means that, "in energetic minds, truth soon changes by domestication into power." Such a developed sensibility is one of the distinctive qualities of Shakespeare, who, far from being a mere "automation" of original genius, "studied patiently, meditated deeply, understood minutely, till knowledge, become habitual and intuitive, *wedded itself to his habitual feelings.*" Accordingly, he possessed the "chief requisite" of the poet:

the ability to "project his mind out of his own particular being," and to arouse in others "that sublime faculty by which a great mind becomes that on which it meditates." This capacity should be distinguished from—is indeed directly opposite to—what Coleridge called "ventriloquism," in which the poet "distributes his own insipidity" by projecting himself upon a phenomenon rather than into it. Sympathetic identification achieves its highest pertinence, of course, in the dramatic portrayal of character. In this sense, particularly, Shakespeare is without rival. Like Hazlitt, Coleridge was fond of comparing him to Proteus, in classic mythology, who could transform himself into diverse shapes of whatever sort: "to *think* ourselves into the thoughts and feelings" of others, whatever their circumstances, "*hic labor, hoc opus;* and who has achieved it? Perhaps only Shakespeare." Milton, by contrast, "attracts all forms and things to himself, into the unity of his own IDEAL," while Wordsworth and Goethe, in another way, are "spectators *ab extra,*—feeling for, but never with, their characters."

Such poets, however, appear external to their subject only when compared with the unique achievement of Shakespeare; and sympathetic absorption, as a fundamental requisite for poetry, has more general implications than the specific needs of the drama. Whether his aim is dramatic or not, the imagination of any poet must have as its complement "the threefold form of sympathy with the interesting in morals, the impressive in form, and the harmonious in sound." For poetry secures its peculiarly human appeal through the active harmonizing fusion of the imagination working in conjunction with the natural imitative and sympathetic capacity of feeling, and transmuting objective conception into emotional participation. It is by combining "a more than ordinary sympathy with the objects, on a more than common sensibility, with a more than ordinary activity of . . . the imagination," that poetry succeeds in its aim of producing "a more vivid reflection of the truths of nature and of the human heart, united with a constant activity modifying and correcting these truths."

• 8 •

The imagination, then, duplicates nature, in which universal and particular develop themselves, by presenting a conception in which the insights of reason have been united with the impressions and judgments of sense and understanding. But it also reconciles its conception "with that which is exclusively human." In this latter function, feeling may itself be viewed as potentiality to be fulfilled through form by the imaginative process. Art implies and rests upon both functions of the imagination. From the former, it secures its objective fidelity to truth. Through the latter, it transmutes truth into actualized response.

Years ago, back in the pantisocratic days when he was only twenty-two and still at Cambridge, he had written to Southey: "The *heart* should have *fed* upon the *truth,* as insects on a leaf, till it be tinged with the colour, and show its food in every the minutest fibre." That ideal remained with him to the end. (And if his own life had appeared to mock it, and of course it had, this was an indictment not of the ideal but of himself.) Art is not only the "mediatress between, and reconciler of, nature and man," in the sense that it makes truth realizable to him. In its capacity of "reconciler," it is also formative: it "assimilates him to Nature," and directs the process of human fulfillment in which "truth . . . changes by domestication into power," and "to *know* is to *resemble.*"

VIII

The First Years at Highgate (1816–1820): The Later Poems; Religious Thought, and the Plan for the *Magnum Opus*

When Coleridge arrived at James Gillman's house on Highgate Hill, April 15, 1816, he was carrying in his hand, said Gillman, the proof sheets of "Christabel." More probably the proof sheets arrived a week or two afterwards (arrangements to publish the poem had only been made on April 12). But that Gillman, writing years later, should associate Coleridge's arrival with the printing of "Christabel" suggests the bustle, the gestures of resolve and reform, made by Coleridge as he began what he desperately hoped would be—and what largely proved to be—a new life. The past fifteen years were to be put behind him. There was to be no more hesitation. If, thanks to Byron's help, John Murray wanted to publish "Christabel," "Kubla Khan," and the "Pains of Sleep," let it be done. He would hand over the proceeds to John Morgan, now so bady in need of help. Coleridge would also want money to pay this young surgeon of thirty-four, James Gillman, who was taking him into his house; and what a warmhearted woman Gillman's wife Anne seemed to be! Yes, he would draw on all the capital he had, with businesslike dispatch. He would also pull together any smaller projects he could, and then turn at once to the central project, the *magnum opus,* he had so long planned.

Highgate at this time was still no more than a small village separated by four miles of open countryside from the city. The place was ideal. There was a garden, and nearby was the beautiful Caen Wood. There were no embarrassing associations with the past. The slate could be wiped clean. He was himself only forty-three and a half—something we forget when we associate Highgate with an elderly Coleridge. Yet the past fifteen years had aged him, and we think back in contrast to the time he first called on the Wordsworths at Racedown, almost twenty years before, and leapt over the gate, as Dorothy said, to meet them. He was trying to do that now with the Gillmans. But at Racedown, when he met Wordsworth and his sister, all paths were still open. Now there was no alternative. He could not allow himself to disappoint these people too. He had begun a drastic reform nine months before, out at Calne in Wiltshire, when he started to dictate the *Biographia*. He could justifiably tell himself that he had made that crucial start pretty much on his own. Granted he had not freed himself from opium. But he had brought it under a kind of control, at least at times. And he had begun to write.

True, within a week or two after arriving at Highgate, he contrived to have laudanum smuggled in to him, as he had warned Gillman he might try to do. He wrote to the innocent Murray asking him to send some books. Would Murray, incidentally, do him a small favor and "dispatch a Porter with the enclosed note [to an apothecary] who is to wait for an answer," and then ask one of the men working for him to "pack up, whatever the Porter brings, carefully with the books"? [1] Still, over the next few months Coleridge was able with Gillman's help to reduce his use of opium to manageability, and by July Crabb Robinson could say that he had never seen him looking so well.

[1] Professor Griggs quotes (*Letters,* IV. 633) an amusing account from a letter of Mary Russell Mitford. Coleridge "put himself under watch and ward . . . gave his money to a friend to keep; and desired his druggist not to trust him. For some days all went well. Our poet was ready to hang himself; could not write; could not eat, could not—incredible as it may seem—could not talk." Then suddenly "he began to mend, he read, he talked." Coleridge "was himself again." Gillman "began to watch within doors and without. The next day the culprit was detected; for the next day came a second supply of laudanum from Murray's well wrapped up in proof-sheets of the 'Quarterly Review.'"

• 2 •

But his feeling of hurry, his desire to proceed briskly, had already begun to conflict with his sentimental heart, his inability to say no. Before he knew it, the yielding Coleridge, always so accident-prone, had signed up his work with a minor publishing firm that was to become bankrupt within three years. This firm (Gale and Curtis) had back in 1812 reprinted his periodical *The Friend.* Coleridge, hoping to capitalize on his past writing, now opened negotiations with them about the republication of *The Friend.* Curtis called on him personally. Coleridge was moved by the high principles of the firm—Curtis had recently entered the clergy. Byron's publishers, the house of Murray, had obvious advantages, but Coleridge thought it more appropriate at this crucial time of resolve to form "a connection with a religious house." He ended by promising Gale and Curtis not only the new general collection of his poems, *Sibylline Leaves* (leaving aside "Christabel," "Kubla Khan," and the "Pains of Sleep," which were published by Murray in May), but also the *Biographia* (printed but waiting for a publisher), and anything else he might publish in the future. Talking with them, he also found himself agreeing to write for them a "Lay Sermon," and began almost at once to work on it. This was conceived partly as a favor to the high-minded publishers, who were trying to establish themselves more firmly. Immediately the project developed into a plan for three "Lay Sermons," the first of which was to be addressed to the "higher classes," the second to the "higher and middle classes," the third to the "working classes." Why should he not throw himself into this task? It would be short. It was in a good cause. It would also help him to get started on his larger work. The result was the uneven, condensed, seminal "lay sermon," with its brave innocence of title, *The Statesman's Manual: or the Bible the Best Guide to Political Skill and Foresight,* published late in 1816.

All through the summer he worked at *The Statesman's Manual,* and if his health became shaky and he went with the Gillmans in September to the Hampshire coast, it was not because of overuse of laudanum. He was really driving himself. At some point in the late summer or early autumn he also wrote, or largely dictated, the fascinating fragment called the "Theory of Life," brief but central to any understanding of his thought in his middle—to some extent his later—years. As with so many of his more interesting works, Coleridge was here serving as escort or helper. The "Theory of Life" was written in order to assist Gillman, who was hoping to write a medical essay. (It proved far too lengthy and philosophical for Gillman to use.)[2] We shall return to this work later, in a short discussion of Coleridge's thought during this period. *The Statesman's Manual* was quickly followed by the second "lay sermon," conventionally called the *Lay Sermon* because of its cumbersome official title, taken from Scripture, "Blessed are ye that sow beside all waters." The third sermon, to the "working classes," was never written. Meanwhile the little publishing house with which he had signed up (now called Rest Fenner, as it underwent a change of hands before its bankruptcy) went ahead with the publication of Coleridge's poems, *Sibylline Leaves* (1817), the *Biographia* (1817), and the unperformed drama *Zapolya* (1817).

The same publishing firm also had thoughts of a new encyclopaedia (the *Encyclopaedia Metropolitana*), which would not be arranged alphabetically in the usual way but according to general subject and, above all, approach. Indeed, Coleridge may have been the principal architect of this new conception of approach and method. He agreed to write for the new *Encyclopaedia* a comprehensive introduction, to make some other contributions, and to supervise and edit the work generally in return for an annual salary that Coleridge understood to be £500 and the publisher somewhat less. The plan soon broke down. Wary of Coleridge's habits, the firm demanded that he leave Highgate and work daily at the premises where the encyclopaedia would be assembled. Coleridge wisely refused to leave Highgate. He ended by writing

[2] Speculations about the date have extended to 1823. But the letter to Gillman (November 10, 1816) plainly refers to the "Theory of Life" and to Gillman's uncertainty whether he could use it.

his *Preliminary Treatise on Method* as a general introduction.[3] It was chopped up and rearranged by the publisher, and Coleridge soon afterwards coalesced parts of it in a new edition of *The Friend* (1818). Needless to say he was distressed, hurt, puzzled, by these difficulties at a time when he was trying to get on his feet—when his real problem was to save himself for anything. How unpredictably, after one had made resolutions about the central anxieties of one's life, these smaller anxieties and obstacles kept sprouting up to complicate the picture!

Well, he would go ahead. He would give more lectures, though this was far from what he really wanted to do. He had expenses that had to be met before he could turn to his serious work. He owed so much to Gillman. He wanted to send money, if he could, to Mrs. Coleridge. The need of funds for the education of his second son, Derwent, also preyed on his imagination. For the Philosophical Society, he signed up for a course of fourteen lectures on literature from the Middle Ages to the present, delivered on Thursday and Friday evenings, from January 27 to March 13 (at the lecture hall in Fleur-de-luce Court, Fleet Street). He conscientiously prepared notes for most of the lectures, for which we have rather full reports. The lectures brought him more financially than any other series he gave, and he was able to meet some of his debts and also send a bonus to his wife. Meanwhile, during the previous summer, he had talked with Ludwig Tieck, who had come out to see him, and had also seen Southey, who was visiting London. Coleridge and the Gillmans then went in September to Littlehampton, where he made the acquaintance of H. F. Cary, the translator of Dante, and astonished Cary's son by his almost verbatim knowledge of the translation after one day's reading of it.

In December, Wordsworth came down from the North to London for a few weeks' visit. Coleridge saw him frequently, but usually in the company of others. Wordsworth was always a little grumpy when he visited London. His dislike of cities, crowds, and traffic increased as he grew older. He wanted to think well of human nature, and, more even than the rest of us, could do

[3] Edited by Alice D. Snyder (London, 1934).

so heartily only when it was not too suffocatingly present. He struck several people during this visit as formal and taciturn. (It was during this visit that Keats met him, and recited the "Ode to Pan," of which Wordsworth remarked "A very pretty piece of paganism.") At a dinner at Charles Lamb's (December 27), Wordsworth's admirer Crabb Robinson wrote in his diary that he was "for the first time in my life not pleased with Wordsworth." Coleridge talked "of painting in that style of mysticism which is now his habit of feeling. Wordsworth met this by dry, unfeeling contradiction. The manner of Coleridge towards Wordsworth was most respectful." As part of the background we should also remember that Wordsworth was not too happy about Coleridge's chapters on him in the *Biographia*. If the criticism was more than generous, the few reservations touched Wordsworth deeply, for they came from a mind that he respected more than any he had known. He was also naturally on the defensive since he was aware that the quarrel of seven years before had become common property because of Coleridge's eloquent and self-justifying advertisement of it.

• 3 •

Throughout this crowded year, Coleridge was also beginning once again to write an occasional poem, and in a very different mode. Perhaps six of the later poems were written at this time.[4] Five years of comparative silence followed. Then a few other poems were written from time to time. If we stop at this point to consider the character of the later poems as a whole, it is partly because at least a third of the more serious poems were written then. A more compelling reason is that what we find revealed in some of these poems is decisively relevant to the self-division in Coleridge that we must discuss in the latter part of this chapter —a subject our limit of space has not allowed us to take up piecemeal.

The relatively few poems that he wrote in his later years are

[4] The dates for the later poems are in most cases speculative. But we could include, under 1817-18, "Limbo," "Ne Plus Ultra," "The Knight's Tomb," "On Donne's Poetry," "Israel's Lament," and "Fancy in Nubibus."

intensely personal. They are what a poet may write when he no longer conceives of himself as a poet at all but is still tempted to write an occasional poem for whatever reason. In other words, these are poems written for no public, poems making no claim, composed to no form or standard, with no reference to any tradition, no interest in any tradition, other than what is engrained in the writer. They consist on the whole of jottings in notebooks and albums, with no thought of publication. Freed thus from the anxieties of self-demand, Coleridge is naturally often trivial, as any writer would be. On occasion, however, the general brilliance of his mind would crystallize and precipitate, as in the famous four-line criticism of Donne's poetry (written around 1817-1820):

> With Donne, whose muse on dromedary trots,
> Wreathe iron pokers into true-love knots;
> Rhyme's sturdy cripple, fancy's maze and clue,
> Wit's forge and fire-blast, meaning's press and screw.

Here Coleridge sums up in an epigram not only the earlier views of metaphysical poetry, for example the views of Dryden and Johnson, but also the twentieth-century praise of metaphysical "wit" as an amalgamation or fusion under pressure. The achievement is typical. In the better verse of Coleridge from 1817 until his death we find a denseness of thought often embodied in an odd, original imagery, frequently homely, occasionally even grotesque. So in "Human Life" man is compared to a "drone-hive strange of phantom purposes," or, in "Duty Surviving Self-love," Coleridge remarks that "Old friends burn dim, like lamps in noisome air." And since philosophy (or philosophical theology) was a prime interest of Coleridge's later years, it is not surprising to find, as a principal element in his poetic language, a philosophically sophisticated use of abstractions. In "Human Life" man is a "Blank accident! nothing's anomaly!" whose "being's being is contradiction," and in "Limbo" Coleridge evokes a "fear" or "future state" which he calls "positive Negation." Such abstractions seem almost substances for him, thick with emotion and meaning. In these poems, with their dense reflectiveness, their odd, often crowded metaphor, their allusion to the technical vocabulary and conceptualizations of Philosophy, Coleridge creates a mode of poetry entirely his own.

The more impressive poems of these years are religious, and the religious feeling is deeply personal. In two visionary poems of extraordinary power, "Limbo" and "Ne Plus Ultra," both apparently written in 1817, we glimpse the appalling spiritual suffering with which Coleridge was sometimes visited. In "Limbo" he speaks as one who has seen, has even inhabited, this "crepuscular" realm on the outmost border of existence—for he conceives it as a state where there is as little of life or being as may be consistent with being at all. Souls dwell in this purgatorial place as prisoners, walled in by horror of that nothing-at-all which surrounds limbo on every side. They are compared to moles whose "negative eye" can see only darkness:

> they shrink in as Moles
> (Nature's mute monks, live mandrakes of the ground)
> Creep back from light—then listen for its sound;—
> See but to dread, and dread they know not why.

Here—typical again of the new style we have mentioned—a severe reductionism treads the brink between compressed meaning and grimly sportive or fanciful image. Moles are "Nature's mute monks,": the devotion of these gray, cloistered creatures is blind, fearful, self-protective, producing only tunneled labyrinths in which the naked soul may hide. The mandrake too, that age-old symbol of man, can live only when its roots are safely in the ground, and according to legend shrieks when it is dug up.

Beneath this play of fancy is the existential dread that this state of "half-being," with man as mole or mandrake, may be all. And what would this mean to the hopeful concept of the "one Life"? "Human Time"—human existence—is conceived of as an old man, looking up from his earthly work in the field, and staring at the skies in the moonlight. But he is blind, his face "eyeless." He may feel, have somehow known, that there is light. But, with his upturned face, he is as unseeing as a statue, and if he turns his uplifted face "moonward" it is only by chance.

But even this blind hope is denied the soul in limbo. For there, if the redemption of man is not believed, hope turns to fear. With their "negative eye" these souls can descry something that comes from beyond limbo, across the mere darkness and nothing that surrounds it, something more terrible, which might be the essence of darkness and which Coleridge calls "positive Negation." From this as from the light the souls also shrink in terror, and one day it will annihilate them. In other words, the souls in limbo, being in a negative state, naturally shrink from light, are helplessly imprisoned, and threatened with still deeper abysses, descending on the negative scale through "blank Naught-at-all" to the final horror of "positive Negation." The poem entitled "Ne Plus Ultra" follows immediately after "Limbo" in Coleridge's notebook. It envisions this negative absolute. The poem takes the form of a litany in which "positive Negation" is identfied with Satan, as Coleridge fuses philosophical with mythological names for the principle of evil:

Sole Positive of Night!
Antipathist of Light!
Fate's only essence! primal scorpion rod—
The one permitted opposite of God!—

One of the names of this being is "The Intercepter," and if one asks what he intercepts, the poem makes clear that he comes between man and God. His "Grasp enorm" intercepts or, as Coleridge also says, interdicts prayer. In other words, in this poem Coleridge evokes an "unrevealable" principle of spritual death.

To keep in mind that Coleridge was familiar with such states makes it easier to understand the special tone of so much of his religious poetry, a tone that can be traced back to "The Pains of Sleep," "The Ancient Mariner," and even to earlier poems. It is as though he has been dreadfully punished and now makes humble and touching gestures of submission. One such poem is "To Nature" (written now or in the next few years), where Coleridge offers as a "sacrifice" to God a certain kind or order of truth. Here Coleridge is saying that he himself can find in leaves and flowers lessons of love and piety. Granted that "the wide world" holds this a mere "phantasy," and the world may be right; but he himself will continue the phantasy. In other words, Coleridge here abandons—at least for this poem—his confidence that the constructions of imagination are revelations of truth, and he also posits a possible separation of nature from God. Nevertheless, through his imagination he will "build" an altar of the field and a "dome" of the sky, so that nature will at least *seem* God's temple. As he thus returns nature to God he may be falsifying nature. But if so, he is only subordinating the discriminations of the intellect to the act of worship. Having done so, he may hope that God will not "despise / Even me, the priest of this poor sacrifice." For it now matters little whether the constructions of the imagination are true or false. What matters is rather the relation of the soul to God. A similar symbolic gesture —to take one more example—is enacted in a poem composed in 1832, "Self-Knowledge." Here again the symbolic gesture lies in the surrender—a giving up to God—of a jewel from Coleridge's intellectual crown, namely, his cherished maxim, "The heaven descended [injunction], *Know Thyself.*" For now he argues that man cannot know himself, and the poem ends, "Ignore thyself, and strive to know thy God."

• 4 •

When his course of literary lectures was finished (March, 1818), the busy Coleridge, still preoccupied with maintaining the momentum begun three years before, turned to his revised edition of *The Friend.* Like *The Statesman's Manual* and the *Treatise on Method,* the new *Friend*—incorporating parts of the *Treatise on Method*—would serve as a preparation for the major effort ahead. As the year wore on, he also planned a series of lectures on the history of philosophy from the Greeks to his own time, which he gave on Monday nights, from December 14, 1818 to March 29, 1819, at the Crown and Anchor Tavern in the Strand. They survived in shorthand notes and remained unpublished until 1949, when they were published under the title of *Philosophi-*

cal Lectures.[5] Meanwhile, he also gave concurrently two courses of literary lectures. Not that he had anything new he wanted to say about purely literary subjects at this point. He was giving these supplementary lectures only for the money. His heart was not in them.

In fact, throughout 1818 and 1819—Coleridge at forty-six and forty-seven—a large inner settlement was beginning to take place in his thinking. The board was being cleared of distractions, of peripheral interests. He was coming to closer grip with the subject to which for twenty years he had felt he could turn if only he had enough time and freedom from personal and financial anxiety. Now he was relatively free—as free as he would ever be. But as he approached the subject more closely, he found that he himself had been changing. The principal interest of the *Philosophical Lectures* is exactly what so disappointed readers when they were at last published—the fact that he is suddenly so reticent when he comes to the "dynamic" and "organic" philosophy that for almost twenty years had seemed so congenial to his thought. The whole of German philosophy is huddled into a part of one lecture instead of the three or four that we should expect in a series of this length. Discussion of Schelling—so eagerly anticipated by modern students of Coleridge—is confined to one hesitant paragraph. He could offer the excuse that he had already used up too much time on the earlier stages of the subject and now had to hasten to a close. But the lectures could have been extended; and in any case, he had never been at a loss, in either his lectures or his writing, to move directly to what was central in his interest if he really wanted to do so.

Plainly something is intervening. An inner portcullis, for some reason, is being dropped on these writers—dropped on the entire movement of thought to which he has been so powerfully drawn. There had been moments before when this had happened. But in the past the porcullis would quickly lift, and he would reach out with open arms and a rush of almost clairvoyant sympathy. To some extent this was to continue to happen. There would always

[5] Edited by Kathleen Coburn (London and New York, 1949).

be second, third, fourth thoughts. This orphan-host, this orphan who so early became host and escort and welcomer, was always to remain eager not only for the security of home but for visits of guests ("the stranger" in "Frost at Midnight"). But, on the whole, the *Philosophical Lectures* mark a decisive turn in the chronology of his thought. For here we are encountering a psychological block so complete, a censorship so strong, that at the moment he finds himself incapable even of summarizing the premises, aims, interests, of a form of thinking that for years has excited (and yet deeply disturbed) him more than any other. How could he start to explain these writers—to interpret what they meant and did—without surrendering to the overwhelming impulse to side with them, to say all that he could so easily begin to say about the "organic" and "dynamic" philosophy? But he was not yet ready. Better, in these lectures, this prefatory exercise, to stay clear of the matter. He could so easily say the wrong thing. Given only another year or two, he would get his bearings.

• 5 •

We may turn at last to the plan of the *magnum opus* and quickly review the background. We have been touching on it indirectly. Only in a far more capacious account of Coleridge's life could we have discussed the background as we really should, tracing the aims, the frustrations and renewed hopes, year by year as they intertwine with other circumstances of his life. Because we are forced to abridge drastically, we have chosen instead to select moments in his complex intellectual life when we could pause, as we have with his poetry or his critical writing, and then focus for a few pages on an essential chapter in the biography of his mind.

The long, never completely abandoned dream of the *magnum opus* was of nothing less than a new *Summa* of theology, morals, psychology, logic, the sciences, and the arts, or rather of a series of works that together might make up a *Summa*.[6] The mention of such a hope naturally evokes a smile. But actually the thought was less impossible than it might seem. For in some respects Coleridge's qualifications were almost unique, not because of any one of them singly but because of the combination. To begin with, probably no one at the time outside Germany was more broadly read in the history of philosophy (though to the confirmed Germanophile this may appear slight praise); and this was something as a start. Secondly, he was a practicing artist with a brilliantly inventive as well as critical mind. He thus possessed a direct and immediate acquaintance with an important range of mental functions denied to the man who knows them only at second or third hand through the filters of hearsay and conventional abstractions. Yet at the same time he was widely, in some ways very concretely, interested in the sciences. Probably no other major modern artist except Goethe (who however was averse to metaphysical speculation) and Thomas Mann has been more so; and conversely, few men so knowledgeable in the sciences, during the last century and a half, have possessed anything like his abilities, at once inventive and critical, in the arts. Fourthly, Coleridge was as gifted a psychologist as any man of his time. Lastly, he was a man of a deeply religious temperament, or at least was becoming so. He really cared to write a *Summa* with an ultimate theological purpose. He really cared to find a unity that would subsume areas of experience of which so many theologies and philosophies often seem only mildly aware. The hunger for unity, the inability to rest content in the vestibule or the aisles, is, in the broadest sense, a religious feeling, a religious need.

On the other hand there were certainly liabilities, and to a

[6] A problem of nomenclature enters here that has naturally confused readers. By convention, and following Coleridge's own tentative reference to it as such, the title *Opus Maximum* is assigned to a specific, comparatively restricted work that actually exists (though in a very unfinished state), is still unpublished except for a few pages, and is scheduled to appear in the *Collected Edition*. Written in the 1820s (see p. 212), it is almost entirely theological. (Presumably these sections were to be supplemented by much else.) The term *magnum opus*, by contrast, refers to the over-all ambition of Coleridge after he returned from Germany (1799).

large extent they were inherent in the very nature of his virtues, his range of sympathies, his inability to say no, his eagerness not only to rescue but to welcome into a home of general meaning the forgotten waif of detail, the overlooked nuance, the apparently unruly and obdurate exception. Of course it was precisely this quality in him that was so valuable. And it need not have been completely inhibiting to a man of such omnivorous curiosity, such readiness of memory and expression, and with a mind that became more excited and resourceful in proportion to the richness of the "multëity" to be combined. The real difficulties began to spawn when he came to *method* and *approach*. For quite commendably his conviction of what should be included went beyond mere diversity of subject matter and extended equally to the widely different approaches that had been traditionally thought appropriate to each. The union desired, in short, would amount to nothing if all that was involved was a two-dimensional, a merely horizontal sweep of subjects as though one were mapping a terrain. What was wanted was rather a union in depth, one that subsumed vertically the procedures and values, the logic and the technical steps, the actual trial and winning of insight. Here Coleridge as a thinker was at his bravest and was also, of course, most vulnerable.

• 6 •

Five major approaches, in particular, were constantly counterpointing in his thought during his middle and to some extent his later years. If we forget the presence of any of them—forget that the hospitality of his mind could exclude none of them—his inner life completely eludes us, and not merely the hopes, frustrations, and conflicts, but also the meaning of much that he actually did succeed in writing. Was not each—he could argue—an important part of the drama of man's effort to understand himself and what lies beyond him? Surely a philosophy honest to the multiplicity of man's experience would seek for a comprehensive ground that would allow one to do justice to them all.

The first three can be mentioned more briefly, in ascending order of the complexities they presented:

(1) The tradition of classical rationalism, from Plato through the Renaissance, with its premise of an ordered, objective reality that transcends our sense experience but can be known through reason.

(2) Curbing the excesses of rampant rationalism, which in its craving for system can so easily cut itself loose from human experience, was the healthful tradition of British empiricism in its more moderate form: empiricism, that is, as it supports or tries to explain what we ordinarily mean by *science,* as contrasted with the "radical" empiricism that, in turning solely on the mind, undercuts itself, as David Hume with such cheerful brilliance had illustrated. And just as Hume was willing to admit that he got out of the way of a carriage when he saw it rushing toward him in the street, Coleridge accepted the fact of science, indeed welcomed it.

Why was the modern philosopher so eager to convince us that we have only one means of knowledge? The radical empiricist and the radical rationalist were always trying to assert as much. Yet amusingly, in order to put across their arguments, their own practice belied their precept, the rationalist taking over premises from the empiricist while the empiricist adopts systematic procedures from the rationalist. Coleridge, for his part, saw no difficulty in uniting the premises of classical rationalism with a moderate, commonsense empiricism, delighting to assert a common ground, an interplay of premises, between Plato and Bacon. Why should there be any difficulty? Did he not have the history of science, indeed the entire practical experience of mankind, on his side? Rigid purities of analysis that ended by denying this large testimony were, as far as he was concerned, of *psychological* rather than philosophical interest, fascinating curiosities of what can happen in our thinking when we are more interested in excluding than including.

(3) The Kantian philosophy, which "took possession" of him, to

quote his famous tribute, "as with a giant's hand." Nothing could be more liberating than this magisterial demonstration that the mind is, at the very least, an active co-partner in the process of knowledge. How much it helped to sweep aside the old dualism of mind and object that had crippled philosophy since the time of Descartes!

Naturally there was room for improvement, or at least for supplement, and to Coleridge improvement usually meant supplementing a thing by engrafting upon it something else or rescuing it into greater breadth of context by giving it family (brothers, cousins, ancestors, possible descendants) as well as environmental roots. Kant, in every other way so admirable, was needlessly cautious in denying—or was he only *appearing* to deny?—the possibility of man's access to ultimate knowledge through reason. That penetrating distinction of Kant's between understanding (*Verstand*) and reason (*Vernunft*)—the understanding directed to the phenomenal world, while reason arranges and interprets the judgments of the understanding in the light of certain universally valid "ideas"—stopped short of where it could and should lead. To Kant the ultimate "ideas" by which reason arranges and interprets the judgments of the understanding were not objects of real knowledge but only necessary hypotheses. The issue, said Coleridge, whether the "ideas" of reason are "regulative" only, as in Kant, or "likewise constitutive, according to Plato and Plotinus . . . is the highest problem of philosophy, and not part of its nomenclature."

In Coleridge's long wrestle with Kant, he seems to have thought of himself as a Jacob condemned, on this one point, to struggle with an angel sent to try him. With his back firmly braced upon the entire classical tradition, and the Hebraic and Christian thinking with which it had combined, he affirmed at every opportunity that reason—as in the Platonic conception of it (*nous*)—is able, as it transcends the experience and judgments drawn from the concrete world, to touch directly a reality to which it is itself the mental analogue or counterpart. From now until the end of his life Coleridge made a great deal of this one crucial difference between himself and Kant, and to such an extent that we could be misled into thinking that it preoccupied him more than any other philosophic issue. To establish his own distinction between "reason" and understanding was "one main object" of Coleridge's periodical, *The Friend* (1809); and twenty-one years later he was still speaking of the distinction as a *Gradus ad Philosophiam.*

The distinction is indeed central to his thought. But on the other hand, the point is one that could be made rather quickly, and he had as well that rich background of support which he cited, again and again, from Plato through the Christian writers of the Middle Ages and the Renaissance. Why then continue to dwell on it as he did, year after year?—for it is not as though he were offering a new epistemological proof. He had two special incentives, the first of which leads directly into the second: (i) It was an important symbolic testimony of intention. For of course Coleridge could never turn his back on the possibility of man's knowledge, through reason, of an ultimate reality—a reality of which reason is, in man, a counterpart. To think otherwise would be a form of impiety. Yes, like Jacob, he would wrestle on behalf of this cause. And if, like Jacob, he was somewhat lamed from this half-martyring encounter with the formidable Kant, he was not unwilling to show the scars or to limp a little in his later duties and efforts. He would have fought the good fight in at least this one respect. (ii) He needed desperately a subject for refinement—for distinction, for philosophical stance, in which he had been reasonably successful—that could distract himself, himself even more than others, from a larger problem that was nagging him more with every year that passed. This larger problem was how to bring together (or rather how to find for them a common ground they could both share)—

(4) The organic or dynamic philosophy of nature—the conception of nature as a unifying process, to which he was so deeply drawn but which, to his distress, was so often dismissed by the religiously orthodox as "pantheism"; and

(5) The Christian religion, to the advancement of which any

magnum opus he might conceive was naturally to be dedicated.

Here, of course, the considerations were on a different plane. For now he was no longer dealing with that exasperating, merely *preliminary* problem which had monopolized, indeed hagridden philosophy ever since Descartes and Locke—the problem of knowledge—of what we *can* know, of *how* we know: a preoccupation (as in the fable of the centipede that stopped to reflect on the workings of its legs) that lowers the sights and inhibits range of movement. Naturally all this was no more than a threshold shuffle to the real concern of philosophy! Not that Coleridge was omitting that ceremony: had he not proved—was he not in fact always proving—that no one could be more conscientious about thresholds, about proper entrances, apologies, and greetings? Who could be more thorough and deliberate in making preliminary distinctions—in accumulating in advance, as Carlyle too roughly said, an array of "formidable apparatus, logical swim-bladders, transcendental life-preservers and other precautionary and vehiculatory gear, for setting out"?

• 7 •

The truth is that, with every year from his late twenties until his late forties, these two final, all-important concerns, each of which appealed to him so deeply, seemed to be developing new areas of conflict or at least new areas of friction. Yet at the same time so much in each of them seemed to come together—come together in comprehensiveness and ideal, in the premium each laid on sympathy, in tenderness and fidelity to the individual. What was wrong? Why this stern and thin-lipped censorship by the religiously orthodox of the dynamic philosophy which they condemned as "pantheism," with the implication that, if you subscribed to it, you were immediately assuming that God could be nothing except a sort of neutral sum total of the universe? Back even in the school days at Christ's Hospital that Lamb described, Coleridge's imagination had been stirred, through Plotinus and the Neoplatonists, by the thought that God could be at once *immanent* throughout all creation and at the same time *transcendent*. Why were people always saying that only one thing or the other was possible?—and with stark oblivion to the interplay of diversity involved in the simplest event of experience —the simplest form of matter itself? Coleridge could take the religious censorship more lightly at first, back in his early twenties. The whole premise behind the "conversation poem" had been the ideal of interconnection, of mutual contribution, of process through synthesis, but usually with the belief (or hope) that this was compatible with some form or other of Christianity. Was not Christianity, above all other religions, one that cherished at once the individual and also the potentialities of union (union through the brotherhood of man, and, in the great symbol of Christ, of union with God)? In his philosophical admirations during his twenties, when he had begun looking for a philosophy that could unify the multiplicity of experience with Christian belief, he had jumped from David Hartley, who finally proved too materialistic, to Berkeley, who proved too specialized in his idealism, to Spinoza. Here at last, in Spinoza, he felt that he had, if not a master to be followed literally, a majestic model of both range and cleanliness of thought (needing only the additional help of a little healthy-minded British empiricism, with its welcome of science and its more psychologically informed recognition of the impulses and needs of the human mind and heart).

But then two things intervened in the troubled decade that followed his return from Germany. One was his reading of Kant, and the other, more gradual, was the growing orthodoxy in his religious thinking and feeling that we have been noticing throughout these years. The former, by itself, seemed at first to create no problems. Rather it opened new vistas. Rightly used—used with some imagination, in a full and honestly admitted context of other considerations—could not the Kantian philosophy help to free us, help to give us a new chance to rejustify the "dynamic" and "organic" conception of process? True, Kant at the same time knocked aside the confident rationalism on which Spinoza's method had rested. Still it was not the systematic rationalism of Spinoza's *approach* that the young Coleridge prized. It was the ideal of unity that had pervaded the thinking of that "God-intoxicated" man, as Novalis called Spinoza. Yes, if Kant closed some doors, he also opened others, and to a universe (when Kant was rightly interpreted) potentially freer than Spinoza's. In fact, was this not already being exemplified, and at this very moment, in that brilliant, divided Germany across the water, of which so many Englishmen, in their reading, their classical education, their trips to Paris and Rome, seemed unaware? Rapid developments in thought were sprouting up there within one university city after another. And at the center of almost every one of them was a gifted man occupied in modifying, or ramifying, the thought of Kant's great seminal *Critiques.* If some were doing this with an ingenious morbid subjectivism (such as Fichte), others were finding means of re-interpreting both the sciences and the arts in a comprehensive spirit, analogous in aim, if not similar in approach, to Spinoza—a spirit at once faithful to objective fact, scientific or psychological, and at the same time "dynamic" in its rediscovery of reality as *process.*

Above all, Coleridge was to begin to feel a deep kinship with that brilliant, star-crossed philosopher, Friedrich Schelling—a man two and a half years younger than himself, whose later intellectual career strangely parallels, in its difficulties and its periods of paralysis, that of Coleridge himself. From Schelling—to a less extent from others—Coleridge grasped at one insight, one reassurance, after another, though later he defensively, and not very nobly, tried to minimize his debt. With Schelling, as Coleridge said, he found a spiritual "coincidence with much that I had toiled out for myself, and a powerful assistance in what I had yet to do."

But what was there "yet to do"? It was—of course—to reconcile the "dynamic" philosophy with Christianity. Schelling, however gifted, had not done that—nor indeed had anyone else. But how to proceed? Back in Coleridge's twenties, as we have noted, the reconciliation of the dynamic and the Christian philosophies had seemed relatively simple. Then in his thirties the complexities increased. It was indeed the *second* interruption to his hoped-for embrace of Spinoza—or rather to the dream of unity that Spinoza represented—that was creating the real difficulty. This was Coleridge's changing conception of the Christian religion itself. He could no longer view it as flexibly as in his Unitarian days. It was a Christianity that had for years become increasingly permeated, first of all, with the traditional Hebraic and Catholic belief in a profound dualism between God and His creation, in the nature of sin, in the smallness of man and his concerns before the infinite; and, secondly, by a growing conviction of the unique function of the Christ. Coleridge had always felt drawn to both of these beliefs. Had not the "Ancient Mariner" reflected this profound sense of the finitude of man, and of the drastic need of the human heart for conversion (itself a mystery) and for the aid of divine grace, however incompletely the poem had suggested this?

But as Coleridge passed into his thirties and forties, as one thing after another happened or seemed to happen to him, he was beginning to experience more deeply what he had only suggested there in the "Mariner," with so little conscious realization of what was involved—the ease with which man can slip into isolation, the fearful nakedness of his brief existence within this vast cosmos, his helplessness, his need. We see this dramatically put in some of the poems he was soon to jot down in his notebooks. Two in particular—"Limbo" and "Ne Plus Ultra"—are as powerful and condensed an expression of cosmic isolation as we can find in English poetry. What more than anything else in his experience had been sweeping him irresistibly to traditional religious doctrine—Hebraic as well as Christian—was its ancient recognition of the helplessness of man without the intervention of divine grace. But how to fit this into the concept of the "one Life" to which he was equally drawn? Why should man especially —as distinguished from a blade of grass, from the dog barking in the barnyard, from the ape chattering in the tree—be singled out in this way, at once so terrible in the possible isolation and so strict in the demand on the individual, so special in the claim on God? Answers were available, of course. But too often they came from men who, if they hungered for unity as much as he himself, construed that unity with a purity, a singleness of interest, altogether different from the unity he himself had in mind. It was like formalism in art. Instead of rising in, with, and through diversity and multiplicity, it was exclusive. It kept out rather than embraced and subsumed. But the greatness of the Christian religion was that it could include as well as exclude.

• 8 •

What was to blame for this growing impasse in his thought between Christianity and the organic, dynamic philosophy? Did it reflect merely a personal division within himself that he did not yet understand psychologically? Or was it something more important? Was there, just possibly, a fundamental division after all—perhaps even an incompatibility—between these two comprehensive views of the world, both of which appealed to him so much and which seemed potentially to have so much in common? He still could not believe that there was a true incompatibility, not at least in general spirit, not when rightly approached.

For of course in his thought of the "one Life" he himself had never been considering "pantheism" in the obvious and crude sense. Who could be sterner than he when he came upon outright examples of it? Or, if not sterner (for he could hardly be that when he thought of men like the gentle and inspired Jakob Boehme, to whom he owed so much), who could be quicker to note when a philosophy was slipping into pantheism? Was Schelling doing that? Well, a salutary corrective could be applied—Schelling's insights could be supplemented. Indeed the very word "pantheism" distressed Coleridge. This is not at all what he had in mind! No, he was never a complete "monist"—one who assumed at the start (and is that not what the pantheist does?) that all is really one substance, one single nature, in which the perceiving mind and the perceived object, spirit and matter, even God and nature, are only different names, at most different attributes. On the contrary, the dynamic philosophy he had in mind was one that presupposed from the beginning a fundamental difference. So in the "Theory of Life" ("Hints Toward the Formation of a More Comprehensive Theory of Life"), the "most general law" from which he proceeds is the "polarity, or the essential dualism of Nature."

What a relief it was to begin that essay on the "Theory of Life," free from the cloggings of conscience by serving once again as helper. For this work was to be written in a good cause, for an honored friend, James Gillman, who was now taking him into his home, and at a time when Coleridge was trying so hard to justify himself. (The essay—as we noted before —was to provide background for a medical discussion Gillman was planning.) Hence Coleridge did not have to speak in his own voice, encountering not only the religious but the epistemological censor in every paragraph. He was all the freer because the man he was now helping was a physician, a scientist, and therefore comparatively removed from theological concerns. The result, though it does not go very far, is the most condensed statement we have of Coleridge's philosophy of nature. (That some of the principal ideas are drawn from German sources is nothing to the purpose, at least at the moment.[7]) We are not speaking of the originality of particular ideas or even particular chains of ideas. Indeed if the "Theory of Life" were no more than an anthology of selected quotations (which it is not), we could justifiably infer something of the dynamic *Natur-Philosophie* he was hoping to coalesce with Christian thought. And in any case, it can tell us something of the drama of his inner debate.

Since he is now trying to proceed with despatch, and feels that he has every excuse for doing so, only a fifth of this fifty-odd pages of the "Theory of Life" are devoted to a preliminary clearing of the ground (and quite effectively) of definitions of life that Coleridge quickly shows to be tautologies. Then he provides

[7] Nor is the fact that, in hastily assembling this essay for Gillman, and pathetically eager to prove to his new benefactor that he would not be completely useless to him, he also directly lifted or paraphrased the equivalent of six pages from Henrik Steffens and three and a half from Schelling (see p. 134).

his own definition, suggested by Henrik Steffens and very much in the spirit of the organicism exemplified by Alfred North Whitehead in our own era. Life is *"the principal of individuation,* or the power which unites a given *all* into a *whole* that is presupposed by all its parts." It follows that "The unity will be more intense in proportion as it constitutes each particular thing a whole of itself; and yet more, again, in proportion to the number and interdependence of the parts, which it unites as a whole." (This is a premise Coleridge applies not only to "life," from the lowest form to the highest, but to every aspect of thought and in particular to art itself.) Or, to put it another way: "The individuality is most intense where the greatest dependence of the parts on the whole is combined with the greatest dependence of the whole on the parts." Proceeding from this definition, he establishes the "essential dualism of Nature" as an assumption that the "tendency to individuate" and to "connect" must presuppose if there is to be anything to "connect." In turn, the former (the "essential dualism") presupposes the latter (the tendency to connect and "individuate") —just as the centrifugal presupposes the centripetal, or "as the two opposite poles constitute each other, and are the constituent acts of one and the same power in the magnet." Concluding this part of his discussion, he states that "In the identity of the two counterpowers, Life *sub*sists; in their strife it *con*sists; and in their reconciliation it at once dies and is born again into a new form."

Then, clairvoyantly anticipating a central premise of modern science, he defines a "thing" as a "synthesis of opposing energies." Some observations on points and lines in space, and on rhythm and pattern in time, are followed by a brief, quasi-symbolic treatment of electricity and magnetism, then metals, crystals, and finally organic life. At each stage in the "ascent" of individuation, the interdependence of part and whole increases. Coleridge pauses especially to talk about insects. They fascinate him anyway, as such a near approach to "mechanism" in the animal world; and he also has some good ideas from Henrik Steffens to insert and develop. In the total organization of insects, the tendency of life, as compared with the higher animals, is *ad extra*, working out toward the "superficies" of their bodies into an almost independent "variety of tools" (their eyes, for example, are not so much *conductors* of light as the "sensorium" itself). Accordingly "the two halves of a divided insect have continued to perform, or attempt, each their separate functions, the trunkless head feeding with its accustomed voracity, while the headless trunk has exhibited its appropriate excitability to the sexual influence." With fish, the direction of the organizing power begins to proceed more *ad intra,*

> with the consequent greater simplicity of the exterior form, and the substitution of condensed and flexible force, with comparative unity of implements, for that variety of tools, almost as numerous as the several objects of which they are applied, which arises from and characterizes the superficial life of the insect creation.

Up to this point the "Theory of Life" has proceeded merrily—at least considering the very special circumstances under which it was written or rather dictated. We should also notice, by the way, that Coleridge somewhat anticipates the belief of modern genetics that evolution proceeds through mutations.[8] In doing so, he not only resolved in advance some of the problems faced by the post-Darwin evolutionists of the later nineteenth century, but laid a basis for what could conceivably have answered some of his uncertainties when he came to the human being. The surprise is that he went as far as he did, without the backlog of investigation of which the natural philosopher of a century and a half later can avail himself.

But at the moment, as he faces the problem of tracing the

[8] See especially Craig Miller, "Coleridge's Concept of Nature," *Journal of the History of Ideas, XXV* (1964), 77-96, which ably refutes the notion that, because Coleridge objected to the cruder pre-Darwin speculations that man was "descended" from the ape (the "oran outang hypothesis," as he called it), he was therefore opposed to the general idea of evolution, and was merely saying in the "Theory of Life" that nature in its different forms exhibits in static form the ascending approximation of nature to spirit. We could add that, even in the "Note on Giordano Bruno," found in his unpublished papers and often vaguely cited as proof that he did not believe in "evolution," he goes on to say that each "step" of creation "must be proceeded by a *process* of growth, and consequently a state of *involution* [concentration of the faculties, completion into a form] and *latency* correspondent to each successive Moment of Development."

progressive individuation *ad intra,* Coleridge becomes uneasy. He is getting closer to man. And to proceed directly to man, in this spirit of dynamic evolution, is not quite what he wanted to do—at least not yet. The essay falls apart. A single page is given to birds, still less to the mammals, and a few sentences to man. Coleridge's voice, even speaking by proxy, deserts him. Of course he could not end the essay thus: If Gillman was to use this as background for a medical discussion, some talk about man was presupposed. Frantically, as if to get back to something that was at least *scientific* in the specialized sense of the word, and at the same time to lift the whole subject to a more abstract and less censorable plane, Coleridge reached out to Schelling's *Zeitschrift für spekulative Physik,* incorporated three and a half pages about a laboratory experiment on magnetism, and then, except for a few general sentences, dropped the whole effort. (Naturally Gillman never used Coleridge's paper.)

• 9 •

Even in this brilliant but hasty essay—relatively free because it could be vicarious—at least one censor intrudes. It is plain that he is not yet ready to talk, or even to provide written materials for another to talk, about what the post-Darwin world was to call "evolution" as it applied to *man.* For the moment there was a bar crossing that path. A certain amount of time would first be necessary, a certain amount of delicacy, judgment, imagination, open-mindedness; there were many considerations yet to be taken into account.[9] Meanwhile, it is also clear that he was at least trying not to think in terms of a simple

[9] Nor was he quite ready to do so four years later (1820), when he was visited by the young Frenchman, Philarète Chasles, and in "many conversations" tried, at Chasles's request, to "reveal to me the main points of his great system." "The material system of life . . . seemed to him to accord with the spiritual mystery." He believed in "progress developing itself"—"vegetation *becoming* animal life in its progress, and the lower animal *ascending* to the higher." Had he spoken even briefly, in one of these "many" talks, of the relation of man himself to the higher animals, we may be sure that Chasles would have mentioned it, if only because any such speculation would have been surprising at the time from a man who also told him of his conviction that "all philosophical doctrines were explained through Christianity."

pantheistic "monism" (nor even voicing it through another). An essential "dualism" was built into the very nature of his concept, was it not? How, in fact, could one even conceive of a truly dynamic union, or rather *process toward union,* without having such a polarity, such an "acknowledged difference," premised at the start? Of course, on second thought (and Coleridge was inclined to second thoughts), one cannot strictly say "at the start." For what precedes and gives that "dualistic" premise? The theologian could retort that such a universe is still "monistic"—a unity simply divides in order afterwards to reunite. Well, how does the theologian's explanation of the origin of evil differ in kind? (The subject, we remember, had years before, back in his twenties, fascinated and then eluded Coleridge as a subject for a major poem.) So much of the problem obviously has to do with the limits and habits of human thinking—the ambiguities in the terms we use. But in any case, for the time being, on that other theological problem, God and nature—God as *transcending* nature, while at the same time becoming immanent: was not Coleridge providing, over and over again, his credentials—in his avowed aims, in his rededications of himself, in his single-handed wrestle with Kant on that "highest problem of philosophy"—the distinction between "reason" and "understanding," the very essence of which involved a transcendent deity?

Plainly there was no choice (the brute fact kept confronting him year after year) except to go back once again to the uncongenial problem of *knowledge* that a century and a half of philosophical thinking had unfortunately thrust into central importance. The frustration wore on him constantly. There was no choice except to clear up first the "communicative intelligence," with all the unnecessary stumbling blocks, the stock responses to traditional terms, the false issues and needless disagreements. What other alternatives were there except to begin from the ground up?—at least if one hoped to find the ground for a new friendship, a new union between Christianity and the dynamic philosophy of nature. Suppose as one alternative he simply leapt over all this preliminary matter of knowledge (which the eighteenth and now the nineteenth century conceived as so important), and with drastic directness started first with traditional Christian theology, readjusting it gradually in order to engraft on it the organic and dynamic philosophy—what, in a passage in the notebooks, he once half-puckishly called "the Iliad of Spinozo-Kantian, Kanto-Fichtean, Fichto-Schellingian Revival of Plato-Plotino-Proclian Idealism." But this was out of the question. It would involve a ruthless tinkering with traditional theology as he went. The second alternative was even more unthinkable—to begin first with the dynamic philosophy, and then bring in the Christian theology as the cap of the pyramid.

No, one must first approach things from a deeper ground, and then, proceeding upward, show the Christian theology (tenderly, protectively) that it had nothing to fear—that its tenets, its premises and aims, were already being provided for—truly explained and justified—within a richer context that would at the same time subsume all that the dynamic philosophy of nature could suggest. Of course there was no alternative except to begin with a comprehensive discussion of the "communicative intelligence"—logic, epistemology, and (increasingly) psychology. Back on June 4, 1803, when he had outlined his plan ("I entitle it Organum verè Organum"), which was itself to be a mere prefatory work, on the use of general intelligence or "practical reasoning" in "real life," he intended to prefix to it three general essays dealing with Aristotelian logic, the philosophy of the medieval schoolmen, and an "Outline of the History of Logic in General"—the last of which was to consist of twelve chapters [10]—

[10] 1. Chapt.—The origin of Philosophy in general, and of Logic speciatim. 2. Chapt. Of the Eleatic & Megaric Logic. 3. of the Platonic Logic. 4. of Aristotle, containing a fair account [of] the " "Οργανον which Dr. Reid in Kaimes' Sketches of man has given a most false, & not only erroneous, but calumnious Statement—as far as this account had not been anticipated in the second Part of my work . . .—5. a philosophical Examination of the Truth, and of the Value, of the Aristotelean System of Logic, including all the after additions to it. 6. on the characteristic Merits & Demerits of Aristotle & Plato, as Philosophers in general, & an attempt to explain the fact of the vast influence of the former during so many ages; and of the influence of Plato's works on the restoration of the Belles Lettres, and on the reformation.—7. Raymund

and all this even before he presents his own "Organum"! The work, he says, is half finished, indeed ready to go to the printer. He was, of course, doing here what he was to do more as the years passed, hoping, by telling others that a work was almost done, to force himself, if only as a matter of pride, to begin on it with dispatch. When this introductory book "is fairly off my hands," he will then be able to "set seriously to work."

So again, a full eleven years later, he announces in his "Principles of Genial Criticism Concerning the Fine Arts," that he is "about to put to the press a large volume on the LOGOS, or the communicative intelligence in nature and in man, together with, and as preliminary to, a Commentary on the Gospel of St. John." Soon afterwards, he gives a detailed description (September, 1814). The work now is to be frankly called "Christianity the One True Philosophy." There will be five treatises on the "Logos, or communicative Intelligence, Natural, Human, and Divine." In later outlines of the same work he decides to include *six* instead of five treatises, beginning now with one on "the History of Philosophy from Pythagoras to the present Day," and concentrating on the "obstacles to just reasoning." And in these treatises he will make more room for the discussion of habits of thought in practical life ("the Bar, the Pulpit, the Senate, and rational Conversation"). He will need also to write on the "science of *premises*" as he takes up the "transcendental" philosophy. There will be separate sections now on the "Mystics and Pantheists," with accompanying "lives of them." For how can one evaluate them except in an organic context that will fairly consider what these men actually experienced, what they lived with and through? There will be a section on Spinoza—also, of course, with a "Life" of Spinoza—explaining, making place, doing complete justice. Much else is to be included. And all this

Lully. 8. Peter Ramus. 9. Lord Bacon—or the Verulamian Logic. 10. Examination of the same, & comparison of it with the Logic of Plato (in which I attempt to make it probable, that tho' considered by Bacon himself as the antithesis & Antidote of Plato, it is bonâ fide the same, & that Plato has been grossly misunderstood.) [11]—DesCartes. [12] Condillac—& a philosophical examination of *his* logic . . ."

is to be only supplementary, or rather only prefatory, to the real concern: the commentary on the Gospel of St. John. There at last he would be able to fulfill the career for which his family had destined him, and fulfill it in a way far beyond whatever hopes they may have had.

• 10 •

In the meantime, certain things had been happening to Coleridge as a mind, a writer, a human being. Chief among them is what we have been noticing all along, since he returned from Germany and went north to Keswick: the twenty-year history of frustration, renewed hopes, further reading, and reconsiderations; the intellectual conflicts followed by the vicious circle of self-doubts, introspective analysis, delays. If we say that we take all this for granted, it should be with some recognition of what it can mean throughout this length of time to have had the principal effort and ambition of one's life frustrated through the very virtues one would assume necessary to its attainment (sympathetic openness, eagerness to include rather than exclude)—virtues one dared not, could not, surrender.

He was caught in some sort of trap that he could not yet understand. Of course he could walk out of the trap if he just stopped caring about too many things. If he had to throw together some sort of comprehensive work, he could do it if he could only be like Christian in *The Pilgrim's Progress* and put his fingers to his ears and start running. A time would come when this would have to be done. But it was not yet. There were too many things clamoring for recognition that should be heard. Granted one could continue this sort of delay forever. Was that what he was doing?

The guiltier and more inadequate he felt, the more he exaggerated the dragon at the gate before which he had been hesitating—the obsession of his own time with epistemology, the theory of knowledge, of what and how we can know. The more this intimidated him, the larger it loomed; and the larger it loomed, the more completely indispensable the conquest of it seemed as the way to win the philosophical respectability—at very least the philosophical acceptance—he so much desired. From now until the end, whatever other interests or habits of anxiety he was able to shed, he continued to show the utmost formal deference to epistemology, and to omit no ceremony to prove to himself and others that he was mindful of its importance. And he became increasingly resourceful, when he did prepare to make an entrance into any philosophical subject, in assembling the proper epistemological tools and weapons to help him, though usually this friendliest of disputants would do no more than brandish them, as if at ceremonial parade. Hence the common (and very mistaken) impression that Coleridge was hopelessly enamored of the preparatory functions of thought. In discussing others we are always, in our haste for explanation, overlooking our own experience and forgetting that habits may be as easily induced by fears and inhibitions as by some original or primitive craving.

Stopping to reflect on his hesitancies, always eager to discover common grounds of feeling and thought, he had for years turned in temporary relief from the abstractions of epistemology to the fertile, uncharted area of psychology, where he felt no immediate burden of self-demand about what had to be done. In the process, this brilliant, defensive mind—so watchful, so richly endowed with diverse interests—had already by his thirties become the most gifted psychological intelligence of his time. This is the Coleridge so prized for the wealth of insights and observations throughout scores of pages in the published works, the letters, the conversations, the notebooks. Even today this treasury of psychological observation is, in its way, unrivalled. For the accumulated analyses of the past century, however, impressive, have repeatedly bumped against a ceiling of intelligence in the raw material provided by the people clinically observable. Here there is no such ceiling. No artist, no scientist, of Coleridge's gifts has been more clairvoyantly aware of the functions of mind involved in what he was doing, however helpless he may at times have been before that awareness. But psychology as he understood it—for that matter, as we ourselves understand it, great as our interest in it may be—was valuable for his larger purpose only as a supplement, an empirical reminder of facts about human nature and human experience that we might otherwise overlook. However inspired, it was by definition reductive—reductive at very least to man, to human impulses and human reactions. Its most ardent advocate could hardly justify it as the principal key in man's objective interpretation of the cosmos, but might even be inclined to dismiss attempts to interpret the objective universe, and man's relation to it, as foredoomed to failure. That was one way of getting rid of a problem. No, whatever Coleridge's other interests, he was forced to return to the time-honored subjects of logic and epistemology, the latter of which rested upon and included the first. He was back in the trap. He had to work his way out of it honestly, in the hard way.

• 11 •

If we lacked Coleridge's own statements of intention or hope, we should be viewing him very differently, and not only during the period we have been discussing but at most periods of his adult life. Johnson, in one of the finest of the moral essays (*Rambler*, No. 2), mentions how much like Don Quixote most of us are, if we only admitted it—leaping ahead in imagination and living "in idea," dreaming of the help we could give to large causes, and planning ambitious projects. "Our hearts inform us that he is not more ridiculous than ourselves, except that he *tells* what we have only thought." Coleridge is in this respect extremely vulnerable. Probably no major writer is more so. And because the capacity for praise within the human heart is very limited, and because all of us are eager to apply standards to others that we do not care to have applied to our own achievements, the temptation to shake the finger and cluck the tongue, to construe the latter half of his life as the failure he feared it might be, has proved irresistible.

But it should be remembered that the design of the *magnum*

opus was very ambitious, and that if Coleridge did not succeed in it, neither has anyone else. We can of course brush it aside as naïve, indeed impossible, in that stern skepticism with which, by showing ourselves difficult to please or convince, we try to invigorate our sense of importance (or to shelter our unimportance). But the assertion that the thing was impossible should be the prerogative of those who have at least tried, or have been animated by comparable ideals. Nor does the experience of mankind suggest that those whose aims are commonly deemed impossible are for that reason less worthy of our admiration than those who are eager to circumscribe the possibilities of thought. And if Coleridge appeared to linger by the door, hesitantly stepping backward (after almost every step forward) into the vestibule of procedure—of epistemology, logic, and definition—the history of philosophy since his own day has done much the same. In this, as in so many other ways, he was to prove a barometer for an intellectual weather to come. But naturally Coleridge himself interpreted his difficulty throughout most of these years in a more personal way, blaming it on illness, lack of time and peace of mind, inability to concentrate because of opium or other habits, or else—very excusably—defending it as necessary until one more bit of real evidence, one more insight, could be added, which might (who knows?) prove to be the keystone of the arch.

In any case, the achievement of the twenty years that followed his return from Germany in 1799 is still extraordinary. We have the great ode, "Dejection"; *The Friend,* the *Biographia, The Statesman's Manual,* the *Treatise on Method*; the lectures on Shakespeare and other literary subjects; the later poems, however few; the wealth of the notebooks. A fraction of what he wrote could have made the reputation of another man. If we have dwelt on his hesitancies in the years of 1800 to 1820, in our summary of the plan of the *magnum opus,* it is because throughout these twenty years they had become so important in Coleridge's own mind. But the biographer need not follow slavishly the misgivings and despairs of his subject any more than the self-congratulatory estimates (of the latter of which, in the case of Coleridge, there are so few except about works unfinished or never begun). We are entitled to expect that the biographer's interpretation of the "inner life" of a man include some realization of what the man did, of what he actually thought.

And during the remaining years of Coleridge's life, still more was done. Lying ahead are not only the *Aids to Reflection* (1825), the posthumous *Confessions of an Inquiring Spirit* (1840), but also the hundreds of pages of theological speculation still unpublished (admittedly fragmentary and uneven), the marginalia scattered throughout hundreds of books, and the richest collection of conversation or table-talk for any English writer since Johnson. Finally there is his immense indirect influence—so memorably analyzed by John Stuart Mill—as, with Jeremy Bentham, one of "the two great seminal minds of England of their age," to whom nineteenth-century England was indebted "not only for the greater part of the important ideas which have been thrown into circulation among its thinking men but for a revolution in its general modes of thought and investigation."

IX

Coleridge at Highgate (1821–1834): The Later Religious Thought; the Final Years

MEANWHILE COLERIDGE'S LIFE AT HIGHGATE was starting to settle into the pattern described by Carlyle in the rough, vivid passages in the *Life of Sterling* that have been anthologized for a century ("Coleridge sat on the brow of Highgate Hill, in those years, looking down on London and its smoke-tumult, like a sage escaped from the inanity of life's battle.") Even before the time Carlyle is recalling (1824-25), Coleridge had begun to pass into legend, at least for younger writers of the day. Hazlitt, in his *Lectures on the English Poets* (1818), had spoken of him with nostalgic reminiscence as "the only person I ever knew who answered to the idea of a man of genius," and his tribute is all in the past tense:

> He talked on forever; and you wished him to talk on forever. . . . His voice rolled on the ear like the pealing organ, and its sound alone was the music of thought. His mind was clothed with wings . . . In his descriptions, you then saw the progress of human happiness and liberty in bright and never-ending succession, like the steps of Jacob's ladder, with airy shapes ascending and descending, and with the voice of God at the top of the ladder. . . . That time is gone forever; that voice is heard no more: but still the recollection comes rushing by with thoughts of long-past years, and rings in my ears with never-dying sound.

In the spring of 1819, when Keats—now twenty-three—met him accidentally, it was with a sense that he had encountered a walking legend. He tells about it in a letter to his brother, George Keats, who had left for America. On a Sunday stroll across Hampstead Heath toward Highgate (April 11), Keats entered a lane and suddenly saw Coleridge approaching with Dr. Joseph Green, a surgeon Keats remembered from his student days at Guy's and St. Thomas's Hospitals:

> I joined them, after enquiring by a look whether it would be agreeable—I walked with him a[t] his alderman-after-dinner pace for near two miles I suppose. In those two Miles he broached a thousand things—let me see if I can give you a list—Nightingales, Poetry—on Poetical sensation—Metaphysics—Different genera and species of Dreams—Nightmare—a dream accompanied by a sense of touch—single and double touch—A dream related—First and second consciousness—Monsters—the Kraken—Mermaids—Southey believes in them—Southeys belief too much diluted—A Ghost story—Good morning—I heard his voice as he came toward me—I heard it as he moved away—I had heard it all the interval—if it may be called so. He was civil enough to ask me to call on him at Highgate.

Typical of Coleridge's growing abstraction of mind is that he himself remembered this meeting—two miles at a slow walk, probably extending to almost an hour—as having lasted only "a minute or so." The mention of nightingales reminds us that, within the next three or four weeks, Keats was to write the "Ode to a Nightingale." This was an unusually good season for nightingales, to judge from a reference in one of Coleridge's letters. He had been taking calomel for the diarrhea that still plagued him (he was still taking some laudanum surreptitiously), and wrote to a friend at Cambridge on May 12—probably within a week of the date of Keats's "Ode": "As to Nightingales—they are almost as numerous with us and as incessant in song as Frogs with you. Ah! (I groaned forth a few nights ago, when qualmy and twitchy from the effects of an Aperient) Ah! PHIlomel! ill do thy strains accord with those of CALomel!"

The Joseph Henry Green to whom Keats refers has an important place in Coleridge's later life. A surgeon of substantial means, appointed at the age of twenty-two Demonstrator of

Anatomy at St. Thomas's Hospital (1813), he studied in Germany, became acquainted with Coleridge in 1817, when Green was twenty-six, and devoted his life thereafter to an attempt to combine medicine and biology with epistemology, ethics, and psychology. He was to become Coleridge's faithful amanuensis, taking down his dictation at least once a week. Later he inherited a large fortune, and, serving as Coleridge's literary executor, retired in order to devote himself to a systematic presentation of Coleridge's religious thought. An eloquent testimony of his devotion is the strenuous course of study he then followed in order to prepare himself for this task.[1] Another younger friend was Thomas Allsop, a young businessman who had heard Coleridge lecture in 1818 (Allsop was then twenty-three), had written Coleridge, had come to know him, and in time put together one of the principal sources of what we know of the later years. (*Letters, Conversations, and Recollections of S. T. Coleridge,* 1836). The historian of English literature of the years 1780 to 1830—we can see the same thing in the America of the period—is repeatedly struck by the interest in letters and the arts on the part of younger men in the middle echelons of the professions and business—George Keats and, among John Keats's friends, Charles Dilke and Charles Brown; or men like Green himself, Allsop, Tom Poole in Nether Stowey, or Crabb Robinson.

Among Coleridge's new friends was Charles Matthews, good as an actor and remarkable as a comedian and mimic. In her memoirs of her husband, Matthews' wife tells of Coleridge's visits to their house in Kentish Town. On a stormy winter evening, when she was ill, he walked down from Highgate Hill to read to her from a new book and talked about it in such a way that she forgot her illness entirely. She thought this typical of a readiness for "compassion" or "pity" that struck her as almost "feminine" in its gentleness. Significantly, she does not use the word "sym-

[1] He read widely in all the sciences, philosophy, and theology, reviewed his knowledge of Greek, learned Hebrew at the age of sixty, and even began to study Sanskrit. He died in 1863, leaving unfinished his *Spiritual Philosophy: Founded on the Teaching of the Late S. T. Coleridge,* which was published posthumously (2 vols., 1865).

pathy," so common at the time as to become almost a cant word. For in his habitual discourse he was now talking almost constantly at a more abstract level than that to which his acquaintances were accustomed. Yet he was the least intimidating of great men, and could only too easily be deflected, partly because of his gentleness.

Particularly fascinating to both of the Matthews was the combination of abstraction of mind with the "simplicity" of Coleridge's character. In their drawing room, they had at one side a mirror that filled an entire wall. When he rose to leave, Coleridge would inevitably start to walk into the mirror. It was not as in those days in Germany when he would cast an uneasy glance at his reflection, wondering what impression he was making. Now he was not seeing himself at all, at least in any concrete sense. He simply moved in the direction in which there seemed the greatest and most open space.

• 2 •

Money continued to be a problem. But gifts from friends made it possible for his second son, Derwent, to enter St. John's College, Cambridge (1820). Any relief Coleridge felt was more than counter-balanced by his distress when the older boy, Hartley, was in the same year deprived for intemperance of his fellowship at Oriel College, Oxford. Hartley, a milder version of some of the father's talents and weaknesses, had quickly slipped at Oxford into a gentle, good-natured Bohemianism. After receiving his fellowship, he forgivably refused to dress for dinner. Worse, he drank heavily—had in fact been found drunk in the gutter of Oriel Lane. Still worse, he was attached to a serving girl. His fellowship was not renewed. Coleridge made frantic, unsuccessful efforts to have the decision reversed. He could not help feeling that the sins of the father were now being visited on the child, and that he himself was deeply guilty in some way. At last he was able to get Hartley a job in a school at Ambleside, in the Lake Country. In a longer biography than this, we could find it psychologically interesting to speculate why Coleridge and Hartley never met thereafter. Each was warm-natured, quick to sympathize. Each was affectionately drawn to the other. Was it that the complexities of life for both were such that each instinctively found it easier to manage his precarious existence by not complicating it further through frequent sympathetic contact with the other?

But in any case it was reassuring that Derwent, a freer soul than Hartley and less troubled by himself and life generally, was now established at Cambridge. Above all there was the pleasure of knowing that his daughter Sara had become as remarkable as Hartley and Derwent had been saying that she was. At Christmas, 1822, Mrs. Coleridge—placid, convinced for years that the separation had been a good thing—visited Coleridge at Highgate for two months with the daughter, now twenty, whose beauty and intelligence captivated everyone.

In the meantime Coleridge's quiet life with the Gillmans continued. Almost yearly now they would go to the seaside at Ramsgate in October. If Gillman had to return early to his work, Coleridge would remain with Mrs. Gillman, who hung over him like a mother hen. He had become a cherished member of the family, and an avuncular friend of the Gillmans' two boys, James and Henry. In December, 1823, the Gillmans moved from their house ("Moreton House") to the place we generally associate with Coleridge at Highgate, No. 3, The Grove. Here at his own request he was given an attic room looking west over Caen Wood. This he used as both a study and a bedroom. On the floor below a parlor was set aside entirely for his own use. There he dictated to his amanuenses—Green in particular, occasionally even Gillman—and received his friends.

During all this time, Coleridge was secretly using more laudanum than the Gillmans knew. An apprentice named Seymour Porter, at Thomas Dunn's apothecary shop in Highgate, has left an account. Coleridge would stop by to have his laudanum bottle filled every five or six days, so that his consumption amounted to a little more than a wineglassful of laudanum each day.[2] It was

[2] See E. L. Griggs, *Huntington Library Quarterly*, XVII (1953-54), 357-378.

not much, particularly when compared to the amount he had taken for years before he went to Highgate. But it was more than the Gillmans assumed he was using; and an uneasy sense of guilt continued to worry him, less because of the use of the laudanum itself (this could be justified or at least rationalized) than at his need for subterfuge, which was so alien to his nature.

• 3 •

Back in 1820 he had written Thomas Allsop a long discussion of four works almost "ready for the press." Most of each was written in one form or another. He had only to assemble them. (1) A book (three volumes of 500 pages each) on the "Characteristics of Shakespeare's Dramatic Art." (2) A "Philosophical Analysis of the Genius and Works of Dante, Spenser, Milton, Cervantes, and Calderón," with a general treatment of the subject. (3) A "History of Philosophy" in two volumes, building on his lectures of the previous year. (4) "Letters on the Old and New Testament." And with these four works out of the way, he would turn to the long-deferred *magnum opus*, "to the preparation of which more than twenty years of my life have been devoted." All that was needed was an annuity, for three or four years, of £250. There was not much prospect of that.

In order to spur himself into activity, and also with the hope of earning some money, he decided early in 1822 to set up a "class" that would meet once a week, and he put an advertisement to that effect in the *Courier*. To these few students he dictated, among other things, the Kantian (and, for Coleridge, obviously preparatory) work in logic, a later copy of which exists in a very unfinished state.[3] He also, very much as a side effort, made plans for a book—it was later to turn into the famous *Aids to Reflection*—in which he would edit, with introduction and notes, selections from the seventeenth-century Scottish divine, Archbishop Robert Leighton (1611-84), whose purity of thought and life he had admired for years. Throughout 1824 the projected work began to

[3] The two manuscript volumes in the British Museum (Egerton 2825, 2826), described by A. D. Snyder, who also prints some selections in *Coleridge on Logic and Learning* (1929), esp. pp. 50-103.

turn into the book we now have. In the same year he was elected a member of the new Royal Society of Literature. It brought with it a stipend of a hundred guineas a year. The obligation to give an annual lecture weighed on him. He could talk forever if he could do so spontaneously. But the burden of a *formal* request, and of a specified deadline, evoked a lifelong fatigue and inner resistance before the demand to perform. How long it had been endured! One could go back almost to the beginning—to Ottery and Christ's Hospital. And was he not already cruelly enough oppressed by a larger self-demand than he had yet been able to fulfill? But he did read an essay (May 18, 1824) on "The *Prometheus* of Aeschylus" ("preparatory to a series of disquisitions respecting the Egyptian in connection with the sacerdotal theology, and in contrast with the mysteries of ancient Greece").

In 1824 he also began to hold his "Thursday evenings," to which so many gifted people in England and from abroad were to come in the years ahead. Conversation, always so tempting as a release, became more so now. For over twenty years he had been noting the possible treacheries of conversation, in any long-range effect on the mind, as well as its undeniable advantages. In his own case, it encouraged—was perhaps one cause of—his principal intellectual weakness: his inability to "do one thing at a time" and to move "consecutively," in a clean-cut and obvious way. He was one of those "talkative fellows," as he had written in a notebook back in the Malta days (December, 1804), who use five hundred more illustrations, images, ideas, than are needed to put across a point, with the result that they "swallow up" his central thesis. "Psychologically my brain-fibres, or the spiritual light that abides in the brain marrow as visible light appears to do in sundry rotten mackerel & other *smashy* matters, is of too general affinity with all things," leading him always to note, share in, justify and refine upon the "*difference* of things" though at bottom he is really "pursuing the likenesses, or rather that which is common." The effect of conversation on him was the opposite of the salutary effect it had on Samuel Johnson. It permitted Johnson, always making place in his serious writing for qualification, to become—thought Coleridge —more "consecutive"—to say the short, sharp things that can never be forgotten: to become, in short, a "drum," as contrasted with the "Eolian harp" that Coleridge as talker thought he himself so often became. Yes, a lifetime of talk had done nothing to remedy his inability to proceed sharply from point to point—to be "consecutive" and constructive. The effect on his prose style was obvious. Take his love of parentheses. He could defend them as part of the actual, organic process of the mind thinking—as "the *drama* of reason." But at other times he thought of himself as similar to the "Surinam toad," the young of which hop out from the mother's back. "I envy dear Southey's power of saying one thing at a time in short and close sentences, whereas my thoughts bustle along like a Surinam toad, with little toads sprouting out of back, side, and belly, vegetating while it crawls" (the remark is itself a parenthesis within a longer sentence).

• 4 •

May, 1825, saw the publication of the *Aids to Reflection,* which was to leave so profound an effect on younger men entering a career in the church. The stimulus of finishing this work may explain the gentle rise in the occasional poems he wrote around this time—though again with no thought of publication.[4] But he was anything but easy in his heart. The major work was still to do, or at least some kind of major work was yet to do, even if he was beginning to retrench his conception of the *magnum opus* and turn more exclusively to theology. Meanwhile the vessel was

[4] Poems of 1825-26 would probably include, besides the specifically dated "Work Without Hope" (February 21, 1825): *"Sancti Dominici Pallium,"* the song "Though veiled in spires," "A Character," "The Pang More Sharp than All," "Duty Surviving Self-Love," and "Lines Suggested by the Last Words of Berengarius." For the frequently anthologized "Constancy to an Ideal Object," tentatively dated 1825-26 by E. H. Coleridge, a letter to J. H. Green (June 11, 1825) in the forthcoming edition of the later letters, indicates, as Professor Griggs points out, a much earlier date, possibly as far back as the Malta period.

becoming increasingly frail. For some time, he told his nephew (1825), "it has been my lot to awake every morning in pain, more or less severe—and to continue in a discomfortable state of feeling for an hour or two." It was probably during this year and the next (1825-6) that he put together the short but important work of Biblical criticism promised in that letter of 1820 to Thomas Allsop cited earlier. The work was found among his literary remains and published six years after his death as *Confessions of an Inquiring Spirit* (1840).

During the years 1825-7 he also continued—perhaps seriously began—work on the three manuscript volumes (together with a fourth as "supplement") to which the title *Opus Maximum* is conventionally but perhaps unfortunately assigned. If I say "unfortunately," it is because of the confusion that results, in the mind of the student, with the twenty-year project of the *magnum opus*. The *Opus Maximum* is more specialized in intent. We have already spoken of the problem of nomenclature.[5] But though the title *Opus Maximum* is appropriated a little too readily to this work, it could be justified in one important respect. It suggests that the major work to which Coleridge is now turning in his fifties (and he plainly thought of this fragment as a portion of that work) is to be primarily theological. In the spirit of Coleridge himself, with his love of distinctions and his interest in symbols, we could say that this change marks the difference in his thought after 1820: that the *magnum opus* represented the hope of a synthesis of arts, sciences, philosophy, through religion; and that in the *Opus Maximum* the concern is more concentrated.

He is now, in whatever years remain to him, working more closely to what he conceives to be the essentials. Poetry and *belles-lettres,* the arts generally, recede rapidly as central interests. He has by no means forgotten them: how could he? But the night was coming. Now at last he must imitate Christian in *The Pilgrim's Progress,* and put his fingers to his ears. If this involved a partial withdrawal from other interests, it was also a

[5] See p. 182n.

concentration on what mattered most. And within these last fourteen years there was a further concentration, so that in the final years of his life he was absorbed mainly in the study of the Bible and commentary on it. It is as though Coleridge, now finding himself in "my decay of life," were resolved to do what he knew he could do, trusting that this more concrete service would still be some "compensation to Thy church for the unused talents Thou hast intrusted to me."

• 5 •

The result is the large, still partly unpublished body of his later religious writing and dictation: brilliant, searching, conservative, boldly speculative and (increasingly) humble—humble before the mystery of the unknown, and the mystery, in particular, of Christianity.[6]

We must speak briefly of this writing now—briefly because already, by the previous chapter, we had exceeded the limits expected for a book in this series. Yet to ignore this writing, which is once again (as in the thirty years that followed his death) beginning to interest a wide group of readers, would be impossible in any biography worthy of the name, however short it must be. Here, in Coleridge's spiritual pilgrimage, we have the true "inner life," or at least the most essential part of it. If we wish to understand and assess Coleridge's career, we must do so at least partly in terms of what mattered most to him: the hope that his life, whatever its failings, might ultimately be religious in shape, intention, meaning.

We should keep in mind that his religious quest was and had been twofold. At least this is true if we also preserve Coleridge's own valuable principle that to distinguish is not necessarily to divide. On the one hand, there is everything that relates to his

[6] Here we include not only the works published by Coleridge himself or the fragments published in the generation after his death, but also (1) the remaining marginalia; (2) the *Opus Maximum* itself, scheduled to appear in the forthcoming edition of Coleridge's works; and (3) the last thirty to thirty-five of the fifty-five *Notebooks*, which are being edited by Kathleen Coburn.

own personal and psychological need—the yearning for religious love and trust, the heart's deep hope for the possibility of prayer and redemption. On the other hand, there is the struggle of the intellect for truth and certitude. In a sense, the continuing effort of Coleridge's life was to bring about a reconciliation and mutual fulfillment, where belief would be equally grounded in the ultimate laws of the intellect and the deepest needs of human nature. Because it must be brief, the discussion that follows necessarily focuses on only some of the crucial points within Coleridge's religious philosophy, taking them up in an expository rather than chronological way.

The central difficulty that had blocked the *magnum opus* was, as we have seen, that of reconciling the "dynamic philosophy" of nature with the Christian dualism of God and the created universe. For the "dynamic philosophy," try as he would to reinterpret it, seemed incorrigibly bent on becoming a pantheistic monism, wherein spirit is the sole substance or being and natural things are steps or stages in its ascending realization. But in such a universe there would be no personal and transcendent God, and hence no possibility of redemption, prayer, and religious love. Moreover, the ascent of the *Weltseele,* or World Soul, through nature implied that man was only the last stage or apex in this process of self-realization, and hence human beings were not different in essence from the rest of nature. But if this were true, how could we speak of man as having a free will, a moral and religious duty, a soul and a future life? And yet, as a science of nature, and as a ground of insight into literature and art, the "dynamic philosophy" seemed valid. Even though, as he preoccupied himself with Christianity, he felt himself moving toward the center, he could not simply abandon what seemed true in other realms. No, the "dynamic philosophy" must also be shepherded into the ultimate philosophic-religious fold.

Repeatedly he kept coming back to the fundamental question of the relation between God and the created universe. We may remind ourselves of the points that would, for Coleridge, be indispensable to any philosophic construction: (1) The reason of nature: that is, the simple question, why does the universe exist? What is its ground in the being of God; or, more anthropomorphically expressed, why did God create the universe? (2) The distinction of God and the universe. For otherwise Coleridge would lapse into the pantheism he was so concerned to avoid. (3) The simultaneous immanence of God, to some extent, within the universe. This traditional Christian belief was equally necessary to Coleridge. Otherwise man would find himself alien and isolated—a spirit in a universe that is merely natural and therefore unrelated to his inmost life. (4) The autonomy of science. He had felt from the beginning that any theology must preserve the possibility of free scientific explanation of nature. There could be no conflict of religion and science. Since for Coleridge, struggling with this last dilemma, "science" meant particularly the "dynamic philosophy," we may quickly review the main notes or highlights of this view of nature that had somehow to be "co-adunated" with Christian faith. There was, in the first place, the notion of all existence as having one substance or essence, what we may call the "*one*-substantiality" of being. (The word is coined in order to contrast with Coleridge's own puzzling and ambiguous word, "*con*substantiality.") In the second place, there was the notion of reality as essentially *process* or *act*. "Objects" or "things" are only phases of energies or forces; they come into existence as "moments" of the dynamic equilibrium of interpenetrating polar forces. And finally, there was the conception of a teleological dynamism in nature as a whole, for the myriad forms of nature seemed plainly to exhibit an ascending scale of being, a direction toward greater organization and individuation.

In the works he himself published during his last ten years, this hope of reconciling the scientific "dynamic" philosophy with Christian belief, which had for years underlain the dream of the *magnum opus,* remains unmentioned. He is there concerned with other questions. But the unpublished writings as well as accounts of his conversations suggest that this was still an essential problem. For years he had felt that he had found the clue in the concept of the Trinity—the orthodox interpretation of the Godhead that itself embodied the ideal of unity persisting through distinction and diversity. How well he could understand the commendable hope and Puritan essentialism of the Unitarian!—had he not himself lived through it, more than taken it for granted, and himself said all that could be said for it? But here, in the Trinity, intelligently interpreted, was the deeper answer he really needed. We can see his intention in the terminology he sometimes adopts. He speaks of (1) *Ipseity* (the unchangeable reality of God the Father); (2) *Alterity,* or otherness—the *Logos,* the Son, the Word—the product, the creation, that is simultaneously *of* the Father and yet by definition different, "other than"; and (3) *Community*—the Holy Spirit, or Love, in and through which creation and God can meet. Only through the Trinity, he thought, have we the possibility of avoiding the pantheism inevitable in the unsupplemented, more naïve uses of the "dynamic" philosophy of science and nature while still making a place for it. And this seemed especially true if he also took as a starting place or fundamental statement the premise that God is "Absolute Will," essential "Causativeness or Act." We should note, by the way, that Coleridge was more than open to the thought—so unorthodox among Christian theologians at the time, but appealing to those of our own day—that the progressive declaration of the *Logos* proceeds throughout the Old Testament. This is indeed the epic of Judaism: the refusal, since the time of Abraham, to accept any God but the highest; and, as man's mental horizon extends and as the standard, the expectation, at once rises and deepens, man's experience of God becomes an experience in and through process.

He brilliantly speculated, time and again, on the profundity of the concept of the Trinity, applying it to every aspect of thought and existence—in logic, epistemology, metaphysics. Inevitably, after seeking to ramify and enrich its potentialities for the questing mind, he simultaneously began to try to deepen the ultimate unity still further and to add a fourth element. If the variety of implication within the Trinity was greater than the run-of-the-mill theologian maintained, so, more deeply, was the unity. He hungered for a philosophic *ground* that could sustain the unity of the "three": an "Identity" logically prior to the "three"—the *ground* of the unity-in-diversity, the *oneness* of the one-in-three. As he sought for ways to explain this, he reached back, for a suggestive symbol, to the ancient Pythagorean concept of the "Tetractys." One of the intellectual potentialities of the "Tetractys" for the Pythagoreans (it was the symbol on which the Pythagorean oath was taken) is that it combined in proportion so much. It consisted of ten numbers arranged as follows:

.

. .

. . .

. . . .

Among its other potentialities, we have *four* units serving as a *base* for a geometrical three that build from it: a base, that is, for an equilateral triangle. Through it, *four* and *three* subsume and demand each other—which was exactly what Coleridge was thinking. Hence the appeal of the symbol in his wrestle with logic and epistemology to establish a still deeper ground of unity that would presuppose and permit an essentially dynamic Godhead. As compared with the more orthodox Trinity, we may note, the Tetractys could suggest an inclination toward modalism, simply because it gives special emphasis to the note of *identity*, as compared to the equal emphasis, within the Trinity, on oneness and difference. This speculation, however, seems unduly rarified. A more significant point is that by the conception of the "Tetractys" Coleridge seems to admit the notions of *potentiality* and *becoming* in the Godhead. Coleridge, however, did not make these extrapolations of potentiality and becoming. They are inconsistent with his formal declarations about the Godhead. And all that the "dynamic philosophy" required as a "ground" was given in the definition of God as Will. For if the essence of the Divine Being is to act, the existence of nature is explained without derogating from God's self-sufficiency. In the same way, as God is essentially an activity, nature also can be conceived of as activity or process. And since the "causativeness," being God's, "is undiminished," the process of nature may be conceived as unending, though, of course, an infinitude of time would only be a human picture language for eternity. As for the teleological ascent of the forms of nature to their apex in man, there was nothing in that to trouble Christian belief, so long as it was also kept in mind that man was not *merely* "natural" but that he was also a spiritual being, a soul.

The "dynamic philosophy," however, also affirmed that all being was one substance, and here Coleridge must part company. God was in nature; but this was very different from identifying him *with* nature. And yet, how to put the difference, and how to find a ground for it in the being of God? Whether they are satisfactory or not, his answers may be quickly stated. From his reading in Neoplatonic philosophy and the Schoolmen Coleridge had long since taken over the notion of the "participation" of created being in the Divine Being, a notion that could explain how created being was not identical with the Divine, and yet not absolutely alien, but the same in a lesser degree. He speaks, then, neither of an identity nor of an absolute distinction, but of a "consubstantiality." The ground of this consubstantiality he discovers in the second person of the Trinity, "Alterity." For the Son or Logos is of God, the same "substance" or "being," and yet also distinct from the Father, and, as Coleridge says, this distinction provides the ground of all other distinctiveness.

So with the problem of "evil." "Original sin"—"moral evil" —is discussed in the *Aids to Reflection* and especially in the *Opus Maximum*.[7] The finite will, created in and through "Alterity," would not be free unless it had a potentiality of affirming itself rather than God. It can, that is, will to be *itself* rather than to be in God. Thus the potentiality of evil is necessary to constitute a free will, though as soon as that potentiality is actualized the will

[7] The problem of "natural evil"—"the origin of EVIL, as distinguished from original Sin"—was also to have been one of the principal subjects of the *Opus Maximum,* but it continued to elude him.

is no longer free. For there can be no freedom in contradiction to God. The point to be stressed—and one relevant to modern theology—is that "original sin" is not something "inherited," as the "Bibliolaters" maintained. It is something built into the very nature of "individuality."

The possibility of "redemption," so important to Coleridge himself, follows in and through the concept of the "Logos" or "Alterity." The Christ, as the "Logos," is at once the prototype of "otherness" from the Father and also of "sameness," and his life is the *exemplum* and key. Here, with a central doctrine of Christianity, Coleridge's sense of personal need and hope coalesced in the most vital way. To a Unitarian, "redemption through Christ" could mean only the efficacious working of Christ's example in forming character. The concept of a distinction or Alterity within the Divine Being, however, made possible for Coleridge the concept of a redemption of all Creation. Since the Logos was the original pattern for Creation, it becomes also the pattern for reconformity. And since man's deformation is in the order of will, his redemption is through an assimilation of his human will with the Divine. Further, since Christ is a mediator who unites in himself the Divine and human natures, this assimilation of wills involves a real change of being, a new sharing for man in the divine life.

• 6 •

Our discussion hitherto has concentrated chiefly on the brilliant and suggestive results Coleridge himself achieved but never published. Some of these conclusions were implicit in notebook and marginal jottings collected by H. N. Coleridge in the *Literary Remains* (1836–9), but for the most part they could not be readily understood by readers who lacked the further clarifications to be found chiefly in the *Opus Maximum*. As a result, Coleridge's more formal theology—however it may now intrigue us—had little impact on earlier generations, and to understand his considerable influence on religious life and thought throughout the nineteenth century, we must naturally concentrate rather on the three connected works that did appear: *Aids to Reflection, On the Constitution of Church and State,* and *Confessions of an Inquiring Spirit.* In these writings English readers found especially (1) a method or approach in apologetics—the argument for Christian belief—that seemed novel and compelling; (2) a profound analysis of the relations between "reason"—including the scientific intellect—and "faith." Here Coleridge clairvoyantly anticipated the central religious problem of the coming century, when faith was to be challenged both by scientific discoveries, such as the theory of evolution, and also by the new critical and historical study of the Bible; (3) a balanced and, for its time, strikingly modern discussion of the claims of the Bible to religious authority; and (4) as part of his social or political philosophy, a new conception of the role of the Church in national life, a conception which helped inspire the Victorian Church with its more urgent sense of mission.

Coleridge's "subjective" method in apologetics appears most clearly in *Aids to Reflection.* Here he assumes the congenial role of benevolent friend, addressing, on this occasion, persons uncommitted to Christianity yet willing to reflect. His first purpose, then, is to summon that activity of reflection which he defines as a looking down into one's own being: "Am I sick, and therefore *need* a physician?—Am I in spiritual slavery, and therefore *need* a ransomer?" To readers acquainted with present-day Christian existentialism, the questions have a familiar ring, but this inward and vitally personal approach was virtually unknown in Coleridge's age. Christian apologetics for at least the previous hundred years had usually begun by mustering empirical "evidences" from without. The same way of arguing from self-awareness continues through the successive steps in persuasion. The teachings of Christ win reverent attention, not—as was the usual argument—because of the miracles Christ performed, but rather because they speak so deeply to the self. Has the inward "experience that [one] needs something" anywhere found an outward answer? "Do the promises of Christ correspond to this self-experience, as remedy to disease—supposing them true?" Only at this point, when a serious hope may have germinated, does Coleridge go on to argue in the more usual way: are "the doctrines said to [have] been taught by Christ . . . logically and metaphysically possible?" And throughout the *Aids to Reflection* Coleridge keeps in mind that Christianity cannot be "proved." One can put forward arguments pro or con; but they cannot be conclusive, and the choice whether to believe or not is not a choice of the intellect merely. Rather it is a total expression of one's personal being, that is, an act of will. In historical terms the primary emphasis on will rather than on reason is a "romantic" element in Coleridge's apologetics, as also in his "idea" of God.

This method of argument indicates how Coleridge handles the central Christian question of reason and faith, their relation and interplay. The problem is, of course, as old as Christianity, but had become newly prominent in Deistic theology. It become even more acute, if only because it troubled more people, throughout the nineteenth century, and it still persists as the central issue within and about Christianity. Both reason and faith claim to be sources of religious knowledge, and the question is to what extent faith may be allowed to go beyond reason, or reason to limit faith. A thoroughgoing rationalist has faith only in reason and therefore argues that one should believe only what the intellect can infer, while a fideist holds that reason by itself can obtain no knowledge worth mentioning. For such a person "all truth," as Coleridge once asserted, "is a species of revelation," a leap of faith beyond reason. As usual, Coleridge sought to mediate rather than militate, acknowledging the truth put forward in each position while rejecting the overemphasis. He insists that "nothing can be allowed as true for the human mind, if it directly contradicts reason," but he equally insists that religious truth "may and must transcend" reason. The revelation given to faith may well be "incomprehensible," but if it is also "absurd," it cannot be revelation. (In fact, his primary definition of faith is "fidelity to our own being," which includes fidelity to "reason.") To denote the faculty or process of mind by which we can and do make decisions in religious questions, including the fundamental decision to believe, Coleridge used the term "higher reason." Neither an irrational nor a merely rational use of the mind, the "higher reason" is, in fact, the integral being of man, the synthesis of will, emotion, conscience, and intellect. The "higher reason," in other words, brings about the total awareness of the self, its situation, and its freedom, to which Coleridge appeals in the *Aids to Reflection*.

A perennial question for Christian thought is the location of authority—whether, that is, we are primarily to believe the Bible, the Church, the individual reason, the conscience, or a less defined inspiration or "inner light." For most Englishmen in Coleridge's time, authority was vested in the Bible as having been dictated by God. Hence the strongest single shake that Coleridge gave contemporary religious opinion was his attack on "Bibliolatry," especially as the attack became concrete and specific in the *Confessions of an Inquiring Spirit*. To believe that the human "penmen" of the Bible were merely scribes or amanuenses of God had led, Coleridge felt, to appalling conclusions, and he urged most of the objections that have become commonplace since. But while denying divine ventriloquism, he did not slide to the other extreme, taking the Bible as a merely human anthology. The Bible, he felt, analyzes and answers our spiritual condition as no merely human document could; the authors of it were not mouthpieces, but we cannot doubt their divine inspiration. The Bible may often be taken literally, as in much of the historical narrative, but it is not literally intended at every point. Neither, on the other hand, can we freely pick and choose within it, adopting as inspired only those passages which suit our taste. Hence Coleridge argues (particularly in *The Statesman's Manual*, 1816) that the Bible should be read as symbolic. Every episode in the Bible carries forward the historical narrative, and the narrative as a whole discloses God's progressive revelation of himself to man. Each episode, then, is an organic part of a process that has inexhaustible meaning to the spirit, and as soon as attention is selectively directed to it, the episode becomes a symbol of the whole. A literal reader ignores the more deeply spiritual meaning, and the Deist or rational allegorist ignores the literal meaning; but the true, reflective Christian will read the Bible as symbol, the infinite idea contemplated in the concrete event. Coleridge's approach to the Bible, then, attempts to preserve the joint authority both of the text itself and the mind that interprets it. He stresses the human elements in the Bible—for example, literary forms and conventions, the intentions of the particular authors, for he believes that a reader can rightly interpret the inspired meaning only when he also understands the human forms in which it is rendered. Especially in the *Confessions of an Inquiring Spirit* he elaborated a crucial distinction between "Revelation" and "Inspiration." His achievement, historically considered, then, was to replace a routine literalism by concepts of general inspiration and special revelation, and in this he led the way for later generations of Englishmen, who, staggered by the results of historical and textual study of the Bible, hurried into the storm shelter that Coleridge had already provided.

The religious thought of Coleridge founded no distinct school or party, though it modified the views of every party. His closest followers were in the liberal or Broad Church group within the Church of England, many of whom would have endorsed the declaration of Julius Hare that to Coleridge they owed "even their own selves." Apart from whatever positions Coleridge supported, his writings gave religious discussion a more philosophic inquiry and a closer contact with spiritual self-awareness and experience. Even more than the generation that followed him, we are beginning to find his writings a perennially valuable example. Here we refer not only to the union of speculative and logical power with (what is so rarely found with it) open and diverse intellectual sympathies. We refer especially to the extent to which this union—already valuable—is further enriched and deepened at every point by our sense of the direct, personal *experience* that, as Richard Niebuhr says, makes Coleridge so unusual and so persuasive to the modern man in quest of religious meaning.

• 7 •

Again, though only as a side interest, Coleridge kept returning to the political situation in England at the time, but in such a way that it was still to leave a deeply suggestive effect on political philosophy. One work in particular should be mentioned, since it not only directly affected an entire generation but has indirectly affected our own period and is once again being actively discussed: *On the Constitution of Church and State* (1830). The whimsy of fate that dogged most of Coleridge's publishing ventures attended this also. Parliament had taken up a series of bills for Catholic emancipation, and Coleridge, though favoring the general purpose, opposed some particulars of the proposed legislation. In order to explain his objections he wrote (as usual at "the request of an absent friend") this work of fundamental inquiry, but the objections were mostly removed by the Bill actually passed in 1829. So far as it was intended to have a timely impact, *On the Constitution of the Church and the State* was outdated before it appeared. But it remains, together with the two "Lay Sermons," the fundamental statement of Coleridge's political philosophy.

At a time when most thoughtful men assumed that a state is originated and held together by the enlightened self-interest of its members, Coleridge's psychological insight told him that a state is also a shared "idea." He stressed, in other words, the role of ideology in creating a genuine "community." An idea is "that conception of a thing . . . given by the knowledge of its ultimate aim," and the ultimate aim of the state is the realization in each of its members of his full humanity. The laborers in an alehouse "discussing the injustice of the present rate of wages" are well enough aware that a human being should be treated as an end, not as a means to an end, though they would not put the idea in this Kantian way. By "full humanity" Coleridge means a capability of moral freedom and responsibility, and the task of a society is to create economic, social and educational conditions that both assure and increase the possibility of a moral life, that is, of being a person as distinct from a thing or instrument in the hands of someone else.

Coleridge envisions the constitution—that which *constitutes*—of any good society as a balance of polar forces, which he calls "permanence" and "progression." He localizes the principle of permanence in the landowners, whether large magnates or small farmers, and finds the counter-principle of progression represented in the mercantile, manufacturing, and professional classes, whose power derives from "movable and personal possessions," including not merely money but also acquired knowledge and skill. It should be stressed that these identifications are simply the concrete application of a theory in the light of English historical experience, and that the same principles or forces could be actuated in any number of ways. The point is only to assure both continuity and change. But there is, or should be, a third force within the state, one that mediates and completes. This is embodied in the thinkers, teachers, and scholars. The functions of this group are to preserve and add to knowledge, and, scattered throughout the countryside as schoolteachers and clergymen, to perform an indispensable civilizing mission. As educators they are directly charged with the ultimate aim of the state, "the harmonious development of those qualities and faculties that characterize our humanity." He calls this group the *clerisy*—that is, the class of learned men, analogous to the "clerks" of the Middle Ages (he also names them the National Church, thinking of the extent to which the Church of England has historically performed this function). For their support, a specific endowment should be set aside. He does not confuse the National Church, in his sense, with religion, that is, the Christian Church, which, he keeps in mind, is not included in the constitution of the state and asks nothing of the state except "protection and to be let alone." The conception of a *clerisy* and the role assigned to it has often been thought Coleridge's most original contribution to political theory.

In its immediate historical context and impact Coleridge's political philosophy could be regarded as conservative in contrast to the way in which it could be viewed by the middle twentieth century. His emphasis on continuity as well as on change involved a protective tenderness for inherited institutions which was altogether contrary to the prevailing utilitarianism of the time. So also was his vision of society as an organic whole rather than an "aggregate" of equal individuals. Meanwhile his stress on moral responsibility as well as rights, his insistence that property is a public trust, his readiness to hedge in the individualist entrepreneur in the name of social ends, set him squarely athwart the dominant laissez-faire economics. His influence was immense. Without Coleridge, there would not have been a truly philosophical conservatism in early nineteenth century England, and it is largely owing to him that the typical Victorian dialogue of conservative and liberal could be so thoughtfully waged. His writings helped nudge John Stuart Mill from simple utilitarianism and liberalism toward a deeper sense of community. He contributed greatly to the intellectual arsenal of Disraeli and his followers, and the major Victorian social critics, Carlyle, Ruskin, Newman, Arnold, worked in the spirit of Coleridge when they urged the importance of spiritual values, and of measuring national greatness not by wealth or machines but by the character of men and the quality of their lives. Meanwhile, to and through such figures as Thomas Arnold, Coleridge gave a new conception of the function of the Church and helped inspire the Broad Church movement.

But in a larger perspective, Coleridge could hardly be termed either conservative or liberal. Like every aspect of his thought, his political philosophy draws its strength from his eclectic and unifying habit of mind, from that undulating, open-armed progression which is so difficult to imitate. Refusing to begin with merely one premise, he looks toward rival parties and assimilates what seems valuable in each while also contributing insights of his own. Unlike many organicist thinkers, he provides no basis at all for totalitarianism, for the individual is the ultimate purpose of the state, though he also insists that the individual must accept a responsibility to the whole society. He agrees with the utilitarians that the commercial and manufacturing classes are—in his time—the progressive element in the society, but he also asserts a positive role for the landowner. He does not believe, with the run-of-the-mill revolutionist, that institutions can completely mold the feelings and opinions of men. For him institutions express the public feeling of the time, but he more than recognizes that, through the "clerisy," society can creatively shape public opinion. He does not believe with Godwin and Paine that mere reason can guide transformation, but neither, with the later Burke, does he stress the value of irrational faith or "prejudice." His ideal, in politics as much as in poetry or logic, is "progressive transition," but transition always toward a moral end.

His point of view, of course, completely satisfied no single party at the moment. But it preserves a perennial relevance. He developed a political philosophy imbued with the English spirit of tactical compromise, yet with no compromise of fundamental principle. It catches up, explains, and protectively justifies, as it were, the English national past and present, while preserving a power of adaptation to changing circumstances. It is in many ways the most finished and—in that one respect—perhaps the most satisfying aspect of his thought.

• 8 •

To linger further on the final years of Coleridge is very tempting. We are all eager to know what a man of his capacity was thinking in the autumn of his life—we speak here particularly of the religious thought—and we are especially eager when it is a man whose experience has included so much. We refer not only to the horizontal span of his talents, interests, reading, speculation—that is taken for granted—but also to the vertical range of emotional and psychological experience that crossed, at times deflected, but in important ways multiplies for us the potential significance of the other. Here is a man whose experience reached a level first of critical and then of religious speculation (and with it always a personal and sympathetic involvement) rarely equaled during the past two centuries, but whose daily life also involved the deepest despair and humiliation—and this not only in dark moments, or even for weeks or months at a time, but for a twenty-year period that cut throughout the heart of his lifetime from his later twenties to his later forties. In our own hunger for meaning we naturally turn to an example so fascinating of the range of what the human being can experience, and begin to think—whatever the defenses of nonchalance or chatter with which we try to shield our nakedness—of what Johnson called the first end and interest of biography, of what "comes *near* to us," of "what can be put *to use*." And aside from this deeply human interest—in part resulting from and through it—is the large historical relevance of at least part of his thought to the nineteenth century, and, far more, to our own and the coming generation.

Another incentive to linger on the later years is the wealth of anecdote. Though some of it is repetitive, all of it is readable. Of the more than hundred accounts of Coleridge written by his contemporaries, over half are concerned with the last fourteen years of his life. Most are by visitors who attended the "Thursday evenings." The diversity of the people who came to the "Thursday evenings" delighted Coleridge, who describes one of them for his old friend Daniel Stuart. Present were two painters, two poets, a clergyman, an eminent chemist and naturalist, a naval captain who had traveled widely, a physician, a major, a colonial chief justice, and a lawyer, together with a group of ladies. There were never less than five or six, and there were often more. Time and again those who came compared his conversation to the flow of a river. Yet they stressed its variety—he could take up anything, give it the fullest justice, but then instinctively began to try to direct it back toward a central flow of meaning. And if he fell into monologue, it was because, as De Quincey said, he was constantly being encouraged by others to do so. Coleridge's principal weakness, said John Wilson, was his "extreme love of sympathy." It was this, "and not pride or vanity, which led him to delight in talking"—an eagerness of "having other minds in communion, as it were, with his own." But if, among those with whom he was talking, there was "the slightest apathy or carelessness displayed, it was curious to see how his voice died away at once."

Whatever his eloquence in talking, his dress had become plainer, even severe, since he had moved to Highgate—"black coat," said Gillman, "black breeches, with black silk stockings and shoes." People who did not know who he was often mistook him for a Dissenting minister, even an itinerant preacher. A few years before (1821), Charles Cowden Clarke, the friend and mentor of

Keats at the Clarke school in Enfield, and by now living much of the time at Ramsgate—where Coleridge went on holiday with the Gillmans—suspected at once that Coleridge was there when Clarke's mother observed that

> she had heard an elderly gentleman in the public library, who looked like a Dissenting minister, talking as she had never heard man talk. Like his own "Ancient Mariner," when he had at once fixed your eye he held you spellbound.

Clarke, who had never met him before, finally encountered him on the East Cliff at Ramsgate, contemplating the sea. Introducing himself as a friend and admirer of Charles Lamb, he was soon convinced that this was

> *the* most extraordinary man of his age . . . [His genius was constantly awake;] like the hare, it slept with its eyes open. He would at any given moment range from the subtlest and most abstruse question in metaphysics to the architectural beauty in the contrivance of the flower.

So with one account after another of the later years. By the middle 1820's, Coleridge's hair—rapidly graying throughout his forties—had become completely white. He walked with a kind of shuffle, his knees slightly bent, and he carried a cane. He still retained the Devonshire accent of his youth. His "r's" were hard. He pronounced the "l" in words like "talk." There was a slight adenoidal difficulty in pronouncing "b's," so that "subject" and "object," as the testy Carlyle said, sounded rather like "sumject" and "omject." As he talked, sitting down or walking about the room, he used snuff, often absent-mindedly, with the result that the grains fell and soiled his neat Spartan dress. At the same time those with whom he talked were infected, said John Lockhart (a sharp and critical witness, difficult to please) with

> the evident kindliness of his whole spirit and intentions—while "he held them with his glittering eye," the cordial childlike innocence of his smile, the inexpressible sweetness of his voice, and the rich musical flow into which his mere language ever threw itself, were subsidiary charms that told even upon the dullest and the coldest. Had it been possible that such a man should ever have taken up the trade of

> a demagogue, either in the pulpit or in the hustings, what power must have been his!

The American novelist James Fenimore Cooper met him at dinner at William Sotheby's (April, 1828) in honor of Sir Walter Scott. The conversation began with a discussion of the Samothracian mysteries and then turned to the multiple authorship of Homer. The range of learning, the "affluence" of both language and ideas, almost hypnotized Cooper:

> When I did look around me, I found every eye fastened on him. Scott sat, immovable as a statue, . . . [and] occasionally muttered, "Eloquent!" "Wonderful!" "Very extraordinary!" Mr. Lockhart caught my eye once, and he gave a very hearty laugh, without making the slightest noise, as if he enjoyed my astonishment.

• 9 •

In the summer of 1828, Coleridge took a trip to Germany with Wordsworth and Wordsworth's daughter, Dora. Thomas Colley Grattan, a friend of Washington Irving, met them in Brussels, and was struck by the ease with which Coleridge could talk with anyone—not for effect but because "he seemed to breathe in words." Everything he touched on seemed to expand into progressively wider circles of meaning. A remark on grammar led to a discussion of the whole philosophy of grammar, then to illustrations from chemistry and then to the theory of colors. From there he began to branch off into the "analogy between natural grammar and colour."

When they settled for a while in Bonn, German visitors flocked to see him. Wordsworth good-naturedly sat silent, watching and admiring his old friend. A. W. Schlegel, one of the visitors, implored Coleridge to speak in English. Whatever Coleridge's fluency in the language, almost thirty years had passed since he had been in Germany. His pronunciation distressed Schlegel, who was himself eager not only to try his English but also to exhibit it before other German visitors who did not know the language but were present because they wanted to see Coleridge.

He was not well when he returned home. Money matters also

continued to prey on his mind, despite the quiet help of friends. He was not paying Gillman all that he should, and his own family had needs for which he still felt responsible. For two or three years he had been contemplating minor projects. With the unworldliness and impracticality so typical of his dealings with publishers, he agreed to contribute occasional verse to the annual "table-books" that had become fashionable. The few pounds he received were more than counterbalanced by the confusions, anguish, and long letters that resulted. A comprehensive edition of his poems (1828) was carelessly assembled and brought little return. (New and corrected editions followed in 1829 and 1834.) His daughter Sara meanwhile married Coleridge's nephew, Henry Nelson Coleridge (1829), which did not wholly please her father. He was uneasy about the marriage of cousins. But he was torn. He would have finally agreed to whatever his gifted daughter wished, and he could hardly help thinking well of this steady, admiring nephew of his. He could also understand his daughter's hunger for stability. In any case, many things that could have disturbed him earlier were beginning to seem less important now.

It is at this time that he wrote or dictated *On the Constitution of Church and State,* which we just discussed in our summary of his later thought as a whole, and to which he devoted—however valuable and influential the work—only a fraction of his mind. In 1830 George IV died and with him, the year following, the annual grants made to members of the Royal Society of Literature. His friend John Hookham Frere made up the loss. Other friends quietly and tactfully helped.

• 10 •

In 1830 his health began rapidly to decline, and he spent most of his time in his attic room. The hypertensive heart disease from which we now know he suffered was already well advanced. Moreover the pain in and below the chest, from the large accumulation of fluid discovered in the autopsy, was becoming severe. Occasionally, in order to distract himself from it, he would walk slowly about his room for several hours, at one time as much as seventeen hours a day. Otherwise he often remained in bed. But visitors continued to appear. However he felt, he usually preferred to meet them in his parlor, on the floor below, and to be as neatly dressed as possible. Only near the end did he abandon the effort and see them in his own room.

Among the visitors (1832) was Harriet Martineau, still famous as one of the great Victorian reformers. She came with a chip on her shoulder. A businesslike soul, with a deep distrust of both metaphysics and conservative religion, the utilitarian Harriet took it for granted beforehand that there would be nothing on which they could agree. "He looked very old, with rounded shoulders and drooping head, and excessively thin limbs. His eyes were as wonderful as they were ever represented to be." To her surprise, he had read some of her works and then,

> after paying some compliments, he avowed there were points on which we differed . . . "for instance," said he, "you appear to consider society as an *aggregate of individuals!*" I replied that I certainly *did.*

He tried then to speak of the "many-sided fact of an organized society," and in the process went up metaphysically into a "balloon." Yet, writing afterwards (and disapproving sternly of what she had heard of his life), she was disturbed at the memory of those "inordinate reflective and analogical faculties, as well as [his] prodigious word power." Reluctantly she had to admit—however strongly she disapproved of the metaphysical tenor of his thought and the "conduct of his life"—that she could see why he should have had such "success as an *instigator* of thought in others."

By the late spring of 1833 he was feeling better, and with Gillman and Joseph Green made a short trip to Cambridge. In August the young Emerson paid him a visit—Coleridge, Wordsworth, and Carlyle were the men Emerson had most wished to see in England. Coleridge began by discussing the limitations of Unitarianism. "When he stopped to take breath, I interposed that 'whilst I highly valued all his explanations, I was bound to tell him that I was born and bred a Unitarian.' 'Yes,' he said, 'I supposed so';

and continued as before." He went on to speak of the Trinity and then the "Tetractys" in a way Emerson could hardly be expected to follow without some preparation. (Joseph Green, after seventeen years of Coleridge's company and free access to the manuscripts, had difficulties in following it.) But the interview, though it seemed "rather a spectacle than a conversation" and left Emerson with the impression that Coleridge "was old and preoccupied" and unable to "bend to a new companion," in no way affected his belief that Coleridge "wrote and spoke the only high criticism of his time."

• 11 •

As the lecture to Emerson suggests—it lasted about an hour—what was most in Coleridge's mind now was what he had only begun upon, in the *Opus Maximum* and the notebooks: the search for a philosophical means by which the mystery of creation (and this would include the *why* and the *how*) could be penetrated in such a way as to answer simultaneously the claims of (1) traditional Christian theology; (2) modern epistemology and logic; and (3) the "dynamic philosophy," with its majestic and—within its theological limits—successful inclusion of the discoveries of science and philosophy.

Yes, this was the real task. Granted that for years he had deliberately retrenched and concentrated his effort—had tried to play more closely to the ground, had focused specifically on Biblical criticism and interpretation, had resolved that, in the years remaining to him, he would learn at last to "do one thing at a time." But could he not just possibly, in the time left, make some headway in resolving what would surely become the central problem to the reflective mind within the next century or two: how, knowing what we do of science and of the human past, do we bring it into a deeper union with the religious aspiration? Back in 1828, just before he took the trip to the Rhineland with Wordsworth, he had written in a notebook a long sketch of what the *Opus Maximum* should ideally be.[8] In it we see him reviving the

[8] Printed in A. D. Snyder, *Coleridge on Logic and Learning*, pp. 3-8.

general aim—if not the extended body—of the *magnum opus.* He would start with the concept of the "Tetractys" as it sustains the Trinity. Then, through the concept of "Alterity"—and the need for difference in and through which "Absolute Will" can *act,* can become "causative"—he would proceed to the "Birth of Time and Nature through the Polarization of Chaos," and then (through discussions of "polar forces" and inorganic life) to the emergence of "vegetable life" and "Animal Life from the Polyp to the primaeval Man." From this he will turn to the drama and direct history of man: the gradual unfolding of Revelation and the potentialities of re-union, or redemption, through the "incarnation of the Logos in Jesus."

How quickly—once he really began to release his ambition—he came back to the old and central problem! Almost he seemed to be returning to some of the premises in the "Theory of Life" written back in 1816. But now there was a difference. He was beginning to understand far better the means of rescuing the dynamic-scientific philosophy through a deeper, more capacious sense of Christian theology. But there must be time to answer logical and epistemological difficulties. And in his outline, which took him three days to write (May 24–27, 1828), he was wryly modest, even self-mocking. Playing with his initials, S. T. C. (always attractive because of their suggestion of businesslike briskness, their lack of claim on him for "high endeavour"), he describes his plan as the *"Esstecean* Methodology, or Philosophy of Epochs and Methods," and inserts as a "motto" a couplet about himself: "Author of tomes, whereof, tho' not in Dutch, / The Public little knows, the Publisher too much." How much of his life had been spent promising the publisher—explaining to him what was about to be sent—and how small the results were for the public!

Of course he could laugh about himself. It would be a real indictment of oneself, as one grew older, if one could not. But the subject was serious enough. If we fold our hands and give up any effort to penetrate the mystery of the unknown, we myopically—and suicidally—remove ourselves as co-partners, in however small a way, in the astonishing, puzzling drama of creation.

• 12 •

Soon after Emerson's visit, Coleridge—aware, with the strange clairvoyance he seemed to possess, that this would be his last winter—wrote the famous epitaph, referring to himself for the last time as "S.T.C." [9]

By the following spring it was obvious to others, as well as to himself, that this long pilgrimage was coming to an end. In May Tom Poole came to London to visit him. That wise friend of forty years thought Coleridge showed "a mind as strong as ever" but "seemingly impatient of its encumbrance." How far away, during the latter half of his life, those days at Nether Stowey had seemed—the garden where he would learn to do useful manual work and grow vegetables for his family, the preaching at the Unitarian chapels, the walks along the Bristol Channel, the "Ancient Mariner." But now those days were returning—they and his early life generally, which had been so open to possibilities or at least seemed so now in retrospect. On July 10, two weeks before Coleridge died, he told his nephew, Henry Nelson Coleridge:

> I am dying, but without expectation of a speedy release. Is it not strange that very recently by-gone images, and scenes of early life, have stolen into my mind, like breezes blown from the spice-islands of Youth and Hope—those twin realities of this phantom world! I do not add Love,—for what is Love but Youth and Hope embracing, and so seen as *one?* I say *realities;* for reality is a thing of degrees, from the Iliad to a dream . . . Yet, in a strict sense, reality is not predicable at all of aught below Heaven. . . . I own I wish life and strength had been spared to me to complete my Philosophy. For, as God hears me, the originating, continuing, and sustaining wish and design in my

[9] Stop, Christian passer-by!—Stop, child of God,
And read with gentle breast. Beneath this sod
A poet lies, or that which once seem'd he.
O, lift one thought in prayer for S.T.C.
That he who many a year with toil of breath
Found death in life, may here find life in death!
Mercy for praise—to be forgiven for fame
He ask'd, and hoped, through Christ. Do thou the same!

heart were to exalt the glory of his name; and, which is the same thing in other words, to promote the improvement of mankind. But *visum aliter Deo,* and his will be done.

Nine days later he suffered a massive attack. Trying to pull himself into clarity, he asked that he be, for a while, completely alone. He wished to concentrate in such time as he had left on the thought of his Redeemer, and "evince in the manner of his death the depth and sincerity of his faith in Christ." On the evening of July 24 he said there were some final words he wanted to dictate to Joseph Green for the *Opus Maximum.* He spoke "with the utmost difficulty":

> And be thou sure in whatever may be published of my posthumous works to remember that, first of all is the Absolute Good whose self-affirmation is the "I am," as the eternal reality in itself, and the ground and source of all other reality.
>
> And next that in this idea nevertheless a distinctivity is to be carefully preserved, as manifested in the person of the Logos by whom that reality is communicated to all other beings.

He then wrote a note in which he asked that some provision be made for the servant, Harriet Macklin, who had been attending him during the last few years. Within another half-hour he fell into a coma, and died at six-thirty the next morning (July 25, 1834), aged sixty-one years and nine months. The autopsy he had requested—discussed earlier in the context of his health generally—was performed, and he was buried in Highgate cemetery (August 2). When Wordsworth heard of Coleridge's death, the thought of their disagreements twenty-five years before, in the darkest period of Coleridge's life, seemed absurdly unimportant. His voice broke as he told the news to a friend: this was "the most *wonderful* man he had ever known." Charles Lamb, who had seen every side of Coleridge since they were boys at Christ's Hospital, tried to tell himself that there was no cause for grief. "It seemed to me that he long had been on the confines of the next world,—that he had a *hunger for eternity.*" But Lamb, who was himself to die before the end of the year, could not bring himself to go to the funeral. "His great and dear spirit haunts me.

. . . Never saw I his likeness, nor probably the world can see again."

Almost immediately Coleridge passed into legend, and has continued to remain there as no other writer in the English-speaking world has done during the last century and a half, leaving one of the most richly diverse legacies of thought and talent in the history of modern experience. "The class of thinkers," John Stuart Mill was to say in a few years, "has scarcely yet arisen by whom he is to be judged."

Index *

* Particular works are indexed under Coleridge, Works.